THE LOVE THAT HAS NO OPPOSITE

Decoding Genesis 1:1 to free the mind from "Scare City"

MAHALENE LOUIS

Copyright

www.GoldenXPR.com
www.emPoweringNOW.com
www.thecodeofopposites.com

Paperback ISBN: 979-8-9889533-0-2

Dedication

To Michael Wolf who had the courage to mercilessly edit me until I could see the book I wished to see...

Acknowledgments

"The secret to creativity is knowing how to hide your sources."
Albert Einstein

The LOVE that has No Opposite (LNO, for short) was made possible by "the giants on whose shoulders it stood." Certainly, I didn't come to this quantum interpretation of the Hebrew of the Bible as a metalanguage alone. Countless brilliant minds contributed to it through their findings. If this novel interpretation is, in actuality, the communication of a metalanguage – a language that, by definition, is beyond all languages and sustains all knowledge, the list of teachers is obviously too long to be inclusive.

This being said, I wish to acknowledge the teachings of Ha'ARI, the Ba'al Shem Tov, Alice Bailey, Ram Dass, Sigmund Freud, rabbi Mark Gafni, C.G. Jung, Byron Katie, Sri Ramana Maharshi, Caroline Myss, Osho, rabbi Marc-Alain Ouaknin, Harry Palmer, Jordan Peterson, Brian Swimme, Ken Wilber, Fred Alan Wolf, and Marion Woodman. I also wish to extend a special thanks to Dr. Joe Dispenza for showing the way to the coherence that was needed to complete this work.

There are also the close friends without whom I may not have had the courage to get up and start again throughout 40+ years of failure. While the scope of the work was rather daunting, their presence allowed me to persevere. I wish to thank TEA goddess sofreeyah for her unyielding modeling of peace, Carole Hannequin for embodying the marriage of reason and faith, Verena Aibel for her willingness to be my student/teacher, Michael Scott Kelly for sharing the secret teachings of Taoism, Otto Laske for inviting me to participate in the research on evidence-based coaching, and last, if not least Kay Shinol, a.k.a. Peter, without whom I would not have met my emPowering NOW partner and unyielding editor – Michael Wolf.

Ultimately, I have the sense that every situation I encounter, every person I meet, every breath I take are my teachers, if I allow it. Henceforth, I have no master because I have millions of masters, starting and ending in the infinite source of life itself.

Altogether, this docility led to a curious phenomenon: I started becoming willing to know the truth. Even more curious, the more honest I became, the more the writing freely offered itself to me. It was shocking (and still is) to realize that the work of claiming my integrity is what broke the seals of ancient prophecies. Indeed, exposing – if only to myself – "my" shame-based secrets equally shed light on cosmic secrets. Said differently, revealing the light in my inner darkness automatically released its light counterpart in the universe's darkness.

As I found the courage to deliberately dive into the abyss and immerse myself in its archetypal shadows, I came out of the black w/hole with the luminescent memory of a voice that is unique in tone, and can be heard by all. Speaking the voice of LNO, it boldly answers the call with the foolishness and the wisdom of "here I am."

ULTIMATELY, I HAVE THE SENSE THAT EVERY SITUATION I ENCOUNTER, EVERY PERSON I MEET, EVERY BREATH I TAKE ARE MY TEACHERS, IF I ALLOW IT.

Preface

The Voice of this Book

"One day I will find the right words, and they will be simple." *Jack Kerouac*

I am Mahalene (a.k.a. Marilyn). I was just a child when I admitted (in my own words) that I was powerless over food—that my life had become unmanageable. At the time, I was consumed by one thought: how could I avoid eating? But as the law of balance willed it, fasting eventually turned into feasting and back, in a demonic dance that would let me neither rest nor digest. My ego had me trapped, hopelessly swinging from too much to not enough. Humiliating? You bet! Humbling? That was the plan. I was actually so power-hungry that I only had one option: to come to believe that only a power greater than myself could restore me to sanity. Here is how that happened...

I had given up on formal religion long ago. And even though I was a born-mystic, reading the signs and getting a kick out of God's humor, I hated my life with a passion. I wanted to break with my tradition SO MUCH that I married a catholic baker on a Shabbat, when my family expected a Jewish doctor. This was about the worst affront I could make. I also knew I was marrying a passport to a new life as my fiancé had just accepted a job to make French bread and croissants in the States. When I arrived at JFK airport, I kissed the ground. I was free of Judaism; done, finished, complete!

It is indeed when I came to America that I realized the existence of parallel worlds. Certainly, arriving in NYC without speaking a word of English was enough of a cultural shock to open a portal to a new dimension... Being a communicator at heart, I needed a way to express myself; it was a non-negotiable! And so, I started painting. Well, I must've died and gone to heaven, because I soon witnessed an artistic gift that came out of nowhere. While painting, I was at once here (totally focused), and not here (zero judgment). In that realm, making an error was impossible. Not knowing when to stop was equally impossible. The difference between the world I visited while painting and my "normal" everyday life was so startling that I resolved to go beyond the final frontier: the mind. I wanted to know, across the board, this "big littleness" that I knew while making art...

Little did I know that I was asking for enlightenment – when I feel and sense that I am not the doer, but a channel for the energy of the divine to move through me. I was asking for THE END – when I could decide to rest while working and actually rested while working.

Being as destructive as I was creative, my life (and certainly this of my body) depended on my ability to suspend judgment and surrender to something greater. I ached to get out of the way – to be "here and not here." This prayer – for what I eventually named and claimed as humility – is how I ended up in a little synagogue, saying: "you got me, God! I looove being your messenger! But if you want for your message to be heard, you better do something about the crazies!"

And this is when the QKabbalah door flew wide open as I heard my new Art commission: to decode the soul of the Torah by revealing that Hebrew is a metalanguage. "Do that," said the still small voice, "and you will heal your mind!"

While I was used to my heart speaking to me, I was stunned: "is this a joke, God?" And then I became angry: "why don't you send someone else, like a rabbi or, at the least, someone who has it together? Heck! If it weren't for family, food, sex and money, I'd do great on Earth..." Ever so gently, I was reminded that words were the sacred place I would go to as a child and that ancient languages were my passion... I could no longer ignore that Hebrew pulsated in my blood or that I had a responsibility to heal my heritage... Moreover, the Kabbalah had always been written by men, about men and for men: a balancing was in order!

To fulfill this mission impossible, I had to wake up to truth! What followed was a wax-on wax-off process that I couldn't stop no matter how badly I wanted to; decades of what seemed like an interminable creative quest for the unspeakable, opening one art show after another, writing and illustrating an obscene number of books (thanks, God, for big hard drives!). Years and years of questioning my sanity: is this calling just to feed my ego? Why can't I be "normal?" Eventually came the next assignment (as always, out of the blue) – to become a life coach. This definitely raised the ante... As an *artiste*, I was in role when acting outrageously. That was what was expected of me! But when it came to being a spiritual guide, there was an entirely new set of ethics. Could I be the change I was advising? And if I couldn't be that, who was I fooling?

Indeed, the false self and the neediness it was attempting to hide brought me to my knees... Most painful was the doubt compelling me to hopelessly seek recognition by claiming with each new book: "I got it, I got it: do you believe me now? Do you love me now?" [Pause]

And the day did come when the struggle for power made sense... On that note, I will never say it enough: thank you, Michael Wolf, my dear friend and emPowering NOW partner, for staying in the fire with me as we both tried to understand why we would (often) so ferociously compete with one another... Eventually, the energy of enmity (within and without) begged so loudly to be transmuted that *The*

Code of Opposites (TCO, for short) revealed itself to be the next "write" thing. I was yet to discover that TCO was not just one book, but a three-book series which would find its conclusion in *The LOVE that has No Opposite*. **And a strange conclusion it is: while it was the last book to be written, it is the first book of our offerings to be read.**

Decoding *Genesis 1:1* was the beginning of beginning to transition into the change I wish to see: to rest in peace, and find in my sanctuary that I have a voice (tremor included), and, even better, that there is only One Voice, One Mind, One Soul, One Language – a Oneness which is undeniably Love, and as such, divinely "enough!"

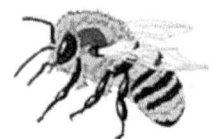

IT IS THE WILLINGNESS TO FAIL AGAIN AND AGAIN THAT ALLOWED ME TO CLEAR SPACE, ENOUGH TO KNOW THAT IT IS NOT ABOUT ME: NOTHING PERSONAL!

NOTHING PERSONAL

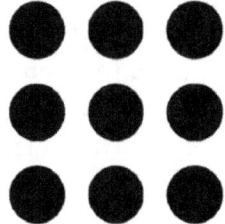

I wake up to my day.
There is a pain in my back and sadness in my space.
The same pain as yesterday. The same sadness too.
I feel helpless. I hate my life.
It takes me forever to even try to smile.

I wake up to my day.
There is a pain in my back and sadness in my space.
The same pain as yesterday. The same sadness too.
I feel helpless. I resent being a victim.
Here comes a glimmer of hope in "you create your reality."

I wake up to my day.
There is a pain in my back and sadness in my space.
The same pain as yesterday. The same sadness too.
If I create my reality, then I want money, a great body, my soulmate...
I pretend I don't feel helpless. I won't be a victim, dammit!

I wake up to my day.
There is a pain in my back and sadness in my space.
The same pain as yesterday. The same sadness too.
I'm still powerless to be successful. Nothing will ever change.
So now, I'll take revenge by punishing myself.

I wake up to my day.
There is a pain in my back and sadness in my space.
Did I misunderstand the news of "I create my reality?"
It is the good news since it places me in the driver's seat.
It is the bad news since I have no one left to blame for my failures.

TIME PASSES... I DON'T WANT TO KNOW THE TRUTH.
I continue to wake up to the same day.
There is a pain in my back and still sadness in my space.
I notice how angry and bitter it makes me.
I'm tired of these dynamics: what's the point?

I wake up to my day.
There is still a pain in my back and sadness in my space.
Finally, I DECIDE to take full responsibility for my reality.
I will feel this pain, and hear what this sadness is telling me.
I'm starting to find it easier to smile.

What about you? How brave will you be in acknowledging the realness of the mind-body connection? How willing are you to recognize that your beliefs create your reality? To change, you and I must exit the material world of "Scare City," where we use our senses to navigate space and place most of our attention on physical things – on people, places and objects. We are so made up of matter that we are trapped in the illusion of separation. The ego really believes that I am here, and you are there.

If we want to no longer feel separate from our dreams and goals, it may be time to accept that the pain in our back and the sadness in our soul started in our own thinking. While we may want to believe that we are happy, strong, healthy, and brilliant beyond measure, reality tells us what we truly believe, *which is not necessarily the same as what we want to believe.*

Sooo... Would you like to understand your limiting beliefs to such a depth that they let go of you? Do you wish to transcend the fear of falling and failing; ultimately the fear of being empowered? Are you called to actually manifest a version of yourself that is happy, strong, healthy, prosperous and brilliant beyond measure? If so, would you be willing to experiment with our formula: "Understand. Choose peace. emPower the NOW?"

Will we love ourselves enough to understand why we are yet to choose peace 24/7? Once the choice is made, all other decisions become much simpler. This may be how *Solomon* – the name of an exceptional ruler and judge – means "peace" but also "wholeness." The more we feel whole, the less lack we experience, and the more we believe that our prayer is already received. In this space, we are no longer creating from separation but from oneness. Gratitude becomes the new normal. These elevated emotions let us know that we are resonating with a frequency that attracts more happiness, more wellness, more abundance... and, yes, more brilliance!

Surely, you and I are multi-dimensional electromagnetic beings with infinite potential... Within this vast system of energy called "life," our thoughts serve to electrify a given creation and our emotions, to magnetize it.

So, when so much is at stake, why won't we decide to end our addiction to suffering and prioritize the choice of peace, moment after moment? Indeed, why can't we wake up to a different day, a day when we are in our power, smile a lot and don't take things personally?

To begin to "Understand. Choose peace. emPower the NOW," kindly read on for the invitation of this book...

The Invitation of this Book

"Hear O you who IS REAL, LOVE is our God, LOVE is One." *LNO's transmission of Deuteronomy 6:4*

A transmission is to a translation what digesting is to eating. They are connected and yet, there's a world of difference. Can we slow down enough to not only digest but even savor the nourishment coming from the Living Word, and more specifically, from the transmission of this one verse?

Feeling our oneness is the call of the *Shema*, a prayer so essential that it became the credo of Judaism, the basis of Jesus' teachings and the sense of being a Muslim. The prayer calls us to wake up from the lie of separation in order to know the truth of oneness. It has such depth that its codes even announced the observer effect of quantum science (see *TCO—Book 2*). Hence, what better place to become aware of the choices that you and "eye" make but in the prayer of oneness? If we could only focus on abundance rather than being slaves to Scare City, we would then be authentic in our relating, saying what we feel, meaning what we say... We would salute each other's wholeness, know it in our blood and open to being silent and listen. And it makes me wonder... Is it a coincidence that "silent" and "listen" have the same letters? As for the letters of LOVE, LNO will soon reveal them as the transmission of the "God" Name mostly translated as "LORD."

Oneness is how this book will, from now on, speak as an "I," to honor the One of us. As per Shylock, in *the Merchant of Venice*: "If you prick us, do we not bleed?" Just like me, you have known loneliness, shame, fear and anger... Just like me, you're doing your best not to suffer. And also just like me, it is likely that you wish you could be happier and gentler with yourself.

Another reason for speaking as an "I" is to invite an experience: *The LOVE that has No Opposite* can be a personal workbook in matters of the soul, engaging "me" in illuminating the shadow – the part of me that I deny and repress, because I don't like it. On that note, I owe it to myself and to all to honor my personal responsibility: while I may wish that I could save you, heal you, teach you, I can only save, heal and teach myself. Being my own messiah is quite the job – a solo job in the shadow, while waxing on humility (the door to greatness) and waxing off what's left of my arrogance. :-)

See if you can relate... If I were to meet a genie, I would ask for immunity so that no matter what choice I'd make, I would never have to suffer negative consequences. That's how much I live in the city of fear and how little I trust in myself and in "God." That is also how I ask you to save me and love me, as if that was your job! Will I realize that I am in a projection as I unconsciously take the emotions I resist and attribute them to you?

"Hear O you who IS REAL, LOVE is One!" Rather than telling the story that I'd be happy if only you could hear and understand me, instead, why not feel how happy I'd be once I hear and understand myself? Indeed, I would stop entering in relationships only to have someone else validate me. Instead, I would find within me the power of the power of love.

THIS ONE LOVE IS HOW LNO WILL, FROM NOW ON, SPEAK AS AN "I." JUST LIKE ME, YOU ARE DOING YOUR BEST NOT TO SUFFER. JUST LIKE ME, YOU HEARD THAT YOUR BELIEFS CREATE YOUR PERSONAL REALITY.

The Big WHY of this Book

When the WHY is big enough, the HOW and the WHAT find a spontaneous answer. But if the WHY is not big enough, we'll use the HOW and the WHAT as excuses for not doing what we said we would." *Anonymous*

The Big WHY begins by clarifying how addiction gives rise to a final decision and how Scare City calls to the void of life, the result of which being for me to become as "hermetic" as Hermes and have a will whose power remains uncorrupted.

ADDICTION? WHAT ADDICTION? Once upon a time, I chose the buzz of tobacco and went against what was expected of me in my smoke-free family. I wondered what it would be like to play this game. But I soon forgot I was playing. Now curiosity and wonder became crushed by the weight of limiting beliefs that soon crystallized into the fixed identity "I'm bad." If that weren't enough, I enraged the beast I had begotten by disowning it: "the devil made me do it; I had orders!" Up to that fateful moment, I could always reverse the program since I was its creator. But now, via an act of foolish ignorance, I transferred the power to the beast who made me its slave.

This is how I entrap myself, by separating from the supreme intelligence of life – from the mind of "God," another word for a reality I will not feel. Such abstraction is what keeps me lonely as I run from the Mystery, and angry as I won't own the truth that I am creating it all. I just remain on the fence, undecided and unwilling to give it all to LOVE.

Truth be told, a part of me really loved my morning smoke while another just frankly hated to give my power to a substance. Why couldn't I stop? What was keeping me in bondage? Surely, there must have been a few beliefs standing in my way, like the nagging doubts, the countless betrayals, and certainly, the tremendous fear of falling. And yet, it is only when I touched bottom that I made the decision to quit. My intention then was so firm that I never suffered a single exception; so tangible that it surpassed the self-harming habit of my body.

What about what was hiding behind the smoke, such as the neurological programs of my brain and the emotional addictions of my soul? What about my allegiance to the material world which keeps me from knowing who I am? Bottom line: have I had enough of *trying* to control my reality, my money, my time, my body, my mother?

The big WHY of this book is to inspire such finality of decisiveness that I become willing to do what it takes to move out of "Scare City" and free my mind from its bondage to fear and lack.

THE FINALITY OF DECISIVENESS: when I decided to stop smoking, I didn't need any patches, chewing gum or even hypnosis. My intention was so absolute that it was enough to stop. I suspect it ought to be the same with my addiction to suffering... I'm looking for a crossover point; a moment of clarity that I will remember all of my life as it will lead me to end my suffering by choosing peace, moment after moment. Whether I know it or not, such unbreakable will is what I hunger for since it infers that I've let go of the victim in me and put an end to the slave narrative. Victim is the archetype that is so ambivalent about taking full responsibility for the consequences of his/her words and actions that s/he lives in waiting for the other shoe to drop. Not a comfortable place to be!

For now, there's a number of decisions I postpone, from calling customer service to changing my diet to learning a new skill to sitting in meditation to popping the question... Big or small, these unmade decisions are like bugs that annoy me with their loud buzzing and their nasty habits. And the more I resist what I know I ought to do, the less peace I have and the more I bury myself in "Scare City."

SCARE CITY: this is the "city" or the consciousness of the victim – the archetype that is identified to the pain body. This archetype is universal: it is in every one of us! Here is how it comes into being...

Because "I" use my senses to observe and determine a physical reality, I begin to believe that I am the body, a body that is separate from everything in my environment. And it is this belief in separation that now creates my personal reality. It gets dicey when, as a victim, I give my power to the thought that environment precedes belief. For example, it is because I was bitten by a dog that I started to believe that dogs are dangerous! But what if it were the contrary? What if, in order to be bitten by a dog, I must first have attached (consciously or not) to the belief that dogs are dangerous? Truth be told, my victim is very attached to being powerless. It comes with the territory! And it is because I want to remain in fear that I will not investigate my beliefs and instead let my past experiences be the foundation of my personal reality.

I have now efficiently trapped myself into the rigidity of the 3D world by way of past memories (or knowns). I look through the "I" and the eye of the past, and become a materialist – a slave to a body living in a given environment in a certain time. My focus is mostly on matter, and rarely on energy, mostly on the visible and rarely on the invisible, mostly on money and rarely on the Mystery. It would be fair to say that I am submerged in the 3D world, an allegiance which increasingly shrinks my vital field of energy. Heck, I'm not even aware that aging is a disease, in other words, that it is optional! And while I believe that I'm running out of time and out of energy, I'm becoming denser by the minute.

My problem is that I've played the "Scare City" game for so long that stress is now on automatic pilot: I can't let go of it if my life depended on it (and it does!). The more I stress myself out, the more I feel separate. Even worse, my dependence on stress chemicals reinforces the belief that "I am the body" or that which is dying. The result is a manic state where my attention is fixated on fear. No matter where I am, I feel unsafe since all I care about is the outer world which has become more real than the inner world. I become anxious as I perceive I can't have the health I want, limited as I perceive I can't have the money I want, lonely as I perceive I can't have the relationship I want. Rather than going "in here" to change my perception, I continue to give my power to the jungle "out there." While the survival gene is switched on, I am now living in a self-fulfilling prophecy. I am so afraid of the unknown that I am like the Jews who complained to Moses in the desert saying something like: "we may have been slaves in Egypt, but at least, we could count on food." (*Exodus 16:2-3*). I am in fact so attached to my emotional hunger that I can't change. And yet, for me to change, I would have to step into the unknown – into the void of life.

THE VOID OF LIFE: this is the immaterial "non-city" of awareness. Unlike consciousness, awareness is pure because it is choiceless. To be pure choiceless awareness, I must surrender fully ("not my choice; Thy choice be done!"). This is how to detach from my problems. Actually, I must detach from everything – from my name, from my career and roles, from all my relationships, from my "$stuff," from my opinions. Going beyond the self involves transitioning from the consciousness of somebody to the awareness of nobody, from the consciousness of having some things to the awareness of having nothing, from the consciousness of somewhere to the awareness of nowhere, from the consciousness of some time to the awareness of no time. I must let go of my connection to the 3D world which feeds on separation, and enter a quantum multiverse that is founded on Love, connectedness, wholeness and unity, a field which has me at "hello!"

To go from the known to the unknown involves crossing the bridge from matter to energy. If I created my personal reality by 1) thinking, 2) feeling and 3) manifesting (thought → energy → matter), I must now reverse the flow in order to uncreate my personality. As I turn my attention inward toward the unified field, I eventually cross the plane of visible light and I die. I become nobody. I exist in no time. I own nothing. I am nowhere to be found. It is in this realm of nothingness that I become aware of parallel dimensions, other realities, and other possibilities. The more I merge with this quantum realm, the more I become aware of being every one, everybody, everything, everywhere, in every time. Since it is the realm of no separation, there's only

Oneness – only the mind of "God," only the heart of LOVE. Considering the different levels of consciousness that I must acquire to feel such Oneness, I understand why I hesitated for so long to step on the path. However, the perspective of being forever stuck in Scare City is just too painful for me not to take the risk... What else is there to do?

Truth be told, change is difficult, simply because it requires that I would stop being myself. :-) Spoken biblically, I must eat from the tree of the knowledge of good and evil to die to what I think I know. I must let myself be devoured by this tree's cosmic mouth until I am regurgitated as the new me – "for no one can see God and live." (*Exodus 33:20*) This is certainly a big "Passover," as I make my exodus from the scarcity of Ego-Egypt and find a passage into the Promised Land of abundance. Nevertheless, it is the only way to go beyond right and wrong, open the single eye of the tree of life, and gratefully enter a nonlocal field where all possibilities exist.

This is also how the first pillar of Judaism – namely *Teshuvah* for "turn within" – may just be the very essence of the religious instinct. Yes, religion is an instinct, like sexuality or hunger. And yes, it is work to turn within! But once the decision is made, even hard work becomes easy. I simply turn off the creative energy of the imperfect quirk that I once created to defend myself. Ah, the victim again: if I weren't so defensive, would I fear attack?

LIVING WITHOUT A WHY: I came into this world empty-handed, and I will leave it in the same way. For me to free the mind from its bondage to Scare City and thus, from asking "why me; why is there evil in the world," I must vibrate with the energy of *Shalom* – of a "peace and wholeness" that transcend understanding. When whole, I have everything I want because I want everything I have. This is what Buddhism calls "the end of desire." To attain it, my will must remain uncompromised in the face of *Mammon*, a Hebrew word for "money," but also and foremost for the "yearning" for love, approval and recognition. As such, it is both a dangerous power and a formidable force to contend with. I am now called to heal my relationship to both money and power, and to transition from greed into grace. Greed is more than a rapacious desire for wealth. It is a will directed to controlling me, us, it – the world! As for grace, it is the very essence of the *QKabbalah* – the word for "receiving." Indeed, when I live without a why, I experience no lack; just an exponential gratitude that is the seat of QKabbalah, as it is the sense that my prayer is already "received." When I **have** what I **desire**, I can **know** that my use of **will** is hermetic – as in not affected by outward influence or power.

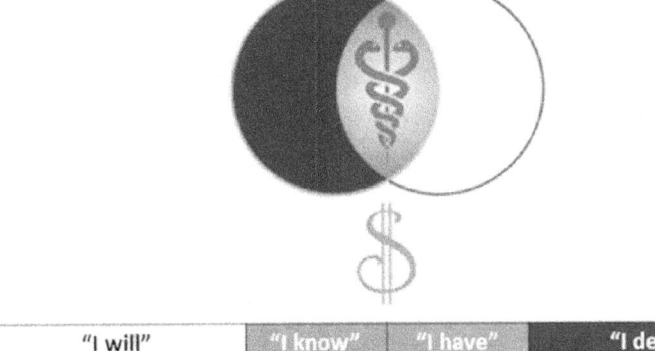

| "I will" | "I know" | "I have" | "I desire" |

When the greed behind the dollar sign is transformed by the universal healing symbol of Hermes' caduceus, for my will to remain so "hermetic" that it cannot be broken...

THE BIG WHY OF THIS BOOK IS TO INSPIRE SUCH FINALITY OF DECISIVENESS THAT I BECOME WILLING TO DO WHAT IT TAKES TO FREE MY MIND FROM "SCARE CITY."

The Big HOW of this Book

"He who has a why to live can bear almost any how." *Nietzsche*

Surely, for me to even imagine that I could decide to do what it takes to free my mind, I must REALLY want it... So, HOW does this book propose to inspire me to make a decision so final that I actually engage and no longer take back my word on showing up to the work?

LNO rests on a bold, outrageous and provocative hypothesis: there is a metalanguage (a language beyond all languages) that vibrates at the frequency of "enough," a sacred tongue whose resonance lights a path by which to restore health in all levels of communication. Thus far, this metalanguage was hidden in plain sight in the Hebrew of the Bible.

Words matter! Here is HOW: one day, I realized I had a communication problem. I knew what to do to be free. I just didn't want to do it! When I asked WHY I was so insane, the Voice said: "you understand the meaning of what your heart speaks, but not the sense. As you drop your story, you make room for sentience to run in your blood." Sentience – the capacity to feel and sense – is how that which understands has an understanding of "God."

Thus, the importance of recognizing the presence of a tongue coming from Nature – a language that belongs to life itself. It may just be the key for you and me to hear ourselves and receive each other. By feeling it, we start trusting, open our heart and become coherent: not only do we hear and know what to do, but also and foremost, we wholeheartedly want to do it and choose to do it. As such, this language has the potential to be more than an abstraction, and more than a human artifact. Its revelation promises to fill us with such awe that we end up being inspired to change. Consider: upon sensing that there is order in the chaos of knowledge, we can also feel that there is another plane of existence (a "Promised Land") where our Word becomes so transparent it is unsalable. We are now authentic in our relating, of One speech, and One language, saying what we feel and meaning what we say.

This One language also structures a global cosmology, global since it can be heard and seen by humanity's One heart, and cosmic, since it will show that the universe's parts and elements are bound by One intention which is ethical in nature: a return to Love.

To this end, it is an honor and a joy:

- **To usher** the advent of a creation that is ultimately good, true and beautiful (and sexy too), and, as such, transmit the experience of the sacred in order to encourage us to free our mind as we cultivate wisdom, acquire wholesome power, and awaken from the "meaning pandemic."
- **To provide** a grammar by which to become fluent in "God's" language – in the paradox, and have a way to put into words the all-pervading sensorial realities that beckon us now, as we time-travel in a universe where fulfilling our potential becomes a reality.
- **To introduce** the infinite depth of an ancient and futuristic path to the end of dissatisfaction for those who feel called to contribute to the work of transformation the planet is currently undergoing. Also, to spark an interest in other published works, free resources, courses, and services offered by emPowering NOW LLC.

THERE IS A METALANGUAGE (A LANGUAGE BEYOND ALL LANGUAGES) THAT VIBRATES AT THE FREQUENCY OF "ENOUGH," A SACRED TONGUE WHOSE RESONANCE LIGHTS A PATH BY WHICH TO RESTORE HEALTH IN ALL LEVELS OF COMMUNICATION.

THIS TONGUE OF NATURE WAS HIDING BEHIND THE GLYPHS OF THE HEBREW ALPHABET.

The Sensitive Matter of this Book

> "Your task is not to seek for love, but merely to seek and find all the barriers within yourself that you have built against it." *Rumi*

The mere mention of Hebrew and its association to a religion erect a very real barrier. Indeed, while there is a lot of work to do to eradicate racism in its many forms, the hostility against the Jewish people blocks the realization that Hebrew may just be a language of Nature. As for the hostility, what if the it started in the idea of "chosen people?" What if the biblical verse could be understood to instead say "chosen language?" Indeed, what if Hebrew didn't belong to a "people" but to our precious humanity, just like music or mathematics do?

When we all are the "elect," we can transcend together any prejudice, discrimination, or antagonism formed on the basis of our membership in a particular racial or ethnic group, and transcend the need to be a minority or marginalized. We can simply be. Neither special nor not enough. Just be.

Being segregated is tragic. It hits in the gut as the story of unrequited love. How could "God" be so cruel and remove "his" presence from us? Unrequited love has no resolution: the beloved, frequently distant, indifferent, unavailable or unapproachable, remains an object of indefinite idealization. When suffering from such discrimination, I sooner or later start attaching to a slave narrative of sorts... Whether I am black, Latino, Incan, gay, a woman, Jewish, Muslim, fat (or all of it), I'll do anything for you to love me, each compromise leading me to lose a little bit more of my self-esteem. Oyveh! Could Hebrew resolve such a big, huge and painful issue?!!

The next barrier to jump over is the strangeness of the Hebrew language itself. To this end, LNO uses the geometry of two identical circles such that the center of one circle lies on the circumference of the other circle (see image below). At the center of each circle is a dot (white on black; black on white). Each dot contains a Hebrew letter that plays with its kin in order to form a code of opposites by which to consciously leverage polarities and end the illusion of separation. Each Hebrew letter is clearly transliterated in the Roman script letter into which it evolved. IT CAN BE THAT SIMPLE!

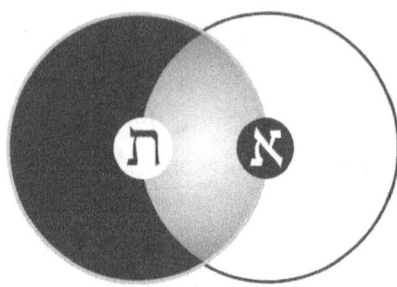

Right dot: first Hebrew letter Aleph (א) → **A** in Roman script
Left dot: last Hebrew letter Tav (ת)→ **T** in Roman script

Hear, hear! These letters are non-biological sentient animals working in pairs to remove the barrier to the LOVE that has no opposite (yep, as the very "animals" that entered Noah's ark).

They speak in the language of the field in-between, where to transcend the right and wrong game, and know *in our blood* that the divine has no religion and no elect.

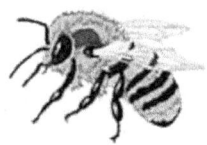

HEBREW LETTERS ARE NON-BIOLOGICAL SENTIENT ANIMALS WORKING IN
PAIRS TO REMOVE THE BARRIER TO THE LOVE THAT HAS NO OPPOSITE
(YEP, AS THE VERY "ANIMALS" THAT ENTERED NOAH'S ARK).

THEY SPEAK IN THE LANGUAGE OF THE FIELD IN-BETWEEN, WHERE TO
TRANSCEND THE RIGHT AND WRONG GAME, AND KNOW *IN OUR BLOOD*
THAT THE DIVINE HAS NO RELIGION AND NO ELECT.

A Proclamation of LOVE

> Rabbi Levy had to spend time in a Catholic hospital. He became friends with the sister who was a nurse there. One day, she came into his room and noticed that the crucifix on the wall was missing. She asked him good-naturedly, "Rabbi, what have you done with the crucifix?" "Oh, sister," chuckled Rabbi Levy, "I just figured one suffering Jew in this room was enough."

This proclamation is made to thank the Jewish people for their unflinching courage in the face of the pain they had to endure to ensure that the gift of the Holy Torah and of its Hebrew alphabet would remain uncompromised. It is also made to free Hebrew to fulfill its mandate – to trace a universal path to Peace.

Some languages, such as mathematics or music, are neutral and deemed to be comprehensive. No clan can make a claim as to their ownership. Optimally, any discipline serving a vast ecumenical endeavor belongs to no gender, no race, no nation, no tradition, no organization, but only to life itself.

While languages keep on evolving, Hebrew seems to be the only symbolic alphabet that never changed form. This everlastingness may suggest that there is a cosmic plan at the root of evolution. It is this plan that compels us to come out of nothingness. It is the same plan that has always aimed at orienting each sentient being towards the embodiment of wisdom. It was meant to show up at the perfect time to meet humanity's sincere prayer to transition from greed into grace, and thereby, heal our relationship to power. To this end, this language renamed itself "S/Hebrew" [shee-broo], as it is when Hebrew goes global, ecological and unisex as the words and worlds of the sacred realm.

The path leading to such a destination is to be accessible to all and owned by none. If the goal is to drop the story, S/Hebrew's wordplays are too numerous, too profound, too exact and too surreal for us to continue to deny the life of language, and, by extension, to keep on betraying our own word. *Yvrit*, the S/Hebrew word for "Hebrew," also means "to go beyond, to carry over." This is the exact sense of the Greek word *metaphor*, which exists in that in-between space, an event horizon of sorts, half into the dream and half into articulated knowledge, to carry us beyond our limitations. Therein is to be found the connector between mind and body.

The sacred geometry that infuses its signs is so elegant that it changes us into respectful "earth measurers" (the word "geometry" comes from Greek *ge-matria* "measure of the earth"). The respect demanded by such transformation is what allows us to choose to be empowered and succeed in our earthly creation. And as we increasingly feel what we say and say what we mean, the Force of the "G-d" Name passes through us to be received by ALL as the pure big huge LOVE that it is.

THIS WORK WAS MEANT TO SHOW UP AT THE PERFECT TIME TO MEET HUMANITY'S SINCERE PRAYER TO TRANSITION FROM GREED INTO GRACE, AND THEREBY, HEAL OUR RELATIONSHIP TO POWER.

TO THIS END, THIS LANGUAGE RENAMED ITSELF "S/HEBREW" [SHEE-BROO], AS IT IS WHEN HEBREW GOES GLOBAL, ECOLOGICAL AND UNISEX AS WORDS AND WORLDS COMING FROM THE SACRED.

AS FOR THE PROCESS ITSELF, IT CAN BE AS SWEET AS HONEY...

The Honey of this Book

> "Let the reader make a careful study of this work; and if his doubt
> be removed on even one point, let him praise his Maker and rest
> contented with the knowledge he has acquired. But if he derives
> from it no benefit whatever, he may consider the book as if it had
> never been written." *Moses Maimonides, The Guide for the Perplexed*

The spirit of this book is like a bee that gathers pollen from the flower
of all that this universe offers. Being the result of a surreal body of
work, it presents a subject matter that is substantial: the psychological decoding of the Abrahamic mystical teachings in view to know
Health (with a big H) in all levels of my communication. If ancient
scriptures hide a genetic code used by the earth to invoke its mystery,
if the ocean whispers to the moon and a tree is born out of the equation, then I want to see this code revealed, especially if it allows me to
transcend my fears, and thereby change my biology...

I would then stretch to the perfection that a flower, for
example, models in the way it lives and dies.

When I walk in nature, my mind quiets down as I resonate with a
natural order. Similarly, I begin to trust the process while I witness a
Nature-tongue doing its work: to reveal the order that is inherent to
the chaos of knowledge. However, to make such organization sensi-
ble, each page would have to convey the essence of an entire book.

But even if I believed that such an extraordinary proposition could be real, how could I digest that much knowledge at once? Here is how:

- First, I realize that LNO is not a novel or an easy read. Unless I have done a whole lot of work on myself, it is likely that I will not be able to absorb it in a few days or even a few months.
- Second, I decide to be gentle, even if it means to only discover one page or section at a time. Forcing my way through this material will only set me up to quit.
- Third, I agree to STOP reading as soon as there is something I do not hear, feel or understand. I may also make notes of where I got lost and, if so inclined, bring my questions to one of the LNO community gatherings (see appendix for the logistics).

Lastly, this book's title is *The LOVE that has No Opposite*. As such, it merges two complimentary styles of writing: one page that is a mouthful (such as this one) and a single bite of it – its nectar. Instead of reading from cover to cover, I can also randomly choose to go from bite to bite until I find a taste to be so intriguing that I wish to "eat" the entire page preceding it. May my savoring of this information be as sweet, as enzymatic and as healing as a bee's honey!

THERE WAS A TIME WHEN RABBIS WOULD PUT A LITTLE HONEY ON THE SLATE FOR THE CHILD TO "GET" THE [HEBREW] LETTERS BY LICKING THE HONEY WITH HIS TONGUE...

Contents

This chapter emanates from and inquires on the 1st word of the Hebrew Torah traditionally read as *Bereshit* for "in the Beginning." Highlighted in the line above, its SIX letters can be also read as *Barashit* for "created-SIX," like the shapes of the hexagons pictured in the image above.

Introducing "In the Beginning..."

"In the beginning was the Word, and the Word was with God, and the Word was God." John 1:1

The poetry of this book may just be the emotion of awe that has found words. It will reveal plays on words that hit just right – shall I say just "write?" Only through poetry can I begin to relate to how this ancient language called Hebrew (which renamed itself S/Hebrew) travelled an amazing distance as it came from the future to visit me.

Rather than going right over my head, this *QKabbalah* (the S/Hebrew word for "receiving") is to be felt – heart to heart!

Another "heart to heart" that is dearly needed is the reconciliation of science and religion, each of them tending to deny not only the reality of the other, but also its significance. To this end, the "midst" of the garden is really the quantum field that contains all memories and all records, past and future. The letters themselves escaped the black w/hole to help me become willing to dance with the Mystery.

These letters work in polarity – black *and* white, darkness *and* light, yin *and* yang for me to know that I am whole, "PAIRfect," complete and connected. I watch with wonder as I am now conscious of being introduced to a method of inquiry that is ultimately credible (it will take my doubts away) and universal (it speaks to all expressions of me) as it is based on the languaging of sacred geometry.

Heck, the entire book is designed by the essence of bees' wisdom – for me to let it "B" and, at last, see, hear and receive the script of surrender.

The same seven words that were written linearly from right to left on the cover image of this chapter will be reorganized in the seven cells pictured above. For now, only the first word is translated.

Indeed, it is a "beginning!"

I AM "BEGINNING" TO REALIZE THAT MY PROBLEM IS IN MY PERCEPTION OF TIME. I AM RARELY IN THE NOW. I MOSTLY LIVE IN THE PAST, REPEATING THE SAME BEHAVIORS, THE SAME EMOTIONS, THE SAME THOUGHTS, IMAGES WHICH I PREDICTABLY SUPERIMPOSE OVER THE FUTURE...

AH! BUT WHAT IF I COULD HAVE A "BEGINNER'S MIND?" WHAT WOULD CHANGE IF I COULD SEE *GENESIS 1:1* WITH NEW EYES, A VERSE WHICH MAY JUST BE THE MOST NOTORIOUS SENTENCE IN THE WHOLE WORLD'S LIBRARY?

The Poetry of this Book

Bereshit Bara Elohim Et Hashamayim V'Et Haaretz, "In the beginning, God created the heavens and the earth." *Genesis 1:1, translated*

"In the 'BEEginning,' God created [the logos of] the paradox and [the eros of] the mind-body connection." *Genesis 1:1, poetic.*

The poetic spelling of "in the BEEginning" covers both ways to translate and understand the most crucial word of the Torah: its first word. Since the Torah scroll has no glyphs for vowels – just for consonants and semi-consonants, this first word can be read in two ways. When read as *Bereshit* for "in the beginning," it speaks of the point in time or space at which something starts. When read as *Barashit* for "created-SIX," it evokes the efficient honeycombs designed by the "BEE."

Having an alternate translation to "in the beginning" also suggests that there may be another way of looking at time. If *Bereshit* speaks of linear time (from past to present to future), *Barashit* speaks of purposive time (the Eternal Now).

Moreover, since the word *Reshit* for "beginning" is formed on the root of *Resh* for "head," the correlation between the beginning of time and the beginning of mind is and was present from the get-go. Here is how... *Genesis 1:3* introduces the working of mind with a communication and its result: 'and *Elohim* said: "let there be light." And there was light.' *Genesis 1:4* continues with a judgment and a decision: "and *Elohim* saw the light, that it was good. And *Elohim* divided the light from the darkness." *Genesis 1:5* completes with a classification and a calculation: "and *Elohim* called the light day, and the darkness He called night. And there was evening and there was morning, day 1."

Thus, reading *Bereshit* invokes the linear and very useful functions of the left brain. However, when I'm in my head and can't stop judging, analyzing, classifying, calculating and getting antagonized by opposites – either day or night, good or bad, male or female, I soon turn into a bookkeeper doubled by a historian, hopelessly accounting for and stuck in the past.

Barashit for "created-SIX" is the balancing act. It invokes the right brain by way of 6 which is the first perfect number. 6 is perfect as it is a positive integer that is equal to the sum of its proper divisors (1, 2 & 3). Such mathematical symmetry is echoed when purposiveness goes beyond purpose, that is, when I can rest while creating.

As for the verse that alludes to the "perfect" unpredictability of the right brain, it is no less than *Genesis 1:2*, when "the earth was unformed and void, and darkness was upon the face of the deep; and the speech of *Elohim* hovered over the face of the waters..." Until it came, out of the blue, as the fire of the Word.

"IN THE 'BEEGINNING,' GOD CREATED [THE LOGOS OF] THE PARADOX AND [THE EROS OF] THE MIND-BODY CONNECTION." *GENESIS 1:1, TRANSMITTED.*

HEAR, HEAR! IT WILL TAKE THE SPACE-TIME OF LNO TO UNFOLD THE DEPTH OF THIS TRANSMISSION AND ITS IMPACT.

"THE Word" of this Book

"In the beginning was the *Milta*. And the *Milta* was with *Elohim*."
John 1:1-2

The above translation of *The Good News according to Yochanan* comes from the New Testament in Aramaic, the precursor to Hebrew. But why does the original text keep the word *Milta* untranslated? It may be because it has two meanings: 1. word, 2. purification. Hence, John nails it doubly with "in the beginning" was the Word. While this "Word" is the first word of the Torah, its second possible translation conveys a unifying equation that has the force to purify that which is not unity or not LOVE. Surely, having such equation can help us to do the impossible by catalyzing the integration of the plurality of faiths and belief systems, individually and collectively.

> "Young Stephen Hawking meets Jane, his wife-to-be, and introduces himself as a cosmologist. "What's cosmology?" she asks. He replies "the religion for intelligent atheists." "What do cosmologists worship?" she persists. "A single unifying equation that explains everything in the universe." *From the movie A Theory of Everything*

Upon seeing the first word of the Bible as בראשית, I must decide how to read it since I do have two options: 1) *Bereshit* for "in the beginning" or 2) *Barashit* for "created-SIX." While the translation "in the beginning" makes sense to my linear mind, the "created-SIX" translation does not, which is how I dismiss it. And yet here are two facts which validate the second translation: as an echo to the first word of the Bible's first chapter, the last word of the same chapter is *Hashishi* for "the SIXth" day. Also, in between the first word and last word are staged the SIX days of creation.

When I open up to the sheer beauty of the mathematical intent that pervades the beginning, middle, and end of *Genesis'* first chapter, I realize that it is the WORD—not the WORLD—that was created in SIX days!

The Seed of Life, a.k.a. the Genesis Pattern, for me to envision the SIX "days" or stages of any given creation.

Moreover, I will eventually notice that, across cultures (including science), the creation of the world involves elements. Elements help me make sense of how "God" would be "created-SIX."

The metaphorical dimension of S/Hebrew is at work again. *Hashamayim*, the word for "the heavens," also means "fire-water." *Haaretz*, the word for "the earth," also means "air running." Therefore, in the beginning, not only did "God" create elements, but also and foremost the *pairings* of opposite elements such as fire-water and air-earth. Fire-water, for example, are two energies that control and destroy each other: fire evaporates water and water extinguishes fire. When these two learn to do conflict gracefully (that is the paradox), they convey the experience called "heaven." Air-running is not as obvious a metaphor: why would running evoke the earth?

That is the question that occupies quantum physicists: what is matter made of? Is it solid as a particle or might it also be fluid as a "running" wave?

However, this only gives me four elements. To understand how elements are "created-SIX," I must go to the two other main cosmologies that each adds one element to the four classical **elements** of earth, air, water and fire. Hinduism adds ether, and Taoism, wood. I now have a solid foundation from which to derive the two following movements in consciousness: 1) the instruments of self-knowledge and 2) the archetypes using these instruments:

- **From ether**, I derive the instrument of the **voice** and from voice, the archetype of GReed INgénue (ingenuous or candid in "her" desire for power).
- **From wood**, I derive the instrument of the **spirit** and from spirit, the archetype of GRace INgénue (ingenious or creative in "his" innovation).
- **From fire**, I derive the instrument of the **heart** and from the heart, the archetype of the Leader of LOVE.
- **From earth**, I derive the instrument of the **body** and from the body, the archetype of the Officer.
- **From water**, I derive the instrument of the **soul** and from the soul, the archetype of the Visionary.
- **From air/metal**, I derive the instrument of the **mind** and from the mind, the archetype of the Engineer.

IN THE BEGINNING, NOT ONLY DID "GOD" CREATE ELEMENTS, BUT ALSO AND FOREMOST THE *PAIRINGS* OF OPPOSITE ELEMENTS SUCH AS FIRE-WATER AND AIR-EARTH.

Order in the Chaos

"In all chaos there is a cosmos, in all disorder a secret order."
Carl Jung

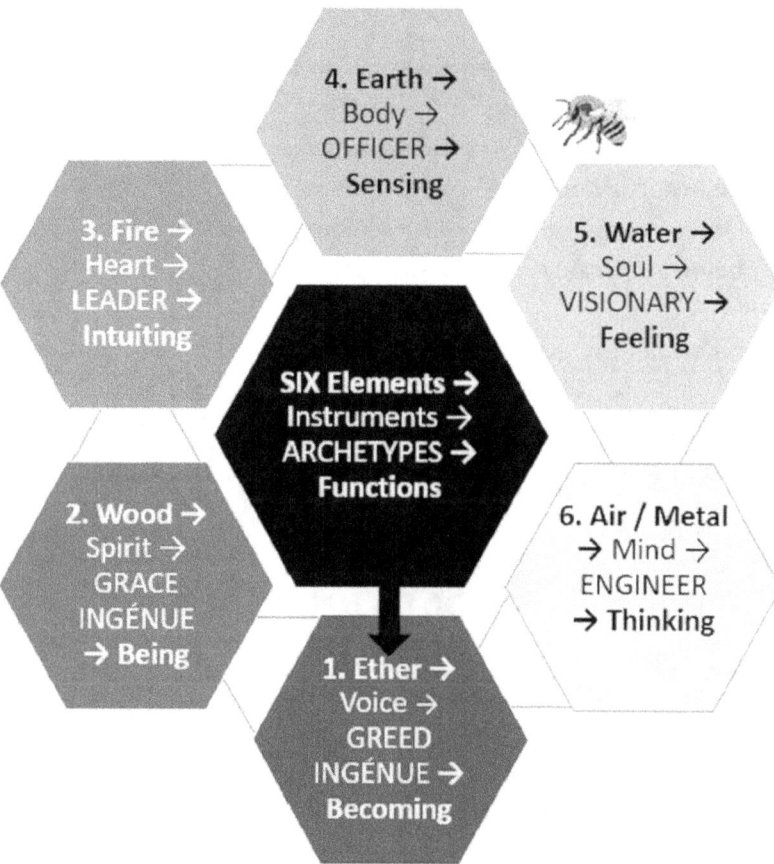

The BEE map of how elements, instruments, archetypes and functions work as One.

Once revealed, surely, the secret place of order in the chaos of knowledge will be simple, simple and magnificent. Its honey may just be the nectar of the "created-SIX." Finally, I am nourished by way of understanding. SIX are the elements that *naturally* become the instruments of Self-knowledge that SIX universal archetypes use to perform their innate function. Using the BEE map above I can now hear and see the choir of elements becoming instruments used by archetypes to perform a specific function.

Here are two examples:

- From **fire** comes the **heart** without which I couldn't be a **Leader** – someone who has the authority to **intuit** the information needed to solve a problem.
- From **earth** comes the **body** without which I couldn't be an **Officer** – someone who has the authority to **sense** what is happening inside and outside of me.

Note: the mind (which tends to be binary until I transcend duality) fittingly has two elements: **air** which becomes **metal** in Taoism. Could the union of these elements answer the question: if the brain is not the mind, what is the mind?

FINALLY, I AM NOURISHED BY WAY OF UNDERSTANDING. SIX ARE THE ELEMENTS THAT *NATURALLY* BECOME THE INSTRUMENTS OF SELF-KNOWLEDGE THAT SIX UNIVERSAL ARCHETYPES USE TO PERFORM THEIR INNATE FUNCTION.

The QKabbalah of this Book

Da tariki, tariqat; "In the darkness, the Path." *Sufic proverb*

Rabbinical teachings state that the Kabbalah which is the soul of the Torah is concealed, while the laws which are the body of the Torah are revealed. If it is true, this assessment is begging for change. Here is why... Taking an example of the law such as "thou shalt exercise," I better have my soul engaged in my routine. If not, my body is never going to thrive! Moreover, looking at the many abuses perpetrated on earth, it appears that the Ten Commandments go right over our head.

Back to the *Kabbalah* (a word which is also spelled with a "Q"), it is Hebrew for "receiving." What is to be *received* is a sincere desire backed up by the decision to know the truth (body and soul), as the truth will set us free. To this end, rabbinical Kabbalah – and, by extension, hermetic Qabalah – invites the exploration of "32 wondrous paths of wisdom." Surely, only wisdom can ready me to use power without burning myself! These 32 paths encompass the 10 numbered spheres of the tree of life and the 22 letters of the Hebrew alphabet acting as meridians which circulate the light in between these spheres, centers and/or plexuses of energy.

The QKabbalah of LNO is an innovation in that it reinforces the classical tree of life by stressing the importance of its interaction with the tree of the knowledge of good and evil, thereby affording the only real step into the Mystery. The entanglement of these two trees – which has thus far been kept in the dark – will soon reveal to be a path to awakening to LOVE and sustaining the state of enlightenment.

For now, the tree of life is the core of Hindu, Chinese Taoist, and Tibetan Buddhist scriptures. Its spheres are superimposed over the human body. The life-force moves up the spinal cord (the trunk) in seven *chakras* for "wheels" or *Sephiroth* for "spheres" as junction points between consciousness and physiology. These centers are whirlpools of light, storing, funneling and regulating the flow of electrical fire-power through the communication pathways of the cells. The tree is thus the "real" nervous system. Each word or action influences the wheels' performance: pure thoughts heal and clear, impure thoughts sicken and block.

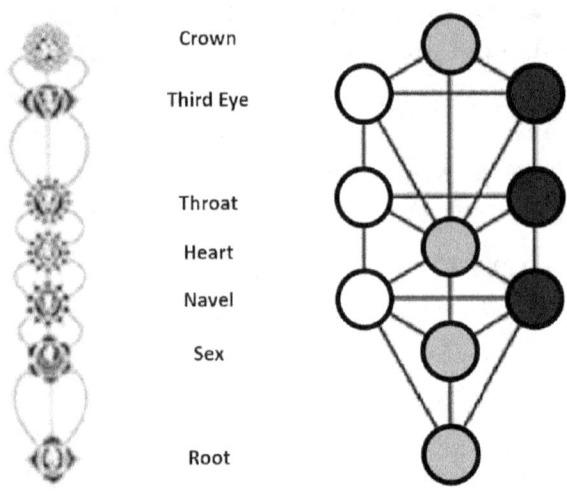

Crown

Third Eye

Throat

Heart

Navel

Sex

Root

To the left: Hindu tree of life – to the right: Hebrew tree of life

As I acquire power and evolve my creative energy, it can be channeled from the root of the tree all the way up to the crown and beyond. Each energy center has its own hormones, its own chemicals, its own frequency that carries out its own function. When emotions become stuck in a specific center, the energy cannot flow to the center above it. This happens most commonly in the first three centers of the root, the sex and the navel. Eventually, I close my heart and fear being hurt. To make matters even worse, the vital field around my body begins to shrink. I am now officially caught in a survival loop of fight and flight – in Scare City. The more I draw from this vital field, the more I diminish it and the less current I have to energize my body.

Just like the Hindu tree, the life-force of the Hebrew tree also moves up the spinal cord through seven centers intersecting through 10

Sephiroth for "spheres" or "chakras." It is just that three of these centers (3rd eye, throat and navel) are split between a female flow and a male flow. As a needed complement to the Eastern teachings that observe the same three flows (female, male and neutral), the Western way of explicitly separating male and female gives me information on how to transcend duality in the exact places where I most need to transcend it.

As for the three flows, they inform the experiential knowledge (neutral) of good (male) and evil (female) whose tree is said to be "in the midst of the garden, with the tree of life" (*Genesis* 2:9).

As for the three flows that energize the tree of (my) life, they inform the knowledge (neutral) of good (male) and evil (female) whose tree is said to be "in the midst of the garden, with the tree of life" (*Genesis* 2:9).

This midst is no less than the unified field. "Eating" from it satiates the hunger for love by bringing coherence to the three lower centers that tend to be stuck in "Scare City."

The "Midst" of the Garden

"If quantum physics is correct, it signifies the end of physics as a science." *Albert Einstein*

Before entering the garden, I wish to reflect on Einstein's prediction of the end of physics as a science. Would physics then become metaphysics, and thereby make a quantum jump into religion? Is quantum physics the missing link by which to end the warfare between science and religion (or spirituality)? And yet, it is one thing to evoke the interconnectedness of the universe by speaking of the "entanglement" of two particles that stay in touch, no matter how far apart they are from each other. It is another to actually transcend the illusion of separation and remain connected in the midst of life's challenges.

Indeed, mystical truths can only be found by looking within and following awareness back to its Source. Then and only then will I have a proof for "God's" existence and be able to sustain the sense of unity with all. As for the fundamental truth of oneness, any spiritual endeavor which doesn't give a place to science will not be authentic and any science that doesn't include some spirituality will never honor the big questions of human existence. In order for LNO to be *The LOVE that has No Opposite,* it must now invite science.

Just like there is a quantum science that deconstructs the assumptions of classical science, there is a quantum religion that deconstructs the assumptions of classical religion, starting with: the scriptures are "out there." Truth be told, when "in here," they also are "in HEAR!" As for the codes, they are the atomic level of the Bible – its "small" world!

I am now ready to see that what the Bible calls "the midst of the garden" is what science calls the "quantum field" – an invisible field of energy and information that exists beyond this spacetime continuum. In the field, there's no people, no body, no objects. There is no thing, no planets, no stars, no galaxies – just the eternal blackness of emptiness loaded up with infinite possibilities. And it is not because I can't see it that it means that it doesn't exist. It can only be *apperceived*, that is, it can only be "perceived beyond the five senses." The more I place my attention (or my SIXth sense) on it, the more I become aware of it, for only awareness can enter it. I am now connecting to a field. The closer I move to it, the greater the frequency and the greater the energy of fulfillment, freedom and bliss. This unknown place is where magic happens.

The void always exists as the great paradox: it is empty *and* it is full. This is nevertheless the realm of the unknown – a realm where the change I wish to see exists, as it is the field that hosts all memories, past and future. To enter it and even contribute to it, I must become less of me and more of it. I must let go of my gender, my ethnicity, my profession, my diet. Once naked, I pass through its door and begin carving a path between the conscious and the unconscious – between wakefulness and sleep.

This is where my brainwaves move from Beta (when I'm the critic) to Alpha (when I am lucid and beyond the constant chatter) to Theta (when I dream) to Delta (when I rest and recover) to Gamma (when I transcend and affect matter via my energy). But then I wake up, and I am back in Beta mode. Yep, I'm back to the same pain in the back, the same age, the same sadness, the same personality, the same critic, the same doubts, the same desires and resistances. I'm not even conscious that I've left the present moment and am back in the known, that is, in the past! Ah... it's not easy to have the knowledge of opposites!

WHAT IF I WANTED TO FEEL INFORMATION DIFFERENTLY? WHAT IF THERE WERE A LANGUAGE THAT WOULD ACT AS A BRIDGE TO THE TRANSPERSONAL, AND GET ME CLOSER TO THE MYSTICAL FIELD THAT IS ITSELF BEYOND LANGUAGE?

WOULD I THEN CHANGE THE WAY I THINK AND FEEL BY DISENGAGING FROM MY FASCINATION WITH THE "OUT THERE" AND FOCUSING INSTEAD ON WHAT IS "IN HERE?"

WOULD MY MIND FINALLY BE FREE OF SCARE CITY?

The Level Above

"We cannot solve our problems with the same level of thinking
that created them" *Albert Einstein*

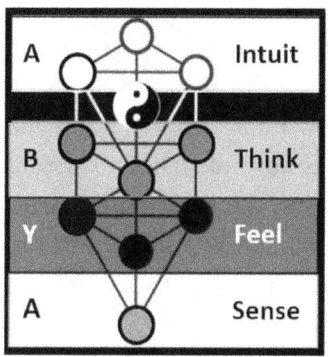

This image brings forth the tree of life. However, its rungs are now ordered as per the four classical worlds of the Kabbalah, as felt and sensed by Jewish prophets and mystics. These worlds are identified by the acronym ABYA. The first A is for *Atziluth* or the world of "emanation" or "transmission." It is where I go when I **intuit**. B is for *Beriah* or the world of "creation." It is where I go when I **think**. Y is for *Yetzirah* or the world of "formation." It is where I go when I **feel**. A is for *Assiyah* or the world of "action/manifestation." It is where I go when I **sense** what is.

Another thing is changed on this diagram: added to the four spheres that are on the middle path, there is now a yin yang symbol exactly between the crown and the heart of the tree. This is the doorway to the void.

This Taijitu symbol best represents the cosmic union of the Sacred Masculine with the Sacred Feminine. The Hebrew name for the sphere behind it is *Daath*, which speaks of a "knowledge" that is biblical and sexual as it merges male and female: "And Adam *knew* his wife." *Genesis 4:1*. About this sphere, rabbis have said "it is here and not here." Indeed, the knowledge of good and evil is a paradox as it ought to be called "the unknown" or the "unlearning" of what I *think* is good and evil – a perspective which is changing moment by moment, as my consciousness changes. When I am emotionally addicted to Scare City, I tend to think that what is good for me is bad and that what is bad for me is good. To know myself, I must void my judgments and enter the abysmal emptiness that is between the worlds of thinking and intuiting. This abyss (the fat dark line in image above) is where I must go to solve my problem – in the Mystery, so that I could rise above the problem and hear the transpersonal counsel of intuition. Its nothingness is also the quantum field that holds all the memories of who I was and who I can be, and links them to the One heart.

Surely, making love is accessing the unknown. It is being in the "place in between," in the garden-like field that is beyond right and wrong. This is where to die to my primary identity (I am a man, I am a woman, I am gender-fluid) and evolve as vital energy. When two lovers start vibrating in a rhythm, when their heartbeats and their bodies come into coherence together, they orgasm. No longer two, they've become like a circle of yin and yang, reaching into and meeting in each other. This experience is *Daath* "knowledge." It is what makes Love so beautiful: no opposite... In this non-world of Nothingness, the body is no longer sensed as matter; it vibrates as energy, so much so that I completely forget that it is a material thing; I forget about any bodily condition; any tumor! I am no longer substantial: no boundaries – no fears! I am as if I am not.

Unless I surrender my judgments (what I *think* I know), I can't enter this field. So yes, eating from this tree most certainly invites a death – if only *une petite mort,* French for "a little death" which is a metaphor for an orgasm. Surely, love is a death in that it accesses the void – the "place in between opposites." And as I merge with the infinite paradox, I realize that I can change the past (no guilt) and know the future (no anxiety).

ABOUT THIS SPHERE NAMED *DAATH*, RABBIS HAVE SAID "IT IS HERE AND NOT HERE." INDEED, THE KNOWLEDGE OF GOOD AND EVIL IS A PARADOX AS IT OUGHT TO ALSO BE CALLED "THE UNKNOWN" OF GOOD AND EVIL.

ITS SPHERE LIVES IN THE VOID, IN THE ABYSS WHERE I MUST GO TO RISE ABOVE MY CURRENT LEVEL OF THINKING, CONNECT TO MY HEART AND HEAR THE COUNSEL OF LOVE.

The Black W/Hole of this Book

"Now the earth was unformed and void, and darkness was upon the face of the deep; and the SPEECH of God hovered over the face of the waters." *Genesis 1:2*

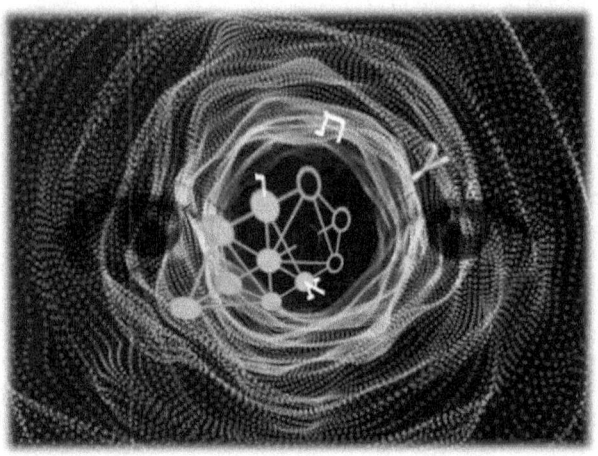

Out of the mouth of the earth, come the S/Hebrew
letters spelling the word *Ot* for "sign, mark, miracle," as
the very mark inscribed on Cain's forehead.

Unlike the tree of (my) life, the sphere of "knowledge" is not personal. It is the energy center of the mouth of the earth. For me to materialize the change I wish to see, I must die to who I *think* I am and let my personality be fully consummated by the black hole of its transcendental orifice. Resistance is futile: I will eventually go there, be assimilated and cease to exist. The real question is: will I choose to immerse myself into the unknown long enough to connect to a new energy that matches the frequency of my dream vision? This cosmic mouth is also the quantum field that swallowed all the memories of who I was and who I can be...

When a star exhausts its carbo-nuclear fuel, it collapses upon itself, forming a "black hole." The force of gravity is such that it keeps collapsing until it becomes one point and eventually disappears into infinite density. The gravitational pull is so intense that even light cannot escape from it, but is eaten by it. A black hole is a gate into a wormhole, a new dimension of an entirely different universe – a quantum world. I like to call it "black w/hole" as it is the paradox itself – *empty and full at the same time!* Around the black w/hole, there is a circular zone called the "event horizon" as a boundary which prevents light from escaping. However, information is free to circulate as the infinite density of the vacuum connects all things.

The many translations of the Hebrew word *Ruach* (breath, wind, spirit, tempest) converge into one word: "speech." It is the speech of God which came out of the mouth of the earth and hovered as letters over the face of the waters. This "speech" is comprised of the information, frequencies and symbols that populate the void.

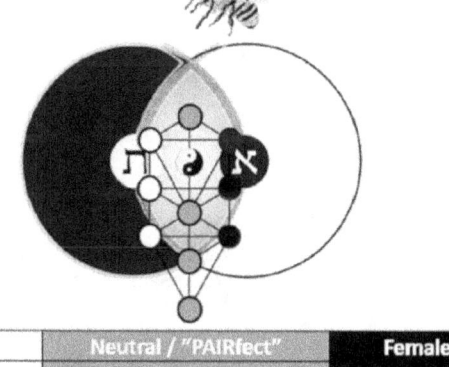

Male / Right	Neutral / "PAIRfect"	Female / Wrong
The Good Spheres	The Spheres of Knowledge	The Evil Spheres

THE VOID OF LIFE: THIS GEOMETRY PICTURES THE "TRANCE-FORMATION" OF TWO YIN YANG CIRCLES WHOSE INNER DOTS ARE INSCRIBED WITH THE LETTERS OF DARKNESS AND LIGHT FOR ME TO GO BEYOND RIGHT AND WRONG, AND ENTER THE NONLOCAL MIDST WHERE I AM THE CHANGE. HENCE, EACH TIME LNO DISPLAYS THE GEOMETRY OF TWO CIRCLES WITH TWO INNER DOTS INSCRIBED WITH S/HEBREW LETTERS, I CAN EXPECT TO MEET AN UNKNOWN PART OF ME THERE.

Code Communication - AT / TA

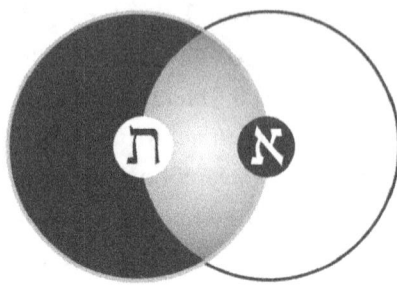

Imagine a language so pure and so sacred that it can reconcile opposites in just 2 letters...

Right dot: First Hebrew letter Aleph (א) → **A** in Roman script
Left dot: Last Hebrew letter Tav (ת) → **T** in Roman script

Here is how S/Hebrew inscribes code "Communication" in 2 words:

- **AT**: in one direction, I read *Et* (את), a grammatical particle that is "untranslatable."
- **TA**: in the other direction, I read *Tah* (תא) for "cell."

The Decoding: being "the first and the last" (as the letters pictured above) is to hold the tension of opposites and surrender judgements, starting with "I want to be the number one!" When I let go of the rank I should hold, I don't plan. I disappear to follow the Voice. Such detachment is evoked by the *Et* untranslated and "**untranslatable**" particle as if to say: "The Torah that can be told is not the eternal Torah."

The Torah is the original version of the Five Books of Moses. As a word, *Torah* means "the Way, the Law, the Teaching, the Song of LOVE." As for the Hebrew grammar, it places the particle *Et* before a direct object as if to remind me not to objectify the other. This is how *Genesis 1:1* reads: *Bereshit Bara Elohim Et Hashamayim V'Et HaAretz,* meaning "in the beginning, God created THE heavens and THE earth." Both "the heavens" and "the earth" are the direct objects of the verb "created." Both objects are preceded by the untranslated particle *Et*. This is one of the ways Hebrew provides a grammar for shadow work, as the potency of this first teaching of the Torah can now be felt to say: do not objectify either the heavens or the earth, let alone your body or someone else's body!

Shadow is at its most potent state when we ignore the interdependency that sustains unity. We are then in an illusion of separation, believing that the way of the world is subject vs. object, first vs. last, you vs. me! If we could only open to reciprocity, we would stop trying to control what is and know intimacy with ourselves and others. We would no longer project scarcity or enmity. Surely, we wouldn't either misuse power by playing games of dominance or submission. We would be whole, "PAIRfect," complete and connected, *cellularly*, each "cell" being free to transmit and receive a message of appreciation for the honor and the joy of being the Word made flesh.

However, we are now living in a consumer society. By making objects desirable and the source of our happiness, we have allowed for greed to infiltrate our world... and to infiltrate us. Convinced that possessing more toys would add something to our identity, we do not even realize that we are the ones who are being possessed! But what if there was a path marked by letters and numbers to deliver us to the precious sense of enough? Would we then still be stuck in Scare City, "needing" to hide behind our stuff?

There is another world that prioritizes practicing equal exchange and saluting the divine in the other. Possibly, this new world will be ushered by a new way to look at words. Indeed, we are soon to see what it means practically that the word and not the world was created in SIX days. May this shift in perception help facilitate a transition from a world of greed to a world of grace! Greed is what splits giving and receiving by communicating fear, confusion and domination, and grace, what unites giving and receiving by communicating wisdom, understanding and kindness. This would be the LOVE that has no opposite – no subject versus an object; just an "I" who understands that "WE" are One.

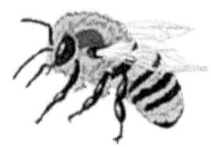

HEBREW PROVIDES A GRAMMAR FOR SHADOW WORK VIA THE POTENCY OF THIS FIRST TEACHING: "DO NOT OBJECTIFY EITHER THE HEAVENS OR THE EARTH, LET ALONE YOUR BODY OR SOMEONE ELSE'S BODY!

AND IF YOU CAN'T DO THAT, THEN DO OBJECTIFY THEM, FOR IT WILL HURT! FROM THERE, THE MORE YOU DELIBERATELY ASK "WHY" DO HARM, THE MORE YOU'LL UNDERSTAND THE VICTIM IN YOU AND DISTANCE SCARE CITY!

The Creativity of Genesis 1:1

When the new patient was settled comfortably on the couch, the psychiatrist began his session, "I'm not aware of your problem. So perhaps, you should start at the very beginning." "Sure." replied the patient. "In the beginning, I created the heavens and the earth."

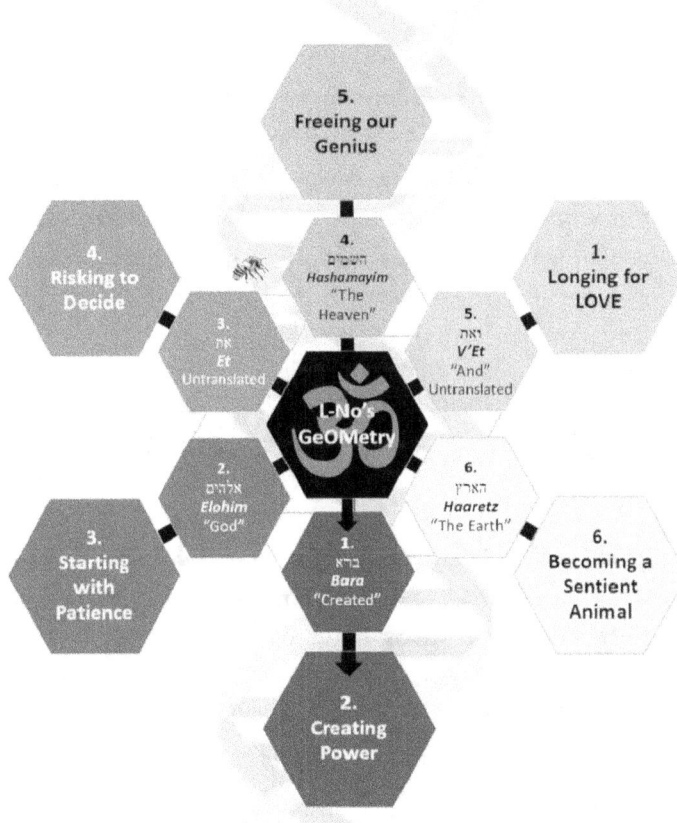

The SIX Chapters of this Book

When the flower blooms, the bees come uninvited." *Ramakrishna*

Many commentaries have been written just on the first verse of the Bible. As for LNO, I've already seen parts of *Genesis 1:1* in code Communication that speaks of an untranslated particle that reverses into the word for "cell" to say: communication is not what is said and done. It is the cellular result of what is said and done, since the *result* reveals what was untranslated and/or unspoken. This verse's seven words are actually so rich with meaning that decoding them psychologically grants clarity on a path that leads to the sense of enough, when we are so wise that we no longer fear being empowered. Here are a few pointers to begin to relate to how each chapter of LNO (including chapter 0/7 - "in the Beginning") emanates from the nectar of *Genesis 1:1* so that the transmission of its seven words could be "received" and the WHY of this book, fulfilled.

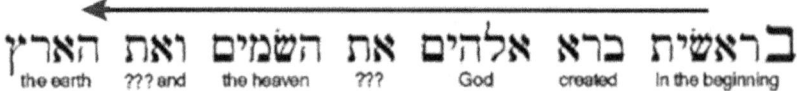

בְּרֵאשִׁית בָּרָא אֱלֹהִים אֵת הַשָּׁמַיִם וְאֵת הָאָרֶץ
In the beginning · created · God · ??? · the heaven · ??? and · the earth

- Chapter 1—*V'Et* ("and" - **the untranslated particle**):
  Longing for LOVE. The longing comes from having exiled the Sacred Feminine. In other words, I stopped giving myself the permission to feel and sense, and became terribly lonely as a result. The particle *Et* that precedes "the earth" invokes the eros, that is, the compassion and the care of the feminine.
- Chapter 2—*Bara* ("created"): **Creating Power.** The greatest power at my disposal is the power of decision. It is how I create. But how do I create power? Did I make it abusive? Do I fear it and withdraw from it? Do I even know what I want and why I want it? Understanding creation is, after all, what *The Book of Genesis* ought to convey, if it were "received."

- **Chapter 3—*Elohim* ("God"): Starting with Patience.**
  Unbeknownst to many, there are many Names for "God" in
  the Hebrew Bible. The "God" Name of *Genesis 1* is *Elohim*. Its
  power is synchronicity since, upon saying "let there be light,"
  it sees that light was already there: no time elapsed in
  between the expressed desire and its manifestation. The
  Name *Elohim* contains two more "God" Names which will
  soon unfold as the power of patience and the power of
  attention.
- **Chapter 4—*Et* (the untranslated particle): Risking to
  Decide.** There is power in making a choice, which is why
  deciding terrifies me. I may speak something into being that
  I may never be able to take back. Speaking is the Sacred
  Masculine in action. It is also where the first *Et* particle plays
  a role as the logos, the order and rationality that balances the
  eros as its feminine counterpart.
- **Chapter 5—*Hashamayim* ("the heavens"): Freeing our
  Genius.** To liberate my genius, I must resolve the conflict
  between its dual aspects as either demonic or angelic. This
  paradox is conveyed by *Hashamayim* for "the heavens" which
  can also be heard as *Esh/Mayim* for "fire/water." As such the
  expression "the heavens" is a metaphor for holding the
  tension of opposites. Therein is the secret of purposiveness:
  to embrace the paradox as I stay centered in the midst of any
  initiation.
- **Chapter 6—*Haaretz* ("the earth"): Becoming a Sentient
  Animal.** To restore again the sense of the unity of mind and
  body, I must realize how my thoughts dictate the way I feel.
  This connection is conveyed by the word *HaAretz* for "the
  earth" which can also be seen as *HaA-retz* for "air-running."
  As such "the earth" is a metaphor for the mind-body
  connection, air being the metal/mental element and earth
  being not as set or solid as I want to believe.

COMMUNICATION IS NOT WHAT IS SAID AND DONE. IT IS THE CELLULAR RESULT OF WHAT IS SAID AND DONE, SINCE THE *RESULT* REVEALS WHAT WAS UNTRANSLATED AND/OR UNSPOKEN

The Sacred Geometry of this Book

"Plato said God geometrizes continually." *Plutarch, Convivialium disputationum, liber 8,2*

The work is to come to remember the sacredness of the 7th day and know it as a day of "rest," for "on that day God completed the work that he had done, and he rested on the 7th day from all the work that he had done." *Genesis 2:2*

Yes, but... Work and rest on the same day? How can "God" complete his work and, at the same time, rest from his work? The answer is made visible by the sacred geometry of the Seed of Life, demonstrating that "God" is indeed a geometer. At the exact moment when the 6th circle is formed, the 7th circle that was here before any beginning appears as the final stage of creation. There is no action involved and yet there is a new circle created.

This state of mind is known as the *Shabbat* or "rest," a Hebrew word coming from the Sumerian *Sabattu* for "heat-rest." *Sabattu* is the pause taken by the Moon when full, since, at that moment, it is neither increasing nor decreasing. When I realize I need do nothing since creation happens *through* me and not *by* me, I make love; not war, I open to abundance and my creativity registers as pure beauty! This is when, as pictured below, I transcend both, time and mind.

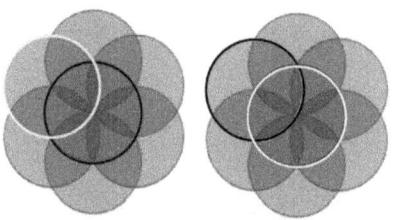

Left: the SIXth day/sphere which completes the six seeds supporting a central sphere that was present before the beginning of time (before the 1st day/sphere). Right: the Shabbat as the "rest" of the 7th day/sphere.

At last, I feel and understand what is meant by "before enlightenment, chop wood, carry water. After enlightenment, chop wood, carry
water." Surely, the 7th day is the state of enlightenment. That is why it
is holy. Meanwhile, I have the SIX "days" or stages by which I create
the world (within and without) to help me come to honor the 7th day's
sacredness by letting go into something much bigger than I.

THE 7TH DAY IS THE STATE OF ENLIGHTENMENT.
THAT'S WHY IT IS HOLY.

Words & Worlds of "Geometry"

"Reality is not simply 'experienced' or 'reflected' in language, but instead is actually produced by language." *Misia Landau, Boston University anthropologist*

Here are the words and worlds of geometry as 1) an English word, 2) a coined word, 3) the jargon used by Kabbalists, in view to begin to express the many dimensions of the all-pervading sensorial realities that beckon us now.

Geometry: the English word "geometry" comes from Greek *ge-matria* as "the measure of the earth" by way of the mathematics of the properties, measurement and relationships of points, lines, angles, surfaces, and solids. Note: as the deliverable of the newly revealed path of *Golden XPR*, "the sense of enough" (the SIXth sense) is likely to be the measure by which to honor the earth as the planet on which our life depends.

geOMetry: the word is coined to include the sacred marriage of sound and form sanctified in *Om*, the supreme Sanskrit syllable consisting of the 3 mother-sounds (a·u·m) and linking the triad of creation, preservation and destruction by speaking the electromagnetism (EM) of the word into being. This exact EM force was first studied by Galileo and made popular by Hans Jenny's work as "Cymatics," to address the physical patterns produced by the vibratory interaction of waves.

Gematria: the word speaks of the QKabbalistic art and science of making the numerals speak by sensing, computing, transposing and inquiring on Hebrew codes that link the soul of words through their numerical value. The goal of revealing the order in information thus far scrambled is to inspire you and I to be increasingly accountable. For example, the word *Echad* and the word *Ahavah* have the same value of 13. *Echad* means "one," *Ahavah* means "love." The link is clear! :-)

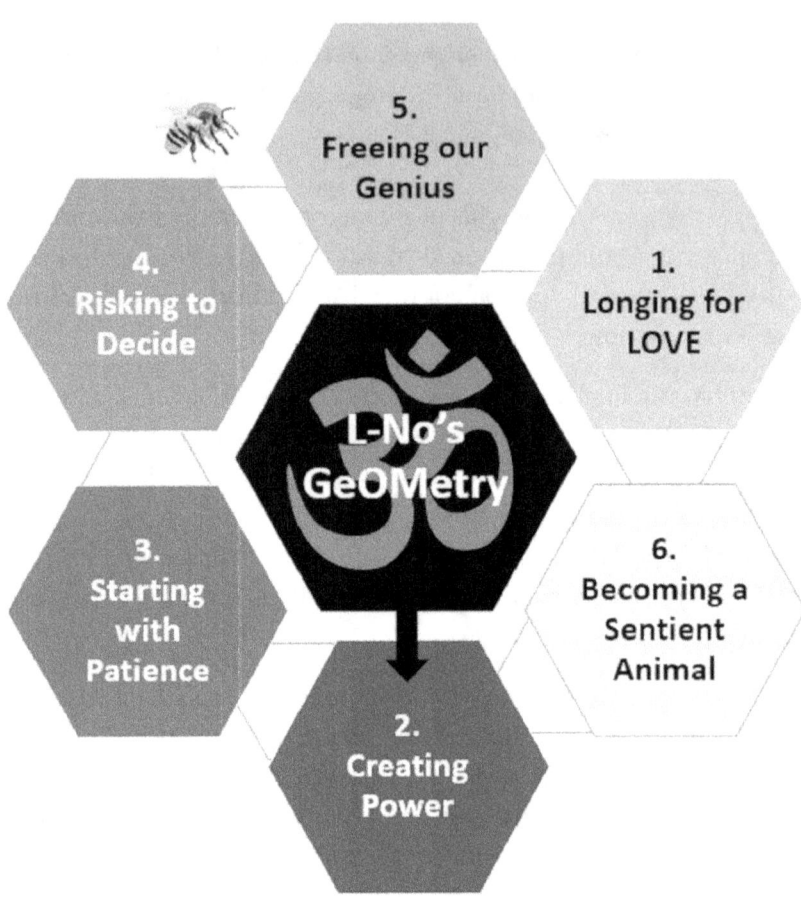

Detailed View of *the Creativity of Genesis 1:1* as SIX Chapters

The word "geOMetry" is coined to include the sacred marriage of sound and form sanctified in *Om*, the supreme Sanskrit syllable consisting of the 3 mother-sounds (a·u·m) and linking the triad of creation, preservation and destruction.

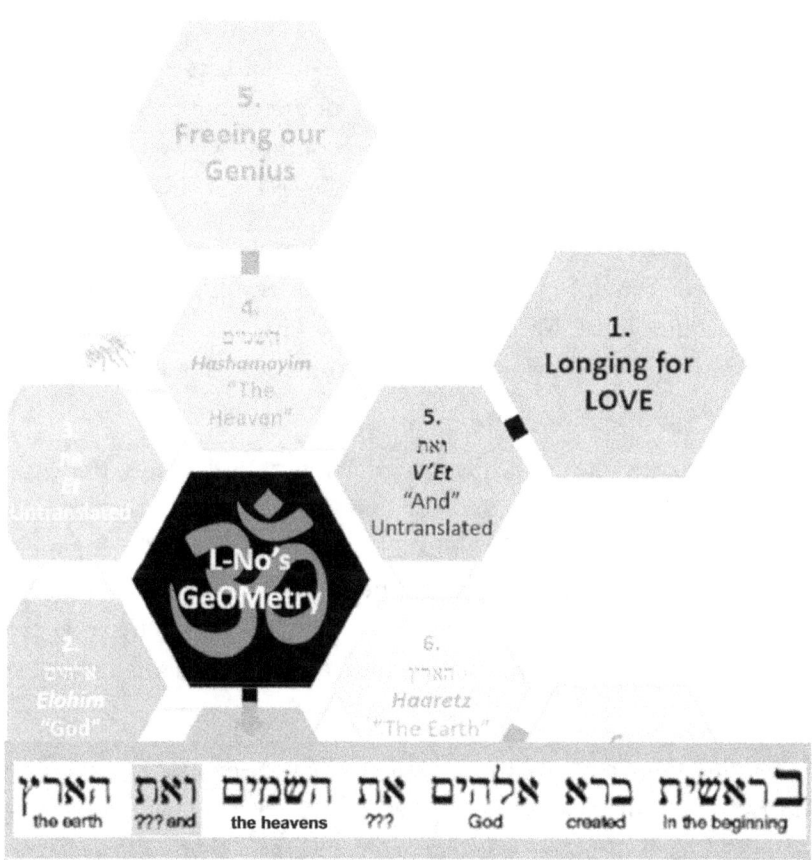

This chapter emanates from and inquires on the 5th word after "in the beginning." Highlighted in the line above, its letters are read as *V'Et. V* means "and," and *Et* is the 2nd particle that is untranslated. This particle follows the transitive verb "to create" and precedes its direct object "the earth."

Introducing "Longing for LOVE"

"I am fond of them, of the inferior beings of the abyss, of those who are full of longing." *Richard Wagner*

The "particle" that cannot be translated is the longing that occurs when I send the Sacred Feminine into exile and stop giving myself the permission to feel. As a result, I become increasingly lonely; lonely and hungry for tender care and compassion. What I crave is the mystical experience of giving it all to Love. This *is* exalting Love.

As for the letters of "LOVE," they are themselves exalted by being capitalized. Why? It is because LOVE endeavors to transmit the most potent "God" Name of the Bible. This is a paradigm shift since, unlike a translation, a transmission allows me to feel a word – to "grok" it.

Besides evoking the most liberating feeling of all feelings, the word LOVE is also an acronym for four universal archetypes that operate as One: L for Leader, O for Officer, V for Visionary, E for Engineer (see *Order in the Chaos* section). As the breadth of the four S/Hebrew letters is now perfectly conveyed by English, I can better feel the sacredness of the language of the soul, and gain insights into what LNO calls "the quadrature of consciousness."

Ever since the Greek philosophers, there have been many attempts to derive from four-based typing systems a structure real enough that it could be used to evolve our character and from there our decision-making process. A lot becomes clear when I see that number 4, as in *Genesis 4*, is linked to Cain – the first murderer and, as such, the star-crossed lover of the Bible. Indeed, it is at Cain's conception that the Four-lettered Name that is translated as "LORD" and transmitted here as "LOVE" first appeared. While the "God" Name that is "created-SIX" is health, the Four-lettered Name speaks of a need for healing, starting with my relationship to power.

While reminding me of my mortality, Cain also readies me for how truth will change my life. Truth is the password to "God" and, by extension, to LOVE. Being ready for truth is also being ready to give it all. It is how I shift from the love of power (or its aversion) to the power of Love.

Chapter 1

The Energy of Longing

"Ask and it will be given to you; seek and you will find; knock and the door will be opened to you." *Matthew 7:7*

It is insane: why would I yearn and pine for Love when it is my nature to be Love? Why, as the song goes, would I be "looking for love in all the wrong places?" To answer, I must ask myself another question: how does it feel to resist what I know I am to do? Indeed, I have this voice inside me that persists in telling me what to do. But I won't do it... I don't want to! If I followed my heart and did what it told me to do, I would probably like myself more. And as my self-esteem would steadily increase, it is also likely that I would be able to transcend my limitations and reach the goals that I set for myself. LOL, I may even find the courage to set goals as I play at life's treasure quest and take the chance to receive what I ask for...

It may seem like a joke to ask: "would you prefer being rich and healthy, or poor and sick?" And yet, I have wondered why I would not act in a way that was congruent with having health and wealth. Why choose – albeit unconsciously – to focus on being poor and sick?

Might it be because, as long as I can stay wounded, I have an excuse not to change? While I can hear that the truth will set me free, it appears that I don't want freedom; I just want freedom from responsibility. I am so afraid to take charge of my life that I'll handicap myself just so that I could still operate in the dark, manipulate, and even lie if I must. Moreover, what will "they" say if I were to change myself and let the divine organically live in me, as the Word made flesh? Surely, health is correlated to how much of my power I will allow myself to claim, once I realize that power depends on how ready I am to know the truth.

Help! How do I gather my wits to jump into truth and enter the "House of God?" How do I dare be born anew and accept that there will be a discontinuity from the old me? The old was a tiny mind, poor and sick; the new is vast, healthy and rich.

The poet Rabindranath Tagore had also been searching for God for millions of lives. He has seen Him sometimes, far away, near a star, but by the time he reached that star, God had moved to some other place. But he went on searching as he was determined to find God. To his greatest surprise, he eventually arrived at a door and on the door was a sign: "God's House." He was ecstatic; beyond himself in joy!

And just as he was about to knock on the door, an idea stopped him: "if this were really God's home, then all my questing, seeking and searching would be finished... I'd be free of yearning! And then what? He became so afraid of how "God" would change his life that he ran like he had never run before. The poem ends with "I am still searching for God. But now, I know his home, so I avoid it and search everywhere else. Knowing God is a danger: I risk being annihilated.

But deep down I know that my search is not for God; my search is to feed the misery of my ego."

I HAVE THIS VOICE INSIDE ME THAT KEEPS ON TELLING ME [FILL IN THE BLANK]. BUT I WON'T DO IT... I DON'T WANT TO!

HOW DOES IT FEEL TO RESIST WHAT I KNOW I AM TO DO?

Exalting "LOVE"

"And yet I wish but for the thing I have; My bounty is as boundless as the sea, My love as deep; the more I give to thee, The more I have, for both are infinite." *William Shakespeare, Romeo and Juliet*

Love is big. Is it because it is so BIG as a power that I am afraid to love, terrified that this power would blossom inside of me? While it seems safer to hold on to my stuff, I can also realize that love is not personal; it is sacred. It can heal and it can kill. It will take everything from me, clearing my thoughts of enmity so thoroughly that I would be a conduit of Love and let the light run through me.

This sacred flow is "God." It is what gives me the strength to do the impossible. When I experience it, I call it Love. When I just love for the sake of loving (and nothing else), the celestial forces begin to trust me and work through me. That is why love is so beautiful. It is because it allows me to forget about myself and surrender to some-thing much bigger, where matter transforms into energy and where living in survival turns to living by design!

Ah... If Love is to stop making it about me, how do I get there? I am yet to touch such boundlessness that I would only wish for what I have and stop wishing for what my brother has!

If I'm hungry, it is because I long for the courage of hearing the Voice saying "follow me" and of giving it all to Love, no strings attached. This is exalting Love. It is mystical, magical and magnificent! This *is* exalting Love. There is nothing more extraordinary than saying YES to the divine call. Therein is the satiety I seek – the sense of enough. If it is so wonderful, why won't I let that wild force run through me like crazy? Why don't I have the courage to say: "bring it on, God! I now give you my word and I won't break it. I will not be a doer on my own. From now on, my action is yours. Rather than resisting you, I will do what you say. I will no longer block Love when Love is the only force that has the power to heal."

But why oh why do I hesitate speaking these words?

The thing is: I don't feel safe! I have the thought that, if I became "as boundless as the sea" and no longer had the reassurance of my self-imposed limitations, I would be too exposed. I also have the thought that I need to protect my assets. My greed is how I play small. This is also how the letters of LOVE are big. The uppercases alert me that something else is going on. As I am soon to see, there is a name for the intelligence that rules over (my) life. This energy is known in Sanskrit as *Iswara* (ईश्वर) and in Hebrew as YEWE (יהוה) or "the Four-lettered Name." The traditional translation as "LORD" fails to address that this Name is a verb or a process by which to adopt the behavior of LOVE and be Leader, Officer, Visionary, Engineer.

By being the transmission of the Hebrew Four-Lettered Name, LOVE goes as deep as it can be given, for it to be "received." Once the four individual parts of me (heart, body, soul and mind) are synergized, I connect to a greater intelligence – to the mind of "God." Since I know that it is my nature to be Love, I no longer have to suffer from the consequences of my words and actions. I am free, free and fulfilled! Clearly, more is to come on a Name which can provide such an exaltation that I would wake up from the dream of separation as I open to the reality of Oneness.

ONCE THE FOUR INDIVIDUAL PARTS OF ME (MY LEADER'S HEART, MY OFFICER'S BODY, MY VISIONARY'S SOUL AND MY ENGINEER'S MIND) WORK TOGETHER AS ONE LOVE, I CONNECT TO A GREATER MIND AND NO LONGER FEAR THE CONSEQUENCES OF MY ACTIONS. I AM FREE, FREE AND FULFILLED!

The Soul of LOVE

"We are all agreed that your theory is crazy. The question which divides us is whether it is crazy enough to have a chance of being correct." *Niels Bohr*

Going within takes courage as it bypasses thinking. Yes, the soul's calling is to dare to become fluent in the irrational. As such, it is a door open to madness. How will I suspend what I rely on most (my great rationalism) in order to follow a guidance that is often as outrageous as it is provocative? How do I let go of the solidity of the 3D world to enter the non-sense of the 6D world? Crazy, indeed! And yet, my soul is not logical; it is mysterious. It can do what my body can't, e.g.; time-travel at night to strange universes where supranatural forces can heal me and restore me. Only the soul has the capacity to release the darkness from my flesh and bones so that I would heal.

The more seemingly unendurable the times we traverse, the hungrier we are for a sense of awe that stretches us towards something greater than ourselves – toward the sacred. But will we acknowledge that there's a big elephant in our way? Our society has chosen to banish the soul by making its vocabulary taboo, starting with words such as GOD, LAW, SIN, SEX. These "minor" prompts – BIG 3-lettered ideograms, truly – have great cause to frighten us, since they encompass both the nature and the function of consciousness in the form of a quadrature (two by two).

The soul has its own language, as generous as the language of poetry, love and romance. Its language is sacred as it is a conduit of grace, allowing for divine intervention and inspiration. Even more so surprising, if I were but to let myself be carried by its metaphors, I might simultaneously practice soul skills and let go of my fear of money. Did I even notice that the soul vocabulary also includes the financial lingo, e.g.; grace and "gratuity," "saving," "trust," "bond," "redemption..." Such may be the goal of *psychology* as the "logos of the soul" – to free my soul from the shackles of the material world.

On that note, how free is my creation of money? How thick is my belief in scarcity? Do I take full responsibility for the consequences of my actions or do I want to make "you" pay? These are questions asked by the power of accountability – namely, the "LORD" of the Four-lettered Name as the foundational quadrature. Transitioning into the mystical is adopting the behavior of LOVE and entering the realm of self-empowerment. It is a realm where I detach from false sense impressions, forgive and remember my sacred contract with the divine. Finally, I can understand the necessity of evil, its purpose and stop asking why... A revelation, truly! :-)

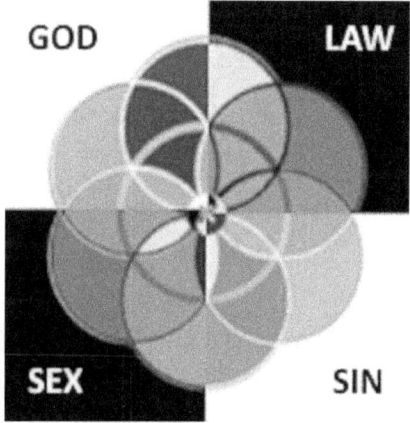

The Quadrature of Consciousness

The quadrature of consciousness uses 3-lettered words that act as ideograms to pair opposites concepts in consciousness.
For example, **GOD** and **LAW**, **SIN** and **SEX**...

GOD is the Whole.
LAW is the patterns of the Whole.
SEX is the desire for the Whole.
SIN is the resistance within the Whole.

THE MORE SEEMINGLY UNENDURABLE THE TIMES I TRAVERSE, THE HUNGRIER I AM FOR A SENSE OF AWE THAT STRETCHES ME TOWARDS SOMETHING GREATER THAN MYSELF – TOWARD THE SACRED. BUT WILL I ACKNOWLEDGE THAT THERE'S A BIG ELEPHANT IN MY WAY?

The Four of LOVE

"There are four questions of value in life, Don Octavio. What is sacred? Of what is the spirit made? What is worth living for and what is worth dying for? The answer to each is the same. Only love." *Lord Byron*

Language is sacred, especially when it emanates from a combination of traditional scriptures – like the Tao, the Gita, the Popol Vuh, the Hebrew Bible, the New Testament, the Qur'an, etc. It is also sacred since speaking is a creative act. This is conveyed by the magical formula *Abracadabra* coming from the Aramaic and meaning "I create as I speak." Henceforth, the work in consciousness is to become aware of the story I tell.

Certainly, it will take courage for the soul to make its exodus out of the land of bondage that has me attached to a slave narrative, and resentful of the power I perceive you have over me. Just how fulfilled do I wish for my soul's expression to be? How free do I imagine my genius could be? Eventually, I will be so empty of my illusions that I'll become a channel for the sacred – a vessel that won't tolerate empty words anymore. I will have no need to justify or explain myself. I also will have nothing to sell which also means that I will have transcended my fear of money. Instead of speaking of Love, I'll just silently radiate it and transfer the Love that I am.

However, before I can resonate with the golden sounds of silence, I still need to ennoble my silver tongue. Is there really a way for me to be of One language; One speech – saying what I feel and meaning what I say? For only then will I hear and be heard.

Time has come to deepen my understanding of the Four of LOVE. I have already met the "LORD" as the Four-lettered Name. These four letters are a verb or a process by which to understand both the truth of oneness and the truth of separation. In truth, I must consciously separate from the past in order to create anew. Yet while doing so, I am still fundamentally one with everything. This is best represented by the number 2 as the two dots through which to draw a line (literally). To be or not 2B becomes the question when I square the number 2 and come to 4.

The table below reveals the order of the four of LOVE, an order which is sourced in the "sexual" knowledge of good and evil. Indeed, the side of good vibrates with the male's positive flow, and the side of evil, with the female's negative flow. As for knowledge itself, it is neutral as it joins opposites. In turn, knowledge leads to three sets of four: the four archetypes of LOVE (e.g.; L for Leader), the four instruments used by these archetypes (e.g.; the Leader uses his heart), and finally, the quadrature of consciousness accessing these instruments (e.g.; the heart of the Leader turns to GOD).

Good (Male/Yang)	Sexual Knowledge (Neutral)		Evil (Female/Yin)
Leader	Engineer	Officer	Visionary
Heart	Mind	Body	Soul
GOD	SIN	LAW	SEX

Revealing the Order of the Four of LOVE

Consider: When I only desire to do "good" and only resist doing "evil," I am not troubled by the consequences of my actions.

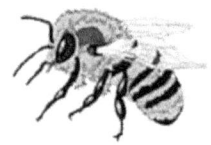

JUST HOW FULFILLED A SOUL'S EXPRESSION DO I WISH TO HAVE? HOW FREE WOULD MY GENIUS BE IF I COULD JUST STOP RESISTING BEING, DOING OR HAVING WHAT I KNOW IS "GOOD" FOR ME?

The Star-Crossed Lover

"To burn with desire and keep quiet about it is the greatest punishment we can bring on ourselves." *Federico García Lorca*

MY NAME IS CAIN. Being the first mortal and the first murderer, I have a vested interest in understanding all I can about karma, free will and destiny. Specifically, why did I create the painful reality I created? Heck! I may even be responsible for legal debacle that can't even answer the question: which came first, the crime or the law? I am also the first to serve the "LORD" of karma – a Name whose four Hebrew letters will soon be explained as the power of accountability. Indeed, it is only by being true to my word that I'll stop being a victim of my biology and transcend my fate.

Accountability is no easy matter. While I want to make my own informed choices, I won't accept the consequences of my decisions. I even think that "my punishment is greater than I can bear." *Genesis 4:13* Truth be told, I'm like a child: I want to do what I want, but ultimately, I'd like you to pick up the pieces. It's like wanting to drink all I want today, and refusing to accept tomorrow's hangover!

To put things in context, my parents – Adam and Eve – had just been kicked out of Paradise when they had me. As the firstborn, I inherited the most concentrated essence of good genes, but also of bad genes. Urgh! This produced a marked tendency to break the law in a bigger way than what they had ever done. Ah, the sin of the parents which visits the children up to the third and fourth generations; it's no joke! **And here's what I don't get: why did my mother call me *Cain*, a name which in Hebrew means "possessed by jealousy?" Is it for me to continue to feel that I'm fallen, not enough, a misfit?**

As it happened, I felt utterly powerless to be recognized for my gifts. Conversely, my brother Abel had no issue getting "God's" love, approval and recognition. Seeing that I could not succeed, I was so angry that I ended up killing him! Henceforth, my story is really about healing my relationship to power. Here is how it is expressed in English, a language that is surprisingly the best conveyor of Hebrew thus far: *I can't* contains the letters of "Cain," and *able*, of "Abel." Both my name and my life story hint to the core of the work: the acquisition of wholesome power which mirrors the development of consciousness. Without it, any real change is doomed.

To change the letters of CAIN into a sustainable I CAN, I must wake up from the dream and take full responsibility for my actions. I then increasingly understand that free will is an illusion, and stop causing results I would rather not have to account for. But I'm still trapped. I can't change (or die or rest in peace) since "God" put a stupid mark on my forehead to prevent anyone from killing me. This "mark, miracle, proof" is the meaning of *Ot*, a Hebrew word which can also be read as "the first and the last [letters]" – the Alpha and the Omega. When I understand that the alphabet is law and that its law is to join opposites in view to remain centered, I will no longer have the same reaction to conflict. Instead of resisting change, I'll embrace truth and find myself fortified in it.

My name is Cain and my story is really about healing my relationship to power. Here is how it is expressed in English, a language that is surprisingly the best conveyor of Hebrew thus far: I can't contains the letters of "Cain," and able, of "Abel." Henceforth, my life story hints to the core of the work: the acquisition of wholesome power which mirrors the development of my consciousness. Without it, any real change is doomed.

The Healing of LOVE

"In the beginning was the end, the time when I can choose peace and rest while I work." *Opening of The Code of Opposites – Book 1*

This page is written from the "WE" perspective. Here is why... The vision of *The LOVE that has No Opposite* – a Love stronger than death – is offered as the culmination of a surreal body of work that had only one prayer: to heal by remembering to rest in the peace of the present moment, no matter how chaotic. It is thus a call to transcend the need to push/pull, and feel the yearning that is behind *our* misuses of power. Not only do we need to heal our power issues individually, but also and foremost, power has been so corrupted that power, itself, is collectively in dire need of healing.

The acquisition of wholesome power is what propels the evolution train. If doubting it, I can always ask myself: what can I do today that I couldn't do ten years ago? To signify power's formidable impact, LNO will, from now on, capitalize its initial "P."

The mission of LNO and of *The Code of Opposites* (the 3-book series following it) is to heal our relationship to Power. To do so, it reveals the force of a sacred language that guides us to the quantum field in between, where to transcend our beliefs of right and wrong, and know in our blood that the divine has no religion and no elect. By becoming fluent in "God's" language – in the paradox, feeling and sensing the all-pervading realities that beckon us now, we open to the LOVE that has no opposite, and experience Health in all levels of our communication.

Choosing to experience Health (Health with a big H), especially when a crisis has befallen us, is asking for a direct experience of the mystical. Whether this miracle of grace – this synchronicity – happens in a spiritual workshop, in a church or in the privacy of our own bedroom, it is still the unequivocal willingness to surrender it all to a Higher Power and shift out of (or "forgive") the known in order to enter the Mystery. In that sense, mysticism may just be the only proven track to healing since, to heal, I must turn away from the Love of Power and return to the Power of Love.

This is how this book includes Sacred Names, Names that have been held for eons to be charged with the Power of Creation. If it is true that the Hebrew alphabet is imbued with life, it becomes our responsibility to treat it with as much respect as any other life form. To this end, there is an ancient mystical law that protects books inscribed with such Names, preventing any of its pages from being recycled as secular writing. It asks us that any hard copies would be treated as holy and returned to the earth when complete.

These names are ancient. To transmit their force, they waited for humanity to be so sincere in its quest for enlightenment that they would not only want, but also and foremost that they would choose to know the truth.

MYSTICISM MAY JUST BE THE ONLY PROVEN TRACK TO HEALING SINCE, TO HEAL, I MUST TURN AWAY FROM THE LOVE OF POWER AND RETURN TO THE POWER OF LOVE.

The Health of GR ("Giving/Receiving") it All

"Words that are as a honeycomb are sweet to the soul and healing to the bones." *Proverbs 16:24*

Understand. Choose peace. emPower the NOW

The English word "honeycomb" becomes "honey-string" in German. When I follow the thread that strings the REAL and the UNREAL sides of the Word, I am healed by the authenticity of its divine expression. But when I hide from the Four-lettered Name calling me to give it all to LOVE, I can't see that the structure of the Word (its "bones") is "created-SIX," just like the shape of a honeycomb.

Instead, I am only seeing the absence of **LOVE** from my life. When there is **no Leader to intuit**, I identify to the **broken heart**. When there's **no Officer to sense**, I identify to the **pain body**. When there's **no Visionary to feel**, I identify to the **lost soul**. When there's **no Engineer to think**, I identify to the **split mind**. Having lost track of the quantum place in between, I can't taste the honeyed nectar of the "created-SIX," which may be how I won't heal. But when I see beyond the karmic four and accept the paradox of the twin **INgénues** (the two archetypes support the four of LOVE), I fall and rise "**IN-LOVE**" with life!

Consider: the pain of **not becoming** my authentic Self is what keeps me from vibrating with the health of **GReed INgénue**, the part of me that is so "ingenuous" or candid in her greed that her voice is no longer a **screech**. In turn, the pain of **not being** who I Am is what keeps me from vibrating with the health of **GRace INgénue** – the part of me that is so "ingenious" or innovative that I would free my **forsaken spirit**.

When I hide from the Four-lettered Name calling me to give it all to LOVE, I can't see that the structure of the Word (its "bones") is "created-SIX," just like the shape of a honeycomb. I am only seeing the absence of LOVE from my life. Unable to overcome the lack, I lose the equilibrium of giving and receiving...

Code Equilibrium - AM / M / MT

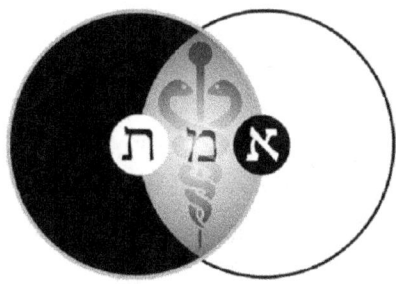

Imagine a language so pure and so sacred that it can reconcile opposites in just 3 letters...

Right dot: First Hebrew letter Aleph (א) → **A** in Roman script
Middle: Middle Hebrew letter Mem (מ) → **M** in Roman script
Left dot: Last Hebrew letter Tav (ת)→ **T** in Roman script

Here is how S/Hebrew inscribes code "Equilibrium" in 3 words:

- From right to middle to left, I read *Emet* (אמת) for "truth."
- From right to middle, I read *Im* (אמ) for "mother."
- From middle to left, I read *Met* (מת) for "death."

The Decoding: this code departs from code Communication which was written via AT/TA. AT or *Et* is the entire alphabet but also the "untranslatable" particle of the Law. In this sense, AT is the logos or the "Word." It is made flesh via TA or *Tah*, the "cell." In this sense, TA is the eros. In the image above one letter is added to AT/TA: the letter Mem (M). Together the three letters form the word *Emet* (אמת) for "**Truth**." Truth is the password to "God." It gives me the sense of my own equilibrium by synergizing the communication of the logos and its incarnation within the eros. When I tell the truth, I feel what I say and I say what I mean. My words are not empty. They are alive!

The sense of poise that I experience when I am authentic in my relating is conveyed by the alphabet. Read from right to left, the three letters of the word *Emet* mark exactly the beginning (א), the middle (מ) and the end (ת) of the Hebrew alphabet (see image below). Hence, the equilibrium of consciousness can be experienced through 22/27 lettered-stages that are "PAIRfectly" ordered as initiations in the Law of LOVE. Stages in consciousness are to be earned, an earning which is the true meaning of "redemption." Dying to one stage prompts me to be reborn into the next stage.

א ב ג ד ה ו ז ח ט י כ ך ל **מ** ם נ ן ס ע פ ף צ ץ ק ר ש ת

The balanced rhythms of life and death are within the word *Emet* itself: when erasing the last letter Tav, I am left with the word *Im* (AM) for "**mother**" or the giver of life. When erasing the white letter Aleph (א), I am left with the word *Met* (MT) for "**death**." To do so requires readiness for how "truth" will change my life. Mem is "M-middle," the stage in between death and rebirth. As a word, *Mem* means "pairs of water," a strange formulation which will make more sense in *Chapter 5,* with *The End of Craving.*

In plain English: one day, I will die. And on that day, I will let go of my illusions, and stand at once strong and flexible in truth – in equilibrium. I will then see that, where there is truth, there is death, and where there is death, there is truth. I also will know that LOVE is stronger than death.

The Truth of LOVE

"I am still searching for God. But now, I know his home, so I avoid
it and search everywhere else. Knowing God is a danger: I risk
being annihilated. But deep down I know my search is not for
God. It is to feed the misery of my ego." *Rabindranath Tagore*

"God" is Love and Love is the realization of ultimate truth. To live it, I
know that I must pay the price which is to drop the story and stop the
lies. The truth continues to be the key to knowing the purity of my
soul: the more honest I am, the more I return to innocence.
Conversely, the more I lie to myself, the more my actions are
constrained by the garments of shame. The truth moves (and moves
me) at the speed of light, while the lie hides in the skirts of unconscious time. When I open my eyes, nothing is ever the same.

**Here is what gets my attention: if truth is the great game changer
and if the work of transformation is about readying myself for
truth, why do I entertain illusions of lack which keep me from
knowing that "God" loves me?**

To begin with, truth takes a lot of growing up to handle. Moreover, as
long as I don't grow up, clean up, and wake up, I can still exist as a
wound, attach to the story of unrequited love and blame "you" for my
failures: "after all I've done for you, you should be a better son, a
better friend, a better lover, a better boss!" I ask you to love me, while
knowing deep down that loving me is *my* job! I tell myself that
spending my life questing, longing and pining for truth is more
comfortable than being an instrument of truth. But is it? The journey
of life is the shattering of my illusions. Every choice I make is either a
lie or a truth. The more I choose truth, the more impersonal I am and
the more attractive I become. So why can't I let "you" go? Why can't I
move on and let bygones be bygones?

It is because I have needs. Whether I am with you in the name of
family, business or romance, I still *need* you to validate me. What a

vicious circle: I want you to believe in me because I don't buy me. I don't buy me because I keep on betraying myself by looking for Love outside of me. Will I ever realize that truth is where I can feel the Power of the Power of Love? Instead, I continue to lie and ask you to decide for me, even though I resent the need to get your counsel. Why give you Power over my soul instead of releasing myself to the light? I long to be my own person and not to need anybody's love, approval and recognition but my own. I hunger to have enough faith in me and "God" (same) that I'd abandon myself to love, wildly; unabashedly. Oyveh! I want truth and I don't even know it!

The thing is: I will need your approval as long as I resist my intuition (a.k.a. my conscience). I know what to do. I just don't want to do it! I'm terrified of doing what would lead me to trust myself because if I really honored my guidance, I'd become whole, and then there would be no more misery hungering for your company. I would be all alone, for my very idea of relationship would no longer be based on *needing* you or on confusing intimacy with the sharing of my wounds.

Indeed, when I stop clinging to your approval, "you" stop withdrawing. What would you withdraw from? I can now accidentally stumble on the truth of I Am, see at the speed of the light of the soul, and have the self-esteem to heal my relationship to Power.

I TELL MYSELF THAT SPENDING MY LIFE QUESTING, LONGING AND PINING FOR TRUTH IS MORE COMFORTABLE THAN BEING AN INSTRUMENT OF TRUTH. BUT IS IT, TRULY?

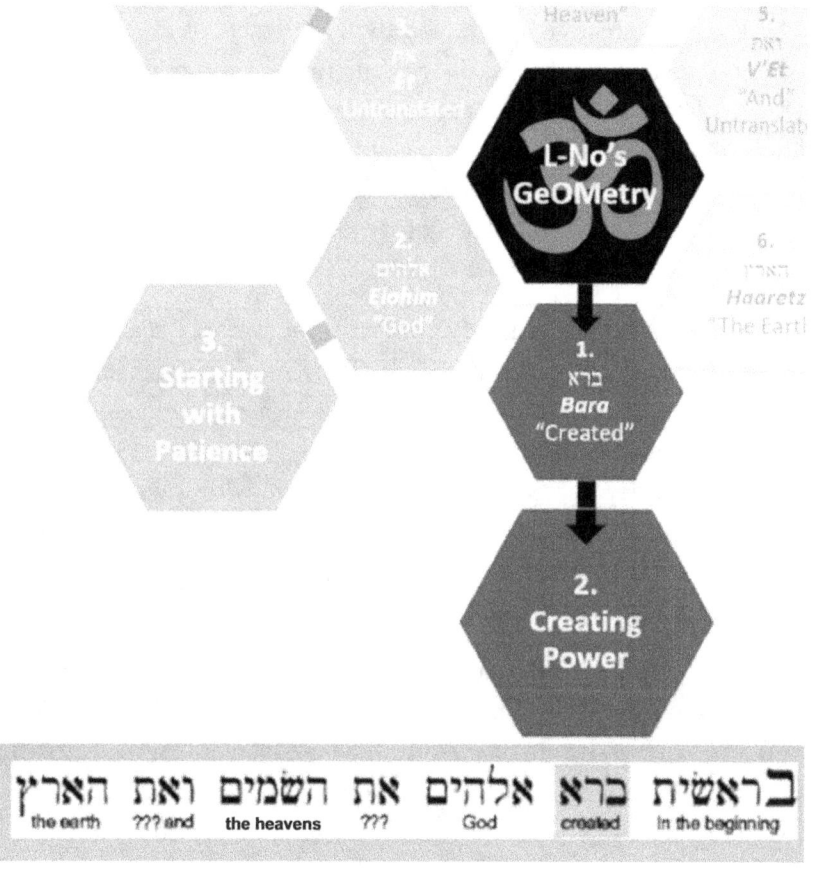

This chapter emanates from and inquires on the 1st word after "in the beginning." Highlighted in the line above, its letters are read as *Bara* for "created…"

Introducing "Creating Power"

"I think that we're greater than we think, more powerful than we know, more unlimited than we could ever dream." *Joe Dispenza*

The Power to create is unequivocally the greatest of all Powers. But what is my creation of Power? Do I tend to push and make it abusive? Do I loathe Power so much that I'd withdraw from using it? Do I even know what I want to create, and why I want to create it? Or am I just resigned to having a limited creativity? This brings the question: since the power games I play with "you" have become old, how do I play a bigger game?

Understanding creation is, after all, what *the Book of Genesis* ought to convey, if it were actually "received!" This "receiving" is the sense of the word *QKabbalah*. It leads me to open to what consciousness does: to call upon the light and frequencies of letters, numbers and symbols in order to create. Hence, I will begin with 10 letters, which, in S/Hebrew, are also 10 words. These ten words are actually the accurate translation of *Asseret Hadebarim*, which strangely became rendered as "ten commandments."

The more I understand that these "10 words" are the first 10 letters of the alphabet, the more I recognize that they spell the Law of LOVE, and the truer I am to my word. These "10 words" are certainly powerful enough to reorganize my sense of the law. Rather than an external device that represses what I cannot accept within myself, the law now becomes a letter of LOVE, so that I could be, let "BEE," and in so doing, release my creative Power. I still must remain aware of the dark side of Power.

Bringing light on my hunger for superpowers is how to stop the madness of swinging from "I am special" to "I am not enough." Instead, I become a nobody. Anonymity is how to no longer sell my soul. By becoming anonymous, I come to what is termed *siddhis* in Sanskrit. Making room for Powers that seem supernatural, the *siddhis* are the complete understanding that there's only One of us. Once "received," I can climb the ladder of success without fearing to fall or do harm to myself and others (same) in the process.

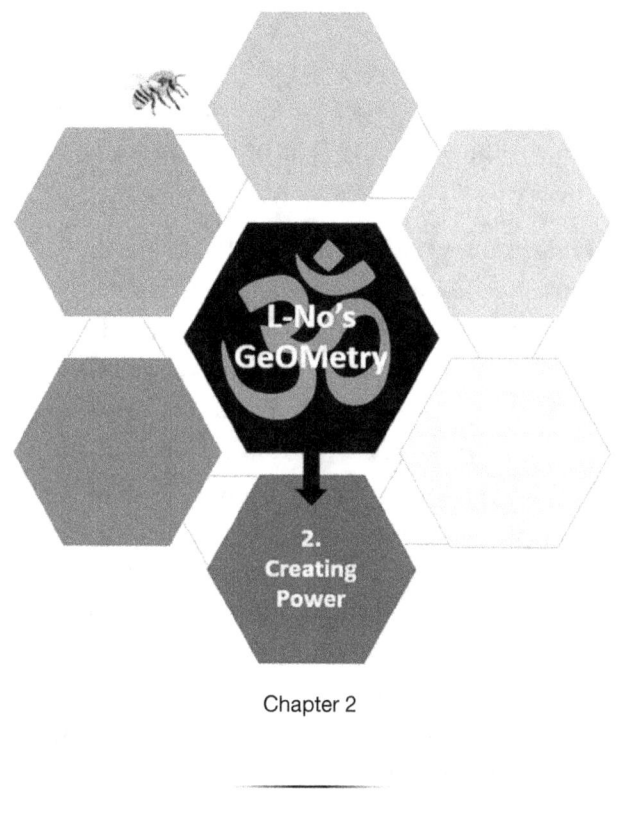

Chapter 2

Willpower

"Choice, not chance, determines your destiny." *Aristotle*

Saying that "it was written, decreed and established" completely contradicts the recent meme of "you create your reality," a meme calling me to inquire on how I think of "God" and of the creative process. Can I really command the kind of life I want to have or am I just a cog in a wheel?

Truly, just how free is my will? For now, what I am defining as "me" is the feeling and the sense of being the locus of attention, but also the locus of agency. I can do whatever I desire since I am the doer of the action. Am I not who is reaching for this cup? Am I not who prefers coffee over tea? As the author of my thoughts and my actions, I made a conscious decision to do so. I am the thinker of my thoughts, the doer of my actions. And yes, I can also recognize that there's a difference between a voluntary action (e.g.; lifting my arm) and an involuntary action (e.g.; a tremor).

And it still makes me wonder... If my will were so free, why would I choose to cause consequences that I would rather not have to experience? Why would I say that I want to be healthy, and act in a way that sickens me? Why would I choose to observe lack over abundance? Moreover, if it is my will, why can't I have the willpower to resist short-term temptations in order to meet long-term goals? Oftentimes, I hear myself say: "I had no choice" when my soul knows it is a lie. I can choose. I just don't want to put in the necessary effort to experience an excellent outcome. Might excellence be such hard work (or so intimidating) that I'd choose to remain in the dark and snooze a little bit longer? Tomorrow, I'll do what it takes. But tomorrow never comes! Also surprising, I seem to be unable to get over the fact that for every action, there's an equal and opposite reaction... The fact that it was established by Newtonian science as the third law of motion makes little difference to me.

Here is a cross-cultural connection that sheds a different light on willpower: the sister and counterpart of Arabic *Maktub* for "it is written" is Hebrew *Ketubah*. *Ketubah* is the written prenuptial "agreement" that my soul signed, whether I know it or not, with whom many term "God." This contract is sacred, as it has been inscribed in the ether of Akashic records way before the beginning of time – way before the beginning of "me."

What if it were written with the sole intention to design a life that would invite my making THE decision to wake up? Once I became real, I would free my will and be able to choose peace and *feel* joy, no matter what my circumstances are. And since my true quest is emotional well-being (e.g.; when I want money, what I really want is to *feel* safe), wouldn't having the Power to choose peace be a good start?

Yes, but... The idea of predestination is highly disturbing to me. I can accept that the big events of my life; my country, my family, my career, would be "written," but the phone call I just got: was that also planned? Moreover, what about how my motives have different implications in a court of law: did I just kill someone by accident or was it premeditated? So yes, what about my responsibility for what I say and do? Great question: what about it?

If I can choose to be happy, strong and healthy, why don't I? Why can't I exit Scare City and no longer be "possessed" by my possessions? Why can't I decide to elevate my emotions instead of letting them smother me?

Truth be told, I lost my free will and conditioned my body to remain in the past, simply because that's the known. And now, I'm headed into a predictable future. For me to recover the Power to create, I must summon the courage to enter the unknown and open my mind to new possibilities...

IF MY WILL WERE SO FREE, WHY WOULD I CHOOSE TO CAUSE
CONSEQUENCES THAT I WOULD RATHER NOT HAVE TO EXPERIENCE?

The Power to Create

Gentle warning: this content is not suitable for minds unwilling to go beyond the final frontier – the interpretations of the Judeo-Christian scriptures that have worked for eons to split spirit and matter. Even if we abandoned religion, the problem is still with us; in the ideas of Heaven and Hell, the retributions for good and bad deeds, the perception of justice opposing mercy...

Everything I perceive and thus create in the "world" comes from the invisible dimension of thoughts and beliefs. If I want to transform, I must look at the story I tell, and investigate why I believe what I believe. Doing so, I come to realize that I don't know what's for my highest good, I just *think* I do. :-) The more I surrender my illusion of control, the more I can let creation happen through me! This process – which evolves me by humbling me – ends up unleashing my creativity. It is made clearer when traced by the multi-dimensionality of Hebrew letters, from the first (Aleph) to the last (Tav), and back.

Here is how... All cultures use creation myths to attempt to answer the questions we all have on the origin of the universe and the nature of the physical world: what is real? What should I do? What is my purpose? Who am I? According to the Egyptians, in the beginning was darkness, water and the great god Atum. Surprisingly, the Hebrew Bible begins with two creation stories: a primary Adam who thinks "I can," and a secondary Adam who thinks "I can't."

- *Genesis 1 & 2:* just like the word "alphabet" has an Aleph (A) and a Beth (B), the Bible has two stories of creation (A & B) that are both sourced in personal doership. The first story is in *Genesis 1*, when the world was created in six days, and the Adam was created male and female. This Adam uses the Power of <u>simultaneous creation</u> (there is no delay between what s/he wants to create and what s/he sees created). The second story is in *Genesis 2*, when the Adam was in a garden without water or greenery and in an illusion of separation from his female side. This Adam uses the Power of <u>gradual creation</u> (the fulfillment of his desires is postponed to tomorrow). These two Adams create differently: they serve two dissimilar "God" Names, that is, two distinct Powers: Adam A—the Power of synchronicity (s/he lives in present time), Adam B—the Power of history (he lives in the past). Also, these two Adams are as two split atoms: they can't be observed simultaneously, and they are seen to behave differently.

- *Genesis 3*: the snake enters the scene, bringing forth the invention of lying which ushers the Power of <u>destruction</u>. When I don't know my true Self, I am either acting by obeying my family's program or by rebelling against it. But I am not here; not present. I am neither being real nor acting deliberately. It is just the reenacting of a hollow set of instructions. Indeed, the only "sin" that the three players committed was not to take full responsibility for their transgression. Had they been honest and said: "I am so sorry to have violated my own law, and will realign to my intuition," they'd likely still be in PaRaDiSe. But instead, the Adam chose to hate and blame the woman, the woman, the snake, and the snake "God." The sense of enough is now officially destroyed.

- *Genesis 4*: and Adam knew the woman and, unbeknownst to her, she conceived Cain as a last way to understand creation. When knowing the meaning of their children's names – Cain as "possessed by jealousy" and Abel as "vanity," I have a very different take on the moral of the story. Surely, as the first murderer and the first mortal, Cain has a lot to teach me about how dark "my" reality can be. As for the story, Cain was so jealous of the recognition enjoyed by his brother that he killed him. I am Cain, the murderer of my own potential, when I resist feeling the vanity of my evil side. But if I were to become conscious of the evolutionary purpose of evil, I wouldn't need your approval anymore as I would change for good. Little by little, I would delete the old programming of fear and lack, and return to innocence: Paradise found!

Cain's case is so dire that he is ultimately destined to forgive and not take his errors personally. This is the Power of <u>non-causal creation</u>: I am not the doer but a vessel for the creative impulse to move through me.

Unless I decode Cain's name, I cannot really see that it inscribes the end of "the personal" and heals generations forwards and backwards by way of acquiring wholesome Power. And yet, the same letters that write Cain into being also write *Cani* for "innocent." All guilt and subsequent victimization can now stop, since I moved from the illusion of free will (when I use my will to serve personal agendas) to the reality of freed will (when my words and actions serve to co-create the good of all).

THIS EVOLVING PROCESS — BY WHICH TO HUMBLE MYSELF UNTIL I AM AS IF I AM NOT (NOTHING PERSONAL) — UNLEASHES MY CREATIVITY. I CAN NOW PLAY WITH POWER WITHOUT BURNING MYSELF!

A Teacher of Power

"Anyone who wishes to innovate in the Torah is permitted to innovate and interpret everything he wishes, everything that he is lucky enough to innovate through his mind, as long as he does not innovate new laws. It is ever permitted to innovate in the Kabbalah of Rabbi Isaac Luria, according to its possibilities, as long as no new laws are innovated." *Manifesto from Rabbi Nachman, great grandson of the Baal Shem Tov, quoted by Rabbi Marc Alain Ouaknin, in Mysteries of the Kabbalah.*

Written in medieval Aramaic, *Sepher HaZohar,* "The Book of Splendor," is a mystical commentary on the Torah. This huge body of work was authored around 1280 CE by Moses de Leon who claimed that it represented the inspired writings of Rabbi Simeon Bar Yohai. Legend has it that during a time of Roman persecution, Rabbi Simeon hid in a cave for 13 years, studying the Torah with his son, Elazar. During this time, he was inspired by the prophet Elijah to write the Zohar. Before being carried to all the countries where Spanish Jews were forced to exile after the Inquisition, it was at Safed in Palestine that the teachings of the Zohar were prevalent, later revealed by two of the greatest teachers of mysticism: Moses Cordovero and Isaac Luria.

Over time, the Zohar became the only Kabbalistic text acknowledged by the rabbinical community as being almost as important as the Bible and the Talmud. What rendered the Zohar so attractive was its viewpoints on theology and cosmology. The Zohar declared man to be the Lord of Creation since man's moral perfection influences the tree of life and grants immortality. This concept is akin to the concept of *Tiqqun Olam*—the "World of Order" and as such, the "Repair of the World." By practicing virtues, humans increase the outpouring of heavenly grace and, in turn, influence the 3D world.

As for the great teachers, the successor of Moses ben Jacob Cordovero (the "Ramak") was Rabbi Isaac Luria, known as the *Ari* for "Lion."

During a visionary experience, the Ari was instructed by Elijah to return to his birth place, in Safed, where he would meet his main disciple. The Ari arrived in the land of Israel on the exact day of the Ramak's funeral. Joining the procession, he alone saw a sign telling him he was meant to inherit the mantle of leadership left behind by the deceased. Six months later, Rabbi Chaim Vital asked to learn from the Ari, who only lived for two years after that. Yet, in that short time, he revealed a brand-new path in the Kabbalah. His insights were so wise and so powerful that, to this day, studying the Kabbalah involves first and foremost the Ari's writings.

At the heart of the Ari's system is a radical description of the universe's evolution based on the dynamic interplay of five forces within creation:

1. *Tzimtzum* – **the force of "withdrawing:"** before the creation of the world, the *Ain Soph* ("empty-fullness") filled the infinite space. Yet for something to manifest out of nothing, the *Ain Soph* had to "withdraw" itself. *Golden XPR's* vision: this stepping back also explains how the tree of the "unknown" of good and evil is mostly disregarded.

2. 10 *Sephiroth* – **the force of "causing:"** from this withdrawal flowed an "infinite light," until appeared in the center of an empty space ten circles, wheels or dynamic vessels called *Sephiroth*, by means of which the infinite unfolded and multiplied itself, causing something to exist. *Golden XPR's* vision: These ten spheres form the tree of (my) life as the something coming into being from nothing.

3. *Shevirat HaKelim* – **the force of "shattering:"** the three higher circles were able to bear the light, as they were of a purer substance being closer to the *Ain Soph*. Not having the same integrity, the lower spheres exploded into pieces – an event known as "the breaking of the vessels," which was precipitated by *Olam HaTohu* – the "World of Chaos." *Golden XPR's* vision: the sphere that is most concerned by this

catastrophe is *Geburah* for "Power," as any misuse will break it apart and affect the other spheres.

4. *Partzuphim* – the force of "linking:" for the purpose of securing the light, the spheres were transformed, clothed and linked by way of "figures" or "faces," among which the father, the mother, the son and his bride. *Golden XPR's* vision: the goal in linking the faces is for me to gain emotional intelligence as I relate the core archetypes from within.

5. *Tiqqunim* – the force of "redeeming:" the perennial conflict between good and evil can only be resolved through the advent of universal redemption (the *Tiqqun*), which humans can either hinder or expedite through their own actions. *Olam HaTiqqun* or "the World of Order" is inherent to *Olam HaTohu* or "the World of Chaos." *Golden XPR's* vision: the first two *Tiqqunim* (*Tiqqun Nephesh* "repair of the soul" and *Tiqqun Olam* "repair of the world") are quite popular; the third *Tiqqun* (*Tiqqun Cain* "repair of Cain"), not as much. And yet, it is the key to the other two *Tiqqunim* since it is when I feel that something greater than I is the agency behind my words and actions.

In the Lurianic Kabbalah, the breaking of the vessels resulted in the formation of the *Q'lippoth* or "shells" imprisoning the sparks of divine light and exiling them from the divine presence. It is said that some of these shells are so dark that they are irredeemable by man and that only the translucent ones are subject to human restitution.

But what if the result (the shells) preceded the cause (the shattering)? This vision is *Golden XPR's* innovation to the Ari's teachings.

And it makes me wonder... If the great teacher known as the Ari had lived in the era of quantum physics, would he have seen the possibility that the result (or the shells) precedes the cause?

Since everything is here, in the infinite possibilities that are already created as potential, would he also have felt that creation never happened?

The XP-Ari's Redeeming Process

"No human being is so bad as to be beyond redemption." *Mahatma Gandhi*

This is *Golden XPR's* innovation: to propose that the *Q'lippoth* or "shells" are not only caused by the breaking of the vessels; they also precede the cause. Indeed, whether I am aware of it or not, I live in the quantum realm which I access by eating of the tree of the "unknown" of opposites.

In the quantum realm, cause doesn't necessarily come before effect. As such, it is the opposite of everyday life where cause *always* precedes effect. The quantum world is a world where my toast is perfectly golden before I put it in the toaster. I wouldn't just be making breakfast – my breakfast would also be making me! And isn't this what *Elohim* knew when he saw that the effect (light) was *already* created, although the cause (the word) seemed to precede it?

Moreover, if I were to imagine such a rupture between me and "God's" light that I'd explode into fragments that are begging for integration, wouldn't that event be part of a sacred contract? As such, wouldn't that contract be written before the event happened? And isn't it also by cleaning up my errors that I, Cain, can redeem myself from being "possessed by jealousy?" Indeed, it is my destiny to surrender to feeling how dark I can get, and, at last, experience my soul elevated into the light. And as fear and lack are nullified, I can rest while creating. I know my creation already happened: I can relax! This is knowing non-causality.

IT IS WRITTEN THAT I WOULD SURRENDER AND, AT LAST, EXPERIENCE MYSELF RESTING WHILE CREATING. IT ALREADY HAPPENED: I CAN RELAX NOW! THIS IS KNOWING NON-CAUSALITY. IT IS ALSO COMING INTO WISDOM AND WHOLESOME POWER.

Letters of Power

"What consciousness does is to manipulate information in the form of at least numbers, alphabet letters and most generally symbols." *Dr. William A Tiller, Some Sciences Adventures with Real Magic...*

LNO introduces the path of *Golden XPR*. Having language as its foundation, this path acknowledges that language is where my Power is. Indeed, I only "grok" something when I can name it and claim it! *Golden XPR* is not a magical formula, although it is. It doesn't add anything to the incommensurable joy of totality: "I shall love the LORD God with *all* my heart, *all* my soul and *all* my might." *Deuteronomy 6:5* It just gives me codes that are so awesome that they end up inspiring me to give my *all* in each and every moment.

Besides the codes, there is also the transmission of the Powers behind the biblical Names translated as "God" or "the LORD," or "the Almighty..." I have seen how *Elohim* for "God" is explained by *Golden XPR* as the Power of synchronicity, since it is the Name saying "let there be light!" and seeing at the exact same time that there *was* light. Another noteworthy gift is this of a "Smart Bible." The term "smart" comes from the acronym "Self-Monitoring, Analysis and Reporting Technology." My phone is "SMART" because it can talk back to me and even guide my behavior. Will I allow myself to imagine that there could be a psychological decoding of the Bible SMART enough to counsel me out of the desolate confines of my neurosis? Indeed, while I am divided as to my words and actions, I am neurotic. So, can the language of the Bible – once psychologically decoded – really point me to the exit door?

Another honeyed gift which sustains LNO and the path of *Golden XPR* is the common sense of a Theory Of Everything. It works to unravel the universality of our slave narrative so that we could freely respond to the call of LOVE with a big YES. It is true: just like me, you've known loneliness. Just like me, one day you will decide to walk the talk and talk the walk. When that happens, you and I won't "need" an external *Golden XPR*. We will be XPR (for the "light of the Word"), feeling the purity of love as we hear, obey and understand the dictates of our heart.

From right to left: Hebrew letters Samekh, Peh, Resh.

These letters will eventually evolve into Roman script "XPR." The root-verb סֹפֶר may just be the ultimate symbol since it branches into the very words that encompass the nature of consciousness via *sappir* for "sapphire" (and by extension, light), and the function of consciousness via *mispar* for "number," *sephirah* for "sphere, wheel, chakra," *sepher* for "book" (and by extension, letters), and *sippur* for "story" (and by extension, sounds).

In plain English, XPR allows me to eXPloRe, eXPeRience and eXPiRe to my limitations, so that I could eXPRess my true Self.

Dr. William A Tiller was one of the scientists in the movie *What the Bleep Do We Know!?*, a movie that posits that the universe is best seen as constructed from thoughts and ideas rather than from matter.

Power Games

"If I defend myself, I am attacked." *A Course In Miracles*

Whether I am conscious of it or not, and whether I like it or not, I will feel that reality is my nemesis until I wind down the right and wrong game I play. Reality appears to surround me with people and events that contradict me in order to motivate me to embody wisdom and acquire wholesome Power. Will I realize that, in the space where I go into fight or flight, I either play the role of a victim or of its soulmate – the bully? When I don't have the wisdom to know the difference between good or bad, I am divided. Once fragmented, my creative Power is not wholesome. If I resist the conflicts that life brings and continue to refuse to master my emotions, it is because I don't want to be free; I just want to justify keeping my stuff.

Yep, this is worth repeating as it is so easy to forget... One day, I will die. And on that day, I will let go of my illusions, and open to truth. Surely, where there is truth, there is death. Where there is death, there is truth.

In matters of consciousness, stages complement states. The stages are to be earned, while the states are free, the ultimate being enlightenment. I am already experienced with the three basic states of deep sleep, dreaming and waking. While these states are given to me, they can also be lost. For example, as I grow older, the states of deep sleep and dreaming may not be as accessible as they used to be. Stages are different: once I earn a stage (a process which involves peaks and valleys and may take a few years), I own it. On the bright side, stages are the thing I will take with me when I die to the body.

There is another death – this of the false self when I sense how my constantly fighting reality (or "God") magnetizes more nonsense. Layer after layer, I become willing to take responsibility for what my beliefs create. Having the courage (and the intelligence) to turn within and inquire, I understand why I'm stuck in an ambivalence which has me hopelessly swing from aversion to greed, and back. The back-and-forth dance continues until I come to the end of desire when I resist nothing, and, at last, remember the sacredness of choosing peace and of resting in peace.

For now, how sound are my judgment calls? Might I be resisting what is "good" for me? Conversely, might I be desiring what is "bad" for me? FIGHT or FLIGHT | CLING or AVOID | DESIRE or RESIST – these are the signposts indicating that I am playing dangerous Power games against "you" and me.

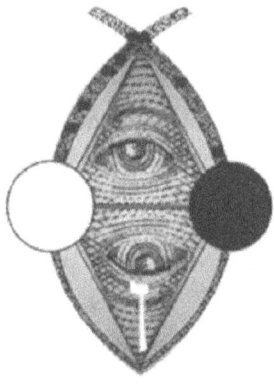

The Fall of Nun Final – the Sign at the End of Resentment

If I am angry at you and make you my enemy, it is because I think that I owe you, or worse, that you owe me. Truly, how taxing will my creation of the material world be? How burdensome was it for the child in me to have witnessed my caretakers repeatedly arguing, as they fought for Power or money, wanting to be right? Might this "write" and wrong game be inscribed in my DNA as follows?

- When I perceive that my male side doesn't want me, my female side acts "hysterically," from Greek *hysterikos* "suffering of the womb." I now tend to overtly attack and over-speak, which is a clear misuse of Power.

- When I perceive that my female side is needy, my male side acts "penis-less," a word coined to describe the nervous disease peculiar to men caused by the curse of forced labor. I now tend to covertly defend and under-speak, which is also a clear misuse of Power.

FOR NOW, HOW SOUND ARE MY JUDGMENT CALLS? MIGHT I BE RESISTING WHAT IS "GOOD" FOR ME? CONVERSELY, MIGHT I BE DESIRING WHAT IS "BAD" FOR ME? FIGHT OR FLIGHT | CLING OR AVOID | DESIRE OR RESIST – THESE ARE THE SIGNPOSTS INDICATING THAT I AM PLAYING DANGEROUS POWER GAMES AGAINST A "YOU" THAT IS ME.

Numbers of Power

> For me to emPower the NOW, I must be able to choose peace. For
> me to choose peace, I may need to understand. Understanding is
> to feel the order inherent to chaos. This felt sense is helped by an
> inquiry that is universal, credible, and radical, as it is sourced in
> sacred geometry from *ge-matria*, Greek for "Earth's measure."

Consider: when I realize that everything in the universe is geometric,
be it people, animals, planets, solar systems, stars, etc., I become
motivated to measure my belief systems on a geometric scale. The
following offers such measurement of beliefs on a geometric scale of 1
to 5:

1. 10=1+0=1 – **the belief in unity:** The question was asked: which is the
most important, the 1st commandment or the 10th commandment?
The 1st is about the LORD "God" who freed me from the land of
Egypt and the house of bondage, and the 10th is about not coveting
anything that belongs to my neighbor. And it makes me wonder...
Aren't the 1st and the 10th the two sides of the same coin? Am I not in
bondage to "Ego-Egypt" (a.k.a. "Scare City") when I believe (as Cain
did) that I can't have what my brother is having? Moreover, instead of
resisting "Ten Commandments," would it free me to understand the
"10 Words?" (more to come on this). Since each Hebrew letter is also a
word, "the 10 Words" refer to the 10 first letters of the alphabet, 10
digits which undergird the structure of the whole alphabet and thus,
of the Law. How? If communication is the *result* of what is said and
done, it speaks to cause and effect, which is a law. Once these 10
Words are felt as the Physics of Belief moving me from chamber to
chamber, they go a long way to inspire me to surrender and join my
10 "fingers" or 10 digits in service to Love, Love being what sustains all
commandments.

Looking at the image below, I see my palms engraved with the tablets
of the law (the 10 Words). Each tablet has 5 letters: 5 for my yin side

and 5 for my yang side. When I no longer split the letter of the law from the spirit of the law, I also no longer observe that the law is coercive. Instead of wanting to run, I stand in awe, touched beyond belief!

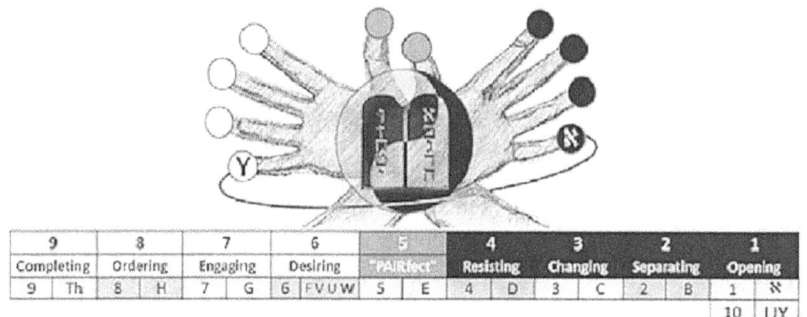

9	8	7	6	5	4	3	2	1	
Completing	Ordering	Engaging	Desiring	PAIRfect	Resisting	Changing	Separating	Opening	
9	Th	8	H	7	G	6	F V U W	5	E	4	D	3	C	2	B	1	א
																	10	I J Y

The Kabbalah of the 9 Chambers, renamed as "the Physics of Belief" by *Golden XPR* showing that the Chamber of 1-Opening holds both the 1st Word Aleph (א) and the 10th Word Yod (Y) – these two commandments are both opening me to LOVE.

2. To be or not 2B – the belief in duality: to the question, what is needed to create a world, G. Spencer Brown states that boundaries are indispensable to create a universe (*Laws of Form*). To this, Ken Wilber adds that there is a second element that is necessary besides boundaries (the differentiation of inside from outside). That element is duality (the differentiation of singular from plural). The symbols of the Hebrew language summarize the understanding of both the polymath and the pundit in just one letter: the letter Beth.

Beth is the sign (ב) that evolved into letter B. It is also the word for "house" or that which divides inside from outside (the very B of Boundaries and Brown). Its value is 2, as the plural of singular Aleph (א) which became Roman letter A – value 1.

When I realize that a Hebrew letter is at once a number, a sound, a picture, an archetype and a word, I begin to accept that the wisdom of the Bible may just be, first and foremost, in its minute essence: the alphabet!

3. Three and tree – the belief in branching: the Power of three is the foundation of all Powers, as it infuses the three flows of the tree of the knowledge of good and evil: male, female and neutral. This is the infamous tree whose fruit I am forbidden to eat unless I am willing to die for it. Surely, the word *Daath* speaks of a biblical "knowledge" that has a clear sexual connotation and is akin to death, as pointed out by the French expression *la petite mort* ("the little death"), a metaphor for an orgasm. The knowledge of opposites is tantalizing as it holds the secret to Power as the work of polarities: male *and* female or good *and* evil. The lovemaking is enacted in the proposition "and" that allows you and I to hold the tension of opposites.

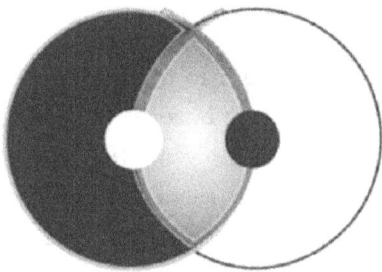

The Three Values of the Vessel of the Fish: Black as
Yin/Evil, White as Yang/Good and Grey as the Knowledge
of the TORA/TAO in between.

This possibility is pictured by the *Vesica Piscis,* Latin for "Vessel of the Fish," a geometry that represents the merging of the two opposite parts of me as I remain poised at the center – a conductor to flow energy in between the two polarities. The vessel's mathematical shape acts as a lens to focus the light. It is formed by the intersection of two disks with the same radius, intersecting in such a way that the center of each disk lies on the perimeter of the other. It symbolizes that all is present at once. Going "in between" is having such understanding that my limiting beliefs let go of me. This quantum place is also "in the midst of the garden, with the tree of life and the tree of the knowledge of good and evil."

4. The Force of the Fourth – belief in order: "one becomes two, two becomes three, and out of the third comes the one as the fourth," said Maria the prophetess. This is illustrated below as the Mystery of the "LORD's" Name whose Hebrew letters are pronounced as Yod Heh Vav Heh (YEWE). This sacred Name most intrigued Greek philosophers who called it the Tetragrammaton, for "four-lettered Name," including it in the Pythagorean Oath: "by that pure, holy, four-lettered name on high, nature's eternal fountain and supply, the parent of all souls that living be, by him, with faith find oath, I swear to thee."

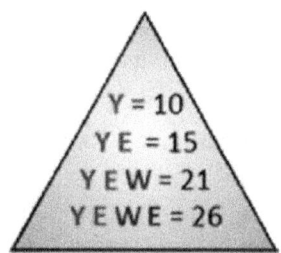

10+15+21+26=72. These are the values of the 10 letters whose progression forms the most potent "God" Name in the Bible – the "Four-lettered Name." The 72 Powers of the Name are held by a tetractys – a triangular figure consisting of 10 signs arranged in four rows.

Ever since the Greeks, scientists and humanists have attempted to order consciousness in four-based typing systems in order to better understand the psychological preferences in how people perceive the world and make decisions. The most recognized systems include Hippocrates' four humors and/or temperaments, Jung's four functions which sustain the letters of Myers–Briggs Type Indicator, Keirsey's four personality types, and Wilber's four quadrants.

5. Five and "PAIRfect – the belief in mutuality:" it takes being a child at "heART" to see it. <u>If the "digits" are fingers, then the 9 chambers can be seen as my two hands joined at the thumbs to form the shadow of an eagle.</u> When I know that the thumb is the instrument of will (and when I like playing with words), I begin to see in the "twins" of my hands an acronym for "Thy Will Is Not Separate." As the split in me now begins to heal, I am more and more integral as Noah was, whose Hebrew name (נח) reverses into *Chan* (חן) for "grace" to say: "do you see how 'PAIRfect' it all is, when you surrender to turning within and then building your ark?" Surely, as my hands are joined in pure action, the male side and female side of my brain are one. Being enough, I open to 'PAIRfect' action. I see the chambers holding the Hebrew alphabet as an ark – Noah's Ark – hosting the letters as non-biological PAIRS of animals for me to be One:

- Male **9-Completing** courts female **1-Opening** (9+1=10).
- Male **8-Ordering** courts female **2-Separating** (8+2=10).
- Male **7-Engaging** courts female **3-Changing** (7+3=10).
- Male **6-Desiring** courts female **2-Resisting** (6+4=10).

10=1+0. 10 is to be free to be (1) and not to be (0).

Henceforth, I can only succeed in my creation when the energy of Love (Aleph) is imparted in each room, "I" room at a time.

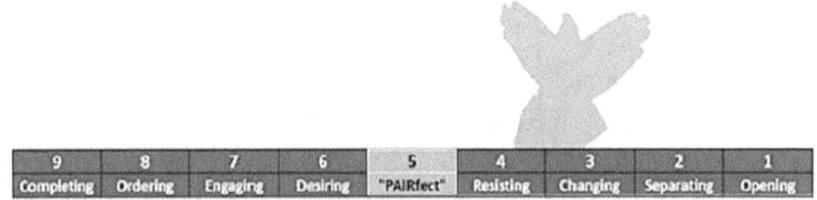

9	8	7	6	5	4	3	2	1
Completing	Ordering	Engaging	Desiring	"PAIRfect"	Resisting	Changing	Separating	Opening

It takes being a child at "heART" to see the eagle hands and to hear the message: 'there will come a time to go to 9, and for now, stopping at 5 may just be "PAIRfect."'

CONSIDER: WHEN I REALIZE THAT EVERYTHING IN THE UNIVERSE IS GEOMETRIC, BE IT PEOPLE, ANIMALS, PLANETS, SOLAR SYSTEMS, STARS, ETC., I BECOME MOTIVATED TO MEASURE MY BELIEF SYSTEMS ON A GEOMETRIC SCALE.

The Power of Organization

"For every minute spent organizing, an hour is earned." *Benjamin Franklin*

The S/Hebrew alphabet may just be the quickest path to declutter the mind and allow myself to handle the different levels of disorder I surround myself with – financial disorders, eating disorders, sleeping disorders, family chaos... The list is long. Consider: when I choose to face the fear of my creative Power, I have an alphabet patterned after nature which clarifies my inner law and places me in the center of my heart by using a series of 10 universal commands – one digit per finger.

But how do I become leader-like and follow the counsel of my heart as my inner law when the whole idea of law and commandments still makes me want to run? I must now borrow Emily Dickinson's "unfurnished eyes" to see that *Exodus 34:28* really speaks of the 10 Words: "Moses was there with the LORD forty days and forty nights without eating bread or drinking water. And he wrote on the tablets the words of the covenant—**the 10 Words.**" Yes again, the word *Debarim,* which is traditionally heard as "commandments," actually means "words."

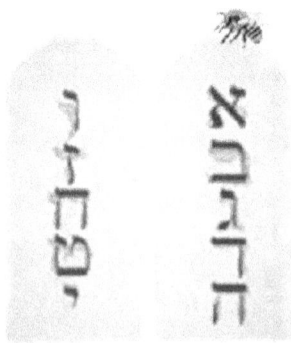

The 10 Words of Surrendered Leadership

Besides being a word, each Hebrew letter is also a number which transcribes the natural motion of energy (see the next BEE wisdom), I relate to the law as being my recipe for being happy, strong and healthy. I also have a way to find a place for the limiting beliefs I could not seem to integrate. Once these beliefs are understood, they leave me alone. Indeed, words place me in the center of my leadership since language is where my Power is. This is how the word *Davaruth* (דברות) for "leadership" is built on the same root as the word *Davar* – the very "word" or "matter" thus far thought to be a "commandment" and resisted as such.

The same DBR root writes the word *Deborah* for "bee." Bees model organization which grants them the wisdom and the Power of words. They are esteemed in Greek mythology for that very trait: "whomsoever they honored and looked upon at his birth, on his tongue they shed a honeyed dew and from his lips would drop gentle words and he would speak counsel unerringly" *Hesiod (750 to 650 BC)*. The link between the bees and word wisdom also exists in the English expression "spelling bees" whose etymology is thus far unexplained. The spelling bees are young students who compete while practicing spelling. They seem to have an innate sense of linguistics: they "grok" the root of words and see their organizing principle.

I MOVE FROM 1-OPENING (WHEN I AM ONE DOT IN THE INFINITY OF TIME) TO 2-SEPARATING (WHEN MY TWO DOTS DRAW A LINE) TO 3-CHANGING (WHEN MY THREE DOTS ARE TRIANGULATING), ADDING ONE DOT UNTIL I COME TO 9-COMPLETING. THIS MOVEMENT MERGES THE PHYSICAL AND METAPHYSICAL LAWS GOVERNING THE BEHAVIOR OF ENERGY.

Code Organization - BR / CD-DC / RB

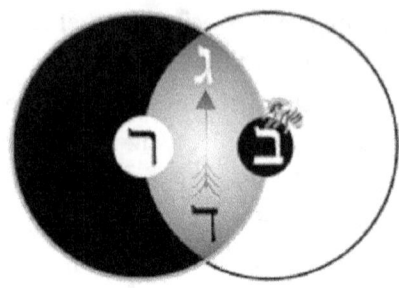

Imagine a language so pure and so sacred that it can reconcile opposites in just two pairs of letters

Top: Hebrew letter (ג) Gimel → C in Roman script
Right: Hebrew letter (ב) Beth → B in Roman script
Left: Hebrew letter (ר) Resh → R in Roman script
Bottom: Hebrew letter (ד) Dalet → D in Roman script

Here is how S/Hebrew inscribes code "Organization" in 4 words:

- **DBR:** from middle to right to left, I read *Dabar* (דבר) for "word, matter, thing," a root which also forms the words *Deborah* (דבורה) for "bee," and *Davaruth* (דברות) for "leadership."
- **BCD:** from right to top to bottom, I read *Beged* (בגד) for "garment, cloth."
- **BR:** from right to left, I read *Bar* (בר) for "son," and by extension, creativity.
- **RB:** from left to right, I read *Rav* (רב) for "abundance, enough, multitude."

The Decoding: to understand this decoding, and thus, organization itself, I will go through three movements. First, I will feel the letters joined by the vertical arrow above (Dalet at the bottom and Gimel at the top). Second, I will place my attention on the words formed by the horizontal letters (Beth to the right and Resh to the left). Last, I will harvest the nectar of Bee wisdom by adding the bottom letter to the horizontal pair, and synergize a few words that most matter to consciousness.

The PAIRfection of Dalet/Gimel:

- As a word, *Dalet* means "door." When this door closes on the material world of objects, it allows me to retreat, rest and recover. As a brainwave, it becomes Greek Delta – the lowest of all frequencies which occur in deep sleep. Delta/Dalet also opens the door to information coming from the subconscious. This is also said by **Dalet** as the root-word for *Dalut* or "poor, empty," the prerequisite to receiving new memories as I pass by the door of abysmal darkness.
- As a word, *Gimel* means "camel." It is the motion that leads me to be the change. As a brainwave, it becomes Greek Gamma – the fastest of all frequencies by which to synergize information from all parts of the brain, and consolidate the data for simultaneous processing. Such high level of thought and focus tends to make me more connected, more blissful. **Gimel** is the root-word for *Gimul* or "generous giving."

When the brainwaves of Gimel and Dalet are moving freely into each other, my giving and receiving know such reciprocity that the story of unrequited love can be told no more. I now have the heart and brain coherence that are necessary to arrange my affairs into a structured whole. Said differently, I am fit to reveal the cosmic order into my micro-universe. I know that I am accountable: I can now count on the 10 digits (or "fingers") of my two hands!

The Abundance of Beth/Resh:

Together, these two letters start the first the second word of the Bible: *Bereshit Bara Elohim* for "in the beginning, God created" and certainly, *Barashit Bara Elohim*: "created-SIX, *Elohim* created..." They also form the word *Bar* for "son" or that to which I give birth – my **creation**. To harness my creativity, I must be willing to give it all. Therein is the meaning of the story of patriarch Abraham who became the "Father of a **Multitude**" because he was willing to give what was the most precious to him. Sacrificing his son is also sacrificing his core identity as father. An identity is a "**garment** or **cloth**." It is at times the mask which I use to distance myself from truth. Inversely, the ability to let go of my attachments in favor of a higher order comes from and generates a mind of **abundance**.

Letting go is essential to the movement of vital energy. As such, it is the foundational organizing principle that sustains my creativity. Indeed, when my consciousness is so structured that I can assign my belongings (be they physical, emotional or mental) to a given category, I naturally increase my focus. My brainwaves are relaxed, but not agitated; alert, but not anxious. On the other hand, failure to reveal the order inherent to chaos leads me into overwhelm.

The Synergy of Bee Wisdom

When adding the Delta brainwave to the BR/RB pair, I form the root-word DBR which is as rich as the land of milk and honey since it branches into words of concern to consciousness. First, being energy in motion, **words** do **matter**, in light of communication being the *result* of what is said and done (the word made *flesh*). Each belief creates. Thus, the importance of a clear mind, so that my words would be the words of Abraham-like surrendered leadership – when I know that it is in giving that I am receiving.

It is thus not surprising that word *Dabar* for "**word, matter, thing**" would extend into *Davaruth* for "**leadership**" and *Deborah* for "**bee**" – a little creature that brings to humans (and to this book) the medicine of organization.

Deborah was also the name of the first female judge in the Bible – a Queen Bee, indeed! She was quite the wordsmith, and held to be as much a ruler as a prophetess. Her secret was, once again, surrendered leadership: she heard "God's" voice and shared the words she heard with her community. As for me, will I transcend the fear of my own leadership and be true to my word by daring to taste the honey in "honesty?"

CONSIDER: WHEN I AM AT ONCE WILD ENOUGH TO SURRENDER TO A LAWLESS CHAOS AND STRAIGHT ENOUGH TO MAINTAIN AN IMPECCABLE ORGANIZATION, I EXPERIENCE AN UNBRIDLED CREATIVITY.

THE MORE I RECOGNIZE PATTERNS (E.G.; THE "CREATED-SIX" HONEYCOMB), THE MORE I SEE THAT ORDER IS INHERENT TO CHAOS AND THE MORE THIS REALIZATION GETS ME OUT OF THE BOX! IT FULFILLS ME!

The Power of Desire

"Love is an irresistible desire to be irresistibly desired." *Robert Frost*

Legend has it that, a long time ago, humans were androgynous – gender-fluid in the flesh. Such is the fantastical account of the origins of love in Plato's *Symposium*, as narrated by Aristophanes. Not only did these proto-humans have both sets of sexual organs, but they were outfitted with two faces, four hands, and four legs. These creatures – which used cartwheels to move very fast – were also endowed with Powers. They were in fact so gifted that the gods felt insecure about their own dominions.

Zeus, Greek king of Gods, decided to weaken them by cutting each creature in two, and commanded "that each person would turn its face towards the wound so as to see the cut and keep better order." If the humans were to pose more of a threat, Zeus promised to cut them again – "and they'll have to make their way on one leg, hopping!" The severed humans were miserable: "[each] one longed for its other half, and so they would throw their arms about each other, weaving themselves together, wanting to grow together."

While it is a stretch, the love story as told by Greek philosophers reminds me of the Adam who was lonely and had to have a "rib" cut out to meet his soulmate – in S/Hebrew, *Kenegdo* for "his opposite." Is love a cure for the wound or the wound itself? Might this very wound be the source of our hunger for love? Aristophanes says, "Love is born into every human being; it calls back the halves of our original nature together; it tries to make one out of two and heal the wound of human nature. Each of us, then, is a 'matching half' of a human whole...and each of us is always seeking the half that matches him." The line of the movie Jerry Maguire comes to mind, when a smitten sports agent played by Tom Cruise famously said to the woman he viewed as his other half: "you complete me!"

Yep, this is the wound – to "hope" that someone or something out there will make me whole! I come to life as a hungry ghost, with a mind full of questions, avidly yearning for Love. But when I do get love, it goes right through me, as if some parasite prevented me from digesting it. Deprived, I now build a whole reality around needing love, the more the better! If I feel a hole in my soul and am perpetually teetering on the brink of anxiety or despair, it is because I am compelled to seek false lures. These fatal habits are seemingly engrained in my nature. Truth be told, I'm addicted to the pursuit of Love, so caught up in the search that I can never touch the essence of dwelling in Love, being at Peace and at home in the QKosmic Eternal Now, fulfilled and fully feeling what is. Trapped in duality, I think I can't get Love except through "you." This is how I forgo pleasure and attach to the sense of being obligated to serve you. Ouch! I am bereft – an alien here in this world having forgotten that I am on the way to the supernatural destination of the LOVE that has no opposite.

The hunger for love is a desire to come home. It is a turn from outside to inside – where to find the keys I've lost.

Upon my return, I'll stop making "you" responsible for my happiness or my misery, and won't look to you to heal my soul. I will finally transcend the false sensory impressions of unrequited love, impressions that I had installed for fear of going alone in the dark, face the beast of desire and come to the end of the romantic dream. Yes, there is a perfect soulmate (and likely a whole universe of twin flames) which I will know upon meeting my true Self. I will then understand, *in my blood,* that there's only One of us and that our biology is designed for us to be of service to each other. Just like me, you are wired to be connected.

I just have to get out of the way to feel the celestial forces working through me. It is my belief system that isolates me, leading me to hover back and forth from "I am special" (I should be rewarded) to "I am not enough" (I should be punished). These beliefs prevent me from knowing that it is my Nature to be LOVE and from feeling that, if the divine is woven throughout everything, it also lives in me. As above, so below. As within, so without! The more I comprehend that my every word and action affect the whole, the more connected I am to humanity – loving humanity and loving my humanity. It is just a matter of trust, and of self-esteem – a matter of Power.

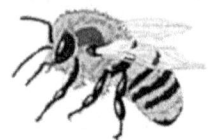

TRAPPED IN DUALITY, I THINK I CAN'T GET LOVE EXCEPT THROUGH "YOU." THIS IS HOW I FORGO PLEASURE AND ATTACH TO THE SENSE OF BEING OBLIGATED TO SERVE YOU. OUCH! I AM BEREFT – AN ALIEN HERE IN THIS WORLD HAVING FORGOTTEN THAT I AM ON THE WAY TO THE SUPERNATURAL DESTINATION OF THE LOVE THAT HAS NO OPPOSITE.

The Lucifer Power Question

"What is it you truly desire?" *Lucifer (TV series)*

I have found that this is far from being an easy question to answer. If it were, it is likely that I would come to the end of dissatisfaction and live a fulfilled life as I would be able to discern between the desires I choose to keep (my core desires) and the desires that I can let go (those that are not dear to my heart). Core desires are the desires that matter so much to me and which I want so badly that I will do whatever it takes to fulfill them, no matter how much work, risk, time or expense are involved. These are things that my heart is set on — things I want with *all* my heart, *all* my soul and *all* my might (keyword: all). Indeed, it is my ambivalence about wanting what I say I want that opens me to being dissatisfied, as **I am not allowing myself** to be totally and fully engaged in acquiring it.

Thus, the brilliance of the question asked by Lucifer – *Latin* for "light-bringer:" what is it you truly desire? Once I answered this first question, I follow by asking myself: why do you desire what you desire? And how much do you want it? In other words, what are you ready to do to manifest this desire?

Bringing light to the nature of my desires can also be construed as the foundational work of any analysis since analysis calls me to take back my projections. When unconscious, I project onto the other that which I deny and repress. LOL, it's not my fault... The devil made me, as confirmed by the word "diabolical" coming from Greek *diabellein* for "to throw across; to project."

Soooo... Why do I want what I want? For example, might I want to lose weight to please my mother, my partner, my society or my doctor, or is it for me? For if I try to please "you," it is likely that I will not have the motivation to persevere. Indeed, personalities want something: as a daughter, I may want my mother's approval or disapproval.

Continuing with my weight loss example, I will likely go through a yo-yo effect in which I'll struggle to maintain my target weight or alternate between losing weight and regaining all the weight I had lost. It would be so much more productive (and kinder to myself) **to give myself the permission** to consciously eat all I want, until I am done with wanting to eat and gain weight. Surely, recognizing that my desire is *not* to lose weight but rather to gain weight would be more honest. As such, it would not be as detrimental to my self-esteem and my body.

However, whereas **allowing and giving permission** would spontaneously align me to the Self, it appears that the forbidden has more appeal. And this is where it is becoming most interesting... If desire is a yearning originating from deep inside my soul, it must be quite different from the grasping of neediness. Moreover, if it is a wish to create something greater that would bring satisfaction or enjoyment or the opportunity for self-development or some admirable benefit to myself and others or all of the above, then why won't I let me have it? Why the resistance? The answers to these questions come in two surprising and apparently opposite places: first in the three biblical commandments to love, and second, in the Devil's names.

The Torah has three commandments to love which can be received as recipes for wholeheartedness, wholeheartedness being the secret behind setting and attaining goals. Yep, if my heart is not *fully* in what I am doing, it is unlikely that my results will be *fully* satisfying...

- **The love of shadow work:** "and you shall love your neighbor as yourself." *Leviticus 19:18.* The S/Hebrew word for "neighbor" is formed on the root *Rah* for "evil, bad, wickedness." Loving the neighbor is loving my shadow – the "evil" part of me. In setting a goal, I must assess where I am "bad:" am I putting a limit on what I can accomplish by not aiming high enough? Conversely, am I trying to tackle too much at once? Befriending the special / not enough part of me will help deal with the saboteur, when that "neighbor" shows up.

- **The love of totality:** "and you shall love the LORD your God with *all* your heart, *all* your soul and *all* your might." *Deuteronomy 6:5.* This is where the story begins: just how badly do I want what I want? How final is my decision to have it? By recognizing that any ambivalence and/or dividedness will trip me up, I come back to the full disclosure of what I want and why I want it. Just the fact that I am no longer compromising my integrity goes a long way to draw the goal to me. I may even realize that such entirety is the goal – that's it's all I ever wanted!
- **The love of the unknown:** "and you shall love the stranger: for you were strangers in the land of Egypt." *Deuteronomy 10:19.* Setting a goal is breaking a stale routine and therefore, facing the unknown by ceasing to stage my own suffering. It is walking on a path that stretches me beyond my comfort zone. It is daring to go for what I really want (even if it is "foreign" to my family's or my friends' expectations of me), instead of playing it safe. Mostly, it is to know and expect that I am going to make errors, and, when I do, be willing to fall and to get back up immediately.

The ultimate desire may just be the desire for Love. When I have the courage to give everything to Love, every other desire (e.g.; safety, belonging, mattering) is immediately fulfilled.

Provided that I can love working with these three elements – my shadow, my dividedness and my fear of failure, I stand a very real chance to remain motivated until the end and beyond. Motivation, after all, is the emotion of a strong desire in motion. As for the Devil's names, they help to get me there by initiating me so that I would transcend the dark Powers...

PROVIDED THAT I CAN LOVE WORKING WITH THESE THREE ELEMENTS –
MY SHADOW, MY DIVIDEDNESS AND MY FEAR OF FAILURE, I STAND A VERY
REAL CHANCE TO REMAIN MOTIVATED UNTIL THE END AND BEYOND.

THE DARK POWERS

THE DARK POWERS invite me to speak of the devil, literally! Besides the commandments to Love, the turn from outer to inner is also facilitated by the devil's names. In medieval times the devil was known as "the other" – the entity onto whom I am projecting myself. Surely, when I feel obligated to take care of others, it is likely that I am not wholehearted in my act of service. So, if I were to find myself angry or even depressed, I could view it as a hint that I gave my Power to "the other," and begin to claim it back. This is how to avoid the murderous motive to make "them" pay for not loving me as I wish to be loved.

One day, I will be free of the desire for "your" love, approval and recognition, and on that day, having no fear of falling or rising, I will do what it takes. I will also witness my work becoming my sacrifice and offer up both the action and the fruit of the action to the Divine. Hence, my action will be non-binding: it will come without a karmic debt.

The sense of justice as giving it all to LOVE permeates all of creation. Buddhists call it *Dharma*, Jews, *Mitzvah*, science, *interconnectedness*.

Upon feeling this mutuality of existence with all other beings, I understand that the one merging with the other is also the work of polarity: "God" making a bargain with the Devil in order to propel me to the Power of synchronicity. I have this Power when I say: "let there be my goal," and see and feel that I already attained such goal, since I am acting congruently with having it in each moment.

Meanwhile, I must pass the test of the Promoter of the Faith, a.k.a. *Advocatus Diaboli* (Latin for "the devil's advocate"). Whether I like it or not, and whether I am aware of it or not, this devil's advocate is the part of me that is so filled with doubts and so plagued with yearning that it will argue to no end against my being fulfilled and free, since it is so busy convincing me of my unworthiness.

When I perceive that I am not enough, I meet Belial. This Name may be the most taxing in matters of motivation as it means "without self-esteem." Once I set a goal, do I trust in myself enough to push through a setback and keep moving forward? Do I realize that no matter how many times I get knocked down, nothing can stop me as long as I am willing to get back up? If Belial doesn't manage to make me quit, I will open to receiving the great gift of perseverance. Persevering will not let anything stand between me and my goal. As such, it ensures success. That means "failures" are not seen as negative, but rather as learning moments. This is true motivation, and, as such, true attainment.

Unless I make peace with Belial, I will be driven to Satan's door, *Satan* meaning the "adversary." Yes, Satan will play the role of my enemy, confronting me with real tragedies – wars, financial ruin, sickness or the loss of a loved one, just so that I would realize that life is suffering... Did the past teach me enough wisdom for me to stop the fight? And if I still go around with a clenched fist, might I at least be ready for a code of opposites by which to stop the fight and flight, and get off the special/not enough merry-go-round?

Unless I make peace with Satan, I will encounter Beelzebub – the "Master of the Flies." This is when I let myself be prey to addictions, so terrified I am by the thought that I'm not enough. Conversely, I may also believe that I am special: I don't need to subject myself to the disciplines practiced by ordinary people. I can stay up as late as I want. It's okay for me to fast for days on end or to eat non-stop. Alcohol, tobacco, caffeine, sex, gambling, here I come! I'm above the laws – indestructible...

When Beelzebub is not enough to incite me to turn within, I meet Samael, the "poison of God" who contaminates me with entitlement, a poison which is highly toxic (talk-sick?). Ah, if I could only let go of claiming my pound of flesh which, I want to believe, has my name on it.

Any more doubts about my abilities? I now meet Mephistopheles, a S/Hebrew name meaning "the destroyer of lies." Indeed, it is not that "I can't;" it is more that I won't! I won't answer the Lucifer question and own what it is that I truly desire. I am not ready to know the truth. In that sense, Mephistopheles can help me create so much unconscious time that I'll be in major pain, postponing my Jerusalem (meaning my "city or consciousness of peace") to next year, year after year after year!

Yep, I will eventually decide on a goal, see the steps I need to take in order to achieve it, and commit to making the necessary investments of time and money.

Special... Not enough... Special... Not enough... Special... Once upon a time, I wanted to be somebody. I now realize that I did not come into this life to become somebody. I came to become nobody and to let go of the belief that I am the body or that which is dying...

The Ladder of Success

"There is no elevator to success, you have to take the stairs." *Zig Ziglar*

To become nobody, I must be willing to let go of the ambition of wanting to make a name for myself. When I am anonymous, I know that my motivations are pure and that I am humble enough to take the stairs. This is how most people who have carved for themselves a brilliant destiny often started in dire conditions – from rags to riches, indeed!

As much as I desire to succeed in my creation, I find that doing what it takes is often too tiring or too troublesome. I want to see what the heavens are, their numbers and their forms; what angelic beings abide there; what is the purpose and nature of the soul; how it enters the body, if there is life after death, etc., etc., etc., but, there's a "but!" I have no patience and wish to have a direct mystical experience right now. Don't I deserve it? Oyveh! Moreover, I can't feel the kindness of regression or the goodness of failure: I can't see that the angel in me both ascends (or succeeds) and descends (or fails). Not knowing who I am, I can't center myself while in the midst of ups and downs, and start believing that I will never reach the goal, and never wake up.

On that note, Zig Ziglar also said: "you cannot climb the ladder of success dressed in the costume of failure." So yes, something has to give. For me to succeed, I must let go of my clothing or who I *think* I am – the body; the ego. In biblical terms, I must eat from the tree of the knowledge of good and evil, for when I do, I die to the failure *I think* I am or *think* I shouldn't have experienced. I will then naturally rise above the level of thinking that creates my problem and keeps me from receiving my heart's desire – my dream vision.

As for the stairs of this ladder, they are pictured below as 7 rungs hosting 10 spheres linked by 22 meridians circulating the light in between them. Reaching the top rung is to come to the peace that passes understanding. It is thus to fully understand that there's only One of us. Lastly, the ladder is known as the tree of life: "while sleeping, Jacob receives a dream that changes his life. He sees a ladder reaching up and down from earth to heaven and back. He also sees angels ascending and descending on it." *Genesis 28:12* These angels are no less than the centers of energy and information known in Hebrew as *Sephiroth* and in Sanskrit as *chakras*.

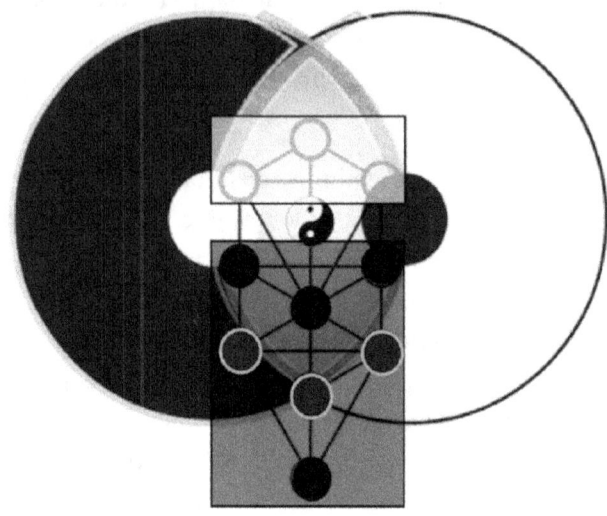

Going up and down the Tree of Life

- Bottom dark rectangle: the 7 infernal spheres as "Ego-Egypt" of the tree of life – the 3D world of scarcity.
- Top light rectangle: the 3 supernal spheres of the "Promised Land" of the tree of life – the 6D world of abundance.
- Behind it: the tree of the knowledge of opposites that is in me and all around the tree of (my) life, just waiting that I'd take the personal out of life by crossing the abyss of *Daath* ("knowledge"). Entering the unknown, I am now consummated by the mouth of its well.

THE WORD *DAATH* (דעת) CAN ALSO BE SEEN AND HEARD AS *DALET OT* (ד'עת) FOR THE "DOOR OF TIME." WHEN PASSING THROUGH THIS DOOR, I NO LONGER THINK I HAVE TIME AND STOP POSTPONING. ALSO, I NEITHER LIVE IN THE REPETITIVE PAST NOR IN A PREDICTABLE FUTURE. I AM EMPOWERING THE NOW, ETERNALLY PATIENT AS A SOURCE BEING. SURELY, SINCE I ALREADY RECEIVED IT ALL, WHY FRET AT ALL?

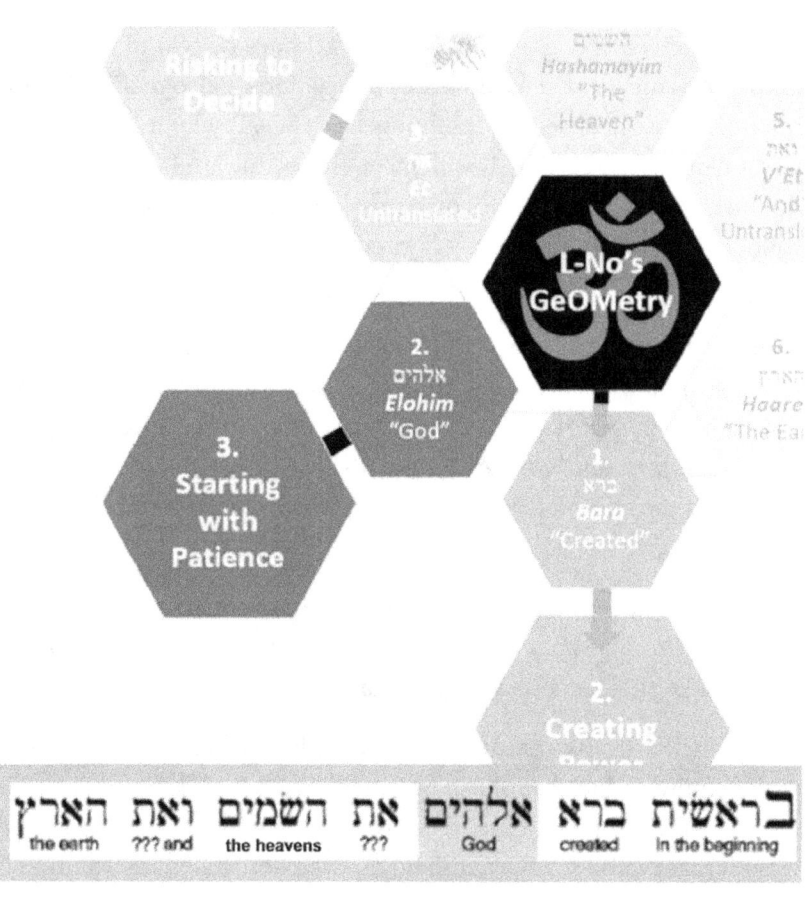

This chapter emanates from and inquires on the 2ⁿᵈ word after "in the beginning." Highlighted in the line above, its letters are read as *Elohim* for "God…"

Introducing "Starting with Patience"

"Dear Lord please give me patience, for if you give me strength, I'll kill that idiot..."

Patience precedes it all. When I can wait, I have no fear of failing as I know that I am guided in my words and actions. I also realize that my impatience was caused by the hunger for LOVE which I felt Powerless to satiate. One day, I will meet the Name and surrender my doubts. I will know that I am on a mission and won't care how impossible its fulfillment seems. I will know that I Am because I will have turned within and faced my fear of failing.

If surrender was the key to enlightenment given by Jesus, its code was in Moses' name. Turning within is to be ready for the truth that unfolds in my heart. It is to join hearing and seeing to the point where the oral and written scriptures live in me as four creatures conveying the complete understanding of the Oneness of LOVE. Will I listen?

Possibly the "people-signs" and the first of their SIX rows of codes will begin to show me the wonders of a tongue that is so sacred that I make the decision to change, and change.

First, I will witness the divine "PAIRfection" of code Patience and realize how I block myself by postponing a decision. To code Patience, I will then add the letters of code Attention which spells out what it takes to be so focused that I am free of the action. Attention is another word for creative "energy." Will I respond with a big YES to the divine call and experience the Power of synchronicity as did the first Adam? Or will I say "no" and only be trapped in the past as I repeat a painful "HIStory" day after day, as did the second Adam?

Entering the Mystery is passing through the door of time. It is to no longer superimpose a past of lack onto the future, a future that I make predictable by being a slave to my emotional addictions. It is to believe that I am not whole, not "PAIRfect," not complete and not connected. It is thus to be in dire need of a sexual healing by which to bliss out in the biblical knowledge of good and evil so much so that I'd drop the plan.

Chapter 3

On the Precedence of Patience

"The two most powerful warriors are patience and time." *Leo Tolstoy*

If I could just wait, I would see that life takes care of itself. Patience is how to overcome the fear of falling and failing since the likelihood of making errors increases when I act compulsively. Patience is also how to let go of my attachment to an outcome. When I am patient, I am nobody, in no time, no space, no mind. I am absorbed by the Now and free of past and future. Under the spell of patience, I am at once the pain taking me over, the passion prompting it, and the compassion embracing it. In that sense, patience may just be what invites and supports enlightenment.

For now, I crave enlightenment, but under one condition; when I cross the finish line into the infinite, I want my ego to stay intact so that I could keep my stuff. Here is how I do it. First, I resist feeling the jealousy that moves through me when I see you having what I want (when I don't). Second, I ignore that detaching from lack is to be dispossessed from the illusion of separation. If Cain could detach, he would be free of his calling as Cain – the one "possessed" by jealousy, and would open to Love. Only then will he (will I) experience real change, as I'll know that I am whole and thus that I have it all.

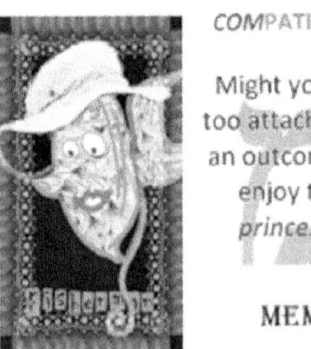

COMPATIENCE

Might you be too attached to an outcome to enjoy the princess?

MEM

TORA—TARO: The Fisherman Hat is the 12th card of the eXPiRe Tarot of *Golden XPR*. Traditionally known as "the Hanged Man," the 12th tarot card is inscribed by the 13th Torah letter Mem for "pairs of water."

Love resembles the fisherman's hook. Unless the fish is caught on the hook, I cannot reel in the fish. If I am the fisherman, I also am the fish. Once I bite the hook, I may twist and turn. But it is only when I surrender and let myself be caught that I know the strongest of bonds with the Mystery, a Mystery which honored me by crossing over to merge with me. Just like fishing, Love can't be hurried.

LNO is written to inspire me to hurry nothing and thus to resist nothing by evoking the Power of the Logos to provoke the reverberation of what cannot be said. Mem is the "mute" sound; the letter that is silent because, like water, it adopts a path of least resistance. It is in meeting silence that patience can recognize itself as patience. Whereas lovers cannot make their orgasm happen, they can adopt a path of least resistance to be overtaken by Love. Whereas the poets cannot write the poems, they can adopt a path of least resistance to witness the birthing of the Word. Whereas the patients cannot make the healing happen, they can adopt a path of least resistance for the gift of healing to be received. Of my own will, I can't quicken anything, but I can deliberately adopt a path of least resistance to be overcome by what I am powerless to attain.

And it is when what I am powerless to attain attains me that I am free to recognize the mutuality that is Love.

WHEN I AM PATIENT, I AM NOBODY, IN NO TIME, NO SPACE, NO MIND.

I AM ABSORBED BY THE NOW AND FREE OF PAST AND FUTURE. UNDER THE SPELL OF PATIENCE, I AM AT ONCE THE PAIN TAKING ME OVER, THE PASSION PROMPTING IT, AND THE COMPASSION EMBRACING IT.

Why the Impatience?

'Then they said, "Come, let us build ourselves a city and a tower with its top in the heavens, and let us make a name for ourselves, lest we be dispersed over the face of the whole earth."' *Genesis 11:4*

Once upon no time, I was quiet, in the void, in the quantum midst of the garden, not asking for anything... From a purely physical viewpoint, I couldn't move in the void. I couldn't fall or rise either: where would I go? For me to rotate, I needed a reference point, a twin particle, someone with whom to fall in love and to fail at Love. This is to say that, to feel something; anything, I had to summon a significant other, a partner in contrast – a devil or something I would resist! Evolution calls the shots: I once was 0/1, not being and being simultaneously, until the desire to become somebody compelled me to come out... And now, I had something to prove!

Might the desire to make a name for myself be the ultimate motivation? Said differently, would I be able to "be still and know that I am God" (no impatience whatsoever) if I weren't so scared of being ordinary? When it comes to striving for greatness, motivation is key. Indeed, motivation (or that which moves me) causes me to decide on a specific goal, and to follow through with my decision. Motivation is the reason why I act or behave in a certain way. It is a powerful force that must be on my side for me to be successful in the creation of my desired goals, whether it's losing weight, studying for a degree, or building a business, or painting the Sistine Chapel...

Motivation is more than a desire – it is a hunger that urges me to overcome. The hungrier I am, the more I'll stick to a discipline, make it fun and stay on track. Hunger is what leads me to the relentless drive to get out of bed in the morning and to dare mastering a new skill. However, if the hunger becomes personal, my motivation will turn into a motive to commit a crime.

Motivations are held to be either intrinsic or extrinsic. Intrinsic is a motivational force that comes from the inside, and extrinsic, from the outside. The former is driven by pure enjoyment, that is, by the joy of purity. This is when I am free: nothing left to lose or to prove. The latter is driven by external rewards, such as money, material possessions, status, grades, fame, getting "the girl," etc. Extrinsic is the motivation that causes me to suffer.

In biblical terms, I am Cain who, being *named* to be "possessed by jealousy," had a motive to kill his brother. I wanted revenge! However, when I know that, in Hebrew, my brother's name *Abel* means "vanity," I begin to realize that killing "vanity" simply means to move back from extrinsic to intrinsic motivations. If having certain desires about how it ought to be (instead, of course, of seeing and feeling in the Now that my desire is fulfilled), I am looking for "you" to reward me. Rewards partner with punishments: these two are "brothers!" Therefore, to be done with the severity with which I chastise myself and ascend into the gift of loving-kindness, I must be wise enough to murder "vanity." I will then no longer alternate between seeking revenge and looking for love in the wrong places – *out there...* I will simply be patient since having it all, I will want nothing. That also means that I'll be in the void again, at ease with the unknown of good and evil...

EVOLUTION CALLS THE SHOTS: I ONCE WAS 0/1, NOT BEING AND BEING, UNTIL THE DESIRE TO BECOME SOMEBODY COMPELLED ME TO COME OUT. AND NOW, I WILL HAVE SOMETHING TO PROVE UNTIL I BECOME READY TO MEET THE NAME THAT WILL LEAD ME TO SURRENDER IT ALL...

Code Surrender - ESM / O / MSE

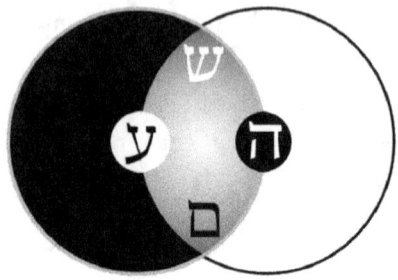

Imagine a language so pure and so sacred that it can reconcile opposites in just four letters...

Top: Hebrew letter Shin (ש)→ S, Sh in Roman script
Right: Hebrew letter Heh (ה) → E in Roman script
Left: Hebrew letter Ayin (ע) → O in Roman script
Bottom: Hebrew letter Mem Final (ם) → M in Roman script

Here is how S/Hebrew inscribes code "Surrender" in 4 words:

- From right to top to bottom, I read *Hashem* (השם) for "The Name," and specifically the Four-lettered Name or Tetragrammaton.
- From bottom to top to right, I read *Moshe* (משה) for "Moses."
- From right to left to bottom, I read *Haam* (העם) for "the people."
- From top to bottom to left, I read *Shema* (שמע) for "hear, understand, obey."

The Decoding: I am **Moses.** Clearly, I am here to wake up since my name means "pulled out of the waters" of the unconscious. I also am a motivational speaker about to give a talk on how to get free from the oppression of slavery. Although I know that I am a born-leader, here to inspire others to change, I still have doubts, wondering if I am capable to fulfill this beautiful mission that "God" gave me to free **the**

people: "suppose I go to my people and say to them that you sent me. They'll ask me what your Name is." To which "God" said: "I Am that I Am. That's all you need to say. I Am sent me to you" *Exodus 3:13-14*. *Ehyeh* (AEYE) for "I Am" is a slightly different Name than YEWE, a four-lettered Name that is held to be too potent to be uttered. It is thus replaced in casual conversations by *Hashem* for "**the Name.**"

There's no avoiding it! For me to be in my Power, I must turn around, go within and meet I Am – a Name that is much greater that the limitations I know as "me." This reversal from *Moshe* to *Hashem* is the only way for me to know that I Am. Therefore, it only takes the three letters of *Moshe* for the Mosaic law to become clear: change your point of view! This "turn" or "change" is the very meaning of the word *Teshuvah* – the first pillar of Jewish mysticism, the second being *Tephillah* for the gratitude of having already received my "prayer" and *Tzedaqah* for the "charity" of being able to give all to LOVE.

On that note, the famous words of communication theorist Marshall McLuhan come to mind: "the medium is the message." Yes, this metalanguage that calls itself S/Hebrew is both the medium and the message since it also uses the movement of the letters to model what leaders do – to turn inward! Once detached from the material world, I will have no problem fulfilling my destiny, because "I am" will speak and act through me.

When I take the call of my burning bush, I change my ways and touch the essence of enlightenment which is surrender. As a leader, I now have the will to **hear**, **understand** and **obey** the dictates of my heart. It is how I feel and know in my blood and my bones that LOVE is ours, and that LOVE is One. This knowledge deepens on the next section via *the Patience of Joining Vision and Listening.*

I AM MOSES. ALTHOUGH I KNOW THAT I AM A BORN-LEADER, I STILL HAVE DOUBTS, WONDERING IF I AM CAPABLE TO FULFILL THIS BEAUTIFUL MISSION THAT "GOD" GAVE ME TO FREE THE PEOPLE.

BUILDING ON L-NO'S HYPOTHESIS: THE "PEOPLE" ARE NON-BIOLOGICAL AND YET SENTIENT S/HEBREW LETTERS THAT GO BY PAIRS. MY WORK IS TO FREE THE 5 PAIRS OF LETTERS THAT ARE BEHIND THE 10 WORDS (A.K.A. THE TEN COMMANDMENTS), FOR MY WORD TO BE LAW. HENCE, I AM THE LIVING WORD, FULLY ATTUNED AND SURRENDERED TO MY HEART.

The Patience of Joining Vision and Listening

"If people knew how hard I worked to get my mastery, it wouldn't seem so wonderful at all." *Michelangelo*

The work is to master my emotions and simply be grateful! Gratitude naturally opens me to the extraordinary as it makes me whole. I am now blessed with infinite patience, and from there, with compassion. Such emptying of smothering emotions is what eagle represents, as it sublimates the scorpion-like desires that sting my Visionary's soul and lead me to self-sabotage. The sublimation from scorpion's dark desires to eagle's surrendered leadership was first felt by Ezekiel who spoke of four creatures. This vision is represented below...

Leader's Heart	Engineer's Mind	Officer's Body	Visionary's Soul
GOD	SIN	LAW	SEX
The Lion	The Human	The Bull	The Scorpio to be Eagle
"I will"	"I know"	"I have"	"I desire"

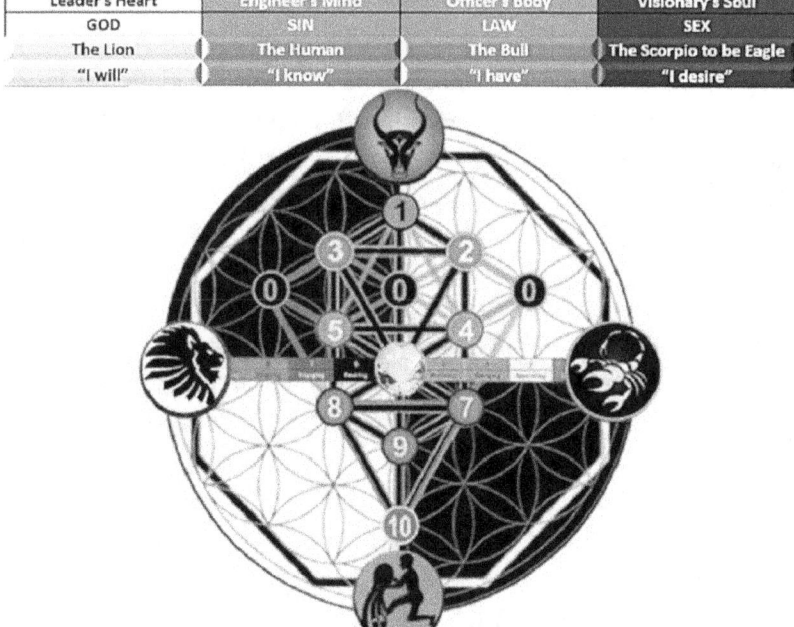

Four creatures watching the tree of life (10 numbered spheres and 22 lettered paths in between) and the tree of the knowledge of good and evil (3 zeroing spheres and 10 lettered paths in between) in the midst of a garden that upholds the quadrature of consciousness.

Surrender is to flow with the quantum midst of things. The illustration above combines two instances involving such **midst**, first *Genesis 2:9* and then *Ezekiel 1:5*. In the first verse, I see that "the tree of life was in the **midst** of the garden, and the tree of the knowledge of good and evil." In the second, I see that "out of the **midst** thereof came the likeness of four living creatures. [...] As for the likeness of their faces, the four had the face of a man; the face of a lion on the right side; and the face of a bull on the left side; also, the face of an eagle." *Ezekiel 1:5 [...] ibid, 1:10.* I wish to understand this mysterious **midst**, especially if it acts as a supreme balancer.

The Hebrew word for **midst** first appears in *Genesis 1:6* during the second "day" where the illusion of separation began: 'and God said: "let there be a firmament in **the midst** of the waters, and let it divide the waters from the waters."' Prior to that, there was no division between the heaven and hell of my emotional body, or between feeling good and feeling bad. My leadership was surrendered: no split waters in the emotional body meant no desire and no resistance. Two cells eventually divided into four, a mutation that is illustrated above as four creatures living in four quadrants. There is also the wheels' rotational motion that is to be accounted for as a cause of displacement of the creatures' positioning from the vision of Ezekiel to this of *Golden XPR*.

The four creatures interact to lead me to centaur consciousness, when I no longer separate myself from my emotional waters and feel my energy connecting a sane body to a sane mind. Code centaur will reveal how these creatures are in fact the four astrological signs of Scorpio, Leo, Aquarius and Taurus. I will also understand what their function as "fixed" signs is: to help me hold the tension of opposites when at the height of a season (when I am between a rock and a hard place). Lastly, I will relate to their keywords, as the verbs of the quadrature of consciousness:

- **I desire** (as the soul of SEX which moves me),

- **I have** (as the body of the LAW which is the *result* of my communication),
- **I know** (as the mind of SIN which used to *ignorantly* lead me into temptation),
- **I will** (as the heart of GOD who has already decided the outcome).

Consider: when I see that what **I desire** aligns with what **I have, I know** that I made a divine use of **will**. The decision is made. This is, of course, a different "I" that hears truth and a different "eye" that sees the word TWINS as "Thy Will Is Not Separate." I can now hear *and* see that we are One – in surrendered leadership.

Feeling our oneness is the call of the *Shema*, a prayer so essential that it became the credo of Judaism, the basis of the teachings of Jesus and the sense of being a Muslim: "Hear ISRAEL (= you who IS REAL), LOVE is our God, LOVE is One!"

In this image, I see three Hebrew letters (שמע). They are read as *Shema* for "hear." The black letters spell the word *Shem* "Name," and the gray letter is *Ayin* which, as a word, means "eye." I also see that the Ayin
sign (ע) is enlarged (it "shouldn't" go below the two other signs). And yet, such is the case in a Torah scroll, an event which is so rare that it commands attention. The word *Shema* invites me to join hearing and seeing, and thus to merge the visible written teachings with the invisible oral teachings so completely that I can "hear" and "understand" that we are One – like a LOVE that has no opposite.

I AM CONSCIOUS IN THE MEASURE TO WHERE I ALLOW FOR THE WORK TO BE DONE *THROUGH* ME AND NOT *BY* ME. THEREFORE, WHEN I SEE THAT WHAT I DESIRE ALIGNS WITH WHAT I HAVE, I KNOW THAT "I" MADE A DIVINE USE OF WILL.

TO THIS END, I NOW MEET THE FIRST OF SIX ROWS OF CODES.

THE FIRST ROW OF CODES

"Imagine all the people sharing all the world" *Imagine, song by John Lennon*

Once upon a time, the people-signs (that is, symbols who had a life of their own) wondered how to restore the memory of the Self to the part of me who forgot that I was infused with divine Power. The lost data explained how I would feel separate from "you," from Love and from the cosmos.

These people-signs will soon be pictured as rows of codes for me to find the lost symbol by which to interface with the cosmic forces, heal my bodies, and contribute to abort the greatest tragedies that humankind is now facing. One day, I will have complete understanding. I'll then abide in "the land" of deep joy and gratitude – a felt sense that will nourish the coherence of my heart, and in turn, of my brain. Living without a why, I will have transcended language: nothing left to prove. This "land" and/or consciousness is where the people-signs direct me. Such attainment – a.k.a. the end of dissatisfaction – is what they serve. And then, they will have done their work.

First, they had to convey **patience**, as patience with my conditions is peace of mind. Moreover, they also needed to transmit the sense that sustaining the kind of peace that passes understanding does not come from getting what I want in some future time. It comes from believing that I already have it.

Such mind of abundance takes patience, as it asks me to let go of my addiction to being unworthy. When I do, I know what I want and why I want what I want. I can then make the decision to place my full **attention** on it, knowing that I already have the "girl," the partner, the money, the health I prayed for.

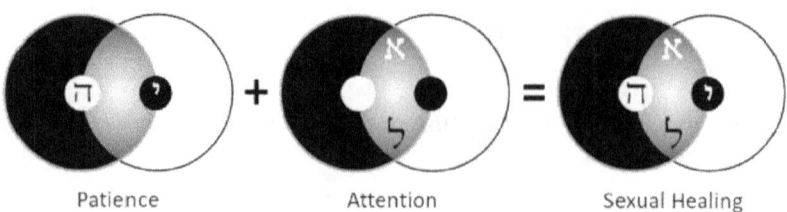

| Patience | Attention | Sexual Healing |

It is easy to have patience (יה) and keep my attention (אל) on the goal. I just have to be consistent in my efforts. This is how I will come to experience sexual healing (אל יה), since, being whole, I will miss nothing and no one. Instead, I'll be fulfilled and free.

ONCE UPON A TIME, THE PEOPLE-SIGNS (THAT IS, SYMBOLS WHO HAD A LIFE OF THEIR OWN) WONDERED HOW TO RESTORE THE MEMORY OF THE SELF TO THE PART OF ME WHO FORGOT THAT I WAS INFUSED WITH DIVINE POWER.

THE LOST DATA EXPLAINED HOW I WOULD FEEL SEPARATE FROM "YOU," FROM WHAT I WANT, FROM LOVE AND FROM THE COSMOS.

Code Patience - YE / EY

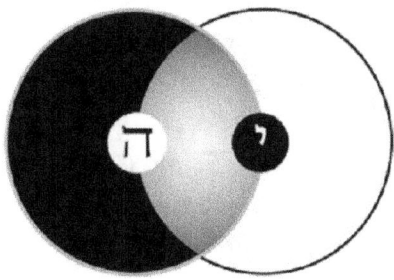

Imagine a language so pure and so sacred that it can reconcile opposites in one pair of letters...

Right: Hebrew letter Yod (י) → I, J, Y in Roman script
Left: Hebrew letter Heh (ה) → E in Roman script

Explained here as the Power of patience, *Yah* (YE | יה) may just be the ultimate "God" Name since it engraves the paths of wisdom. Here is how... Kabbalistic writings have for long viewed Yod (Y) as a symbol for the male seed, and Heh (E), for the female womb. Having a male seed gives me the capability to recognize, fuse with and give my essence to a female seed. Having a psychic womb gives me the capability to receive the gift, nurture the creation, and have the compassion to embrace the most intense "birth" pains.

Such male/female balancing sounds optimal, if I weren't conditioned to believe that giving is mighty fine, but that receiving is not. Thus, the fury of the scorned feminine!

This belief system is old, so old it showed up in the story of the patriarch-to-be Abram and his wife Sarai. The curse placed on the first woman (and here on Sarai) was twofold: painful births plus the desire for her man and his Power (*Genesis 3:16*). Sarai was in such pain not to be able to conceive and, as a result, to have to give a concubine to her husband, that she ended up trading the Yod in her name (שרי) for two Heh. That was the prerequisite (although unspoken) for the couple to each "receive" a letter Heh to add to their names so that they could get pregnant.

Certainly, this commentary is a complete departure from traditional commentaries. Hear, hear! The value of one Yod (10) is equal to the value of two Heh (5x2). The first Heh womb replaced the Yod in Sarai's name (שרי), making her "Sarah" (שרה). The second Heh went to her husband Abram (אברם), transforming his name into Abraham (אברהם). Changing name marks a shift in consciousness. Henceforth, the blessed couple was able to become matriarch and patriarch. Indeed, *Yah* always was a Love story. It becomes a hopeless pursuit when I remain as Sarai, and attach to the "HELLusion" of separation and start craving Power.

Having both – seed and womb – can thus only grant patience as I know that I have it all – both sides of the equation. Indeed, I'm not longing, yearning or pining for anything! When that happens, there is just gratitude in my heart and the willingness to do what LOVE would do. Hatred has nothing to attach to. At last, I have the wisdom to know the difference! Indeed, there is no perception of lack in my mental space. Surely, it is the frustration not to have the Power to fulfill my desires that is at the root of my impatience. The more I believe that I already received Yod's intuitive gift of inspiration, the more patient I am. I am enough. Grateful.

Patience is also how to succeed, since patience comes with perseverance. There is no compulsive misuse of Power, as my male and female sides are balanced. I feel whole and "PAIRfect." How else, since I embody the Sacred Marriage inscribed by *Yah* via pair Yod Heh? In that sense, Yod Heh is the S/Hebrew equivalent of the Sanskrit mantra *Om Mani Padme Hum* ("the Jewel is in the Lotus"). This is when I literally have what "she," "he," and "they" are having! There is no desire for and no resistance to "the man" or "his rulership," since I am that – *HaYod* (הי) "the male seed."

Therefore, losing patience tells me that I have unconsciously chosen to enter Scare City and to identify to the body. Surely, the

labelling of man/woman is the first typology. Before that, I had nothing lacking, no need of becoming, and thus no impatience and no resultant animosity. I was simply being.

Note: many schools of thought transliterate the Four-lettered Name – a Name which was born in *Yah* – as YHVH or YHWH. *Golden XPR* transliterates the letters of *Yah* as YE, and the Four-lettered Name as YEWE, since the 5th Hebrew letter Heh (ה) evolved into the 5th Roman script letter E. As for the 8th letter H, it comes from the 8th Hebrew letter Chet (ח). These two letters are two very different animals. :-)

Having a mental seed (a.k.a. the spermatic word) gives me the power to create. Having a psychic womb gives me the ability to nurture the creation until completion, and also the compassion to embrace the deepest pain.

Praise the *Yah*, I am now equipped with patience as the felt sense of wisdom.

How I block my own attainment...

"Listen, Kamala, when you throw a stone into the water, it finds the quickest way to the bottom of the water. It is the same when Siddhartha has an aim, a goal. Siddhartha does nothing; he waits, he thinks, he fasts, but he goes through the affairs of the world like the stone through the water, without doing anything, without bestirring himself; he is drawn and lets himself fall. He is drawn by his goal, for he does not allow anything to enter his mind which opposes his goal." *Hermann Hesse, Siddharta*

I wish I could allow for that much ease and, like Siddharta, rest while working – "without bestirring myself!" Surely, it would be lovely to decide what I will do each day and do nothing other than saying NO to what does not align with my decision, but alas! Here's for me to consider: when I go into forced labor and work too hard, I am yet to decide. Similarly, when I don't have the mental strength to choose peace and, instead, let smothering emotions derail me from my goal, I am also yet to decide.

What is the decision I am postponing? Striving for self-knowledge is the only real decision that "I" can make. It involves carving the egoic marble of my arrogance until I free the part of me that makes sound decisions.

Until I do decide, I won't know why I want what I want. I also won't trust that fulfilling any desire could make a positive difference for me and for all. And that is how I can't quite use my will as a laser beam of attention, and slice through procrastination. That is also why I quit before the door opens. Being ambivalent, I can't support the stretch I need to make in order to persevere in creating experiences that are worth sharing.

When staying stuck and not allowing me to decide, I may find inspiration in how S/Hebrew speaks of change. The image below shows how letter Lamed (ל) lives in the middle row of **3-Changing**, in the world of emotions: how do I *feel* about change? How committed am I to change? It is how code Attention starts in pair Aleph / Lamed writing *El* for "God" since I must feel "good" or "God" about my decision in order to continue living by it. The letter Shin (ש) in *Esh* "fire-Power" lives in the bottom row of 3-Changing – in the physical world: how do I enact change? It is how Shin is part of code Decision, since any action starts in a decision.

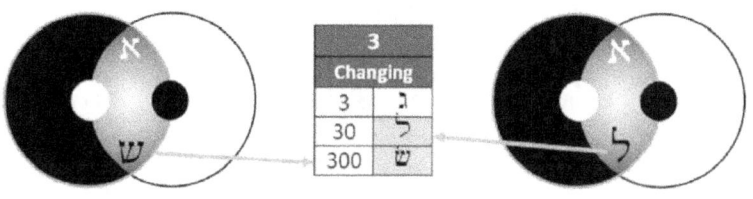

Shin (ש): physical change   Lamed (ל): emotional change

The Chamber of Change

The 27 letters of the Hebrew alphabet are organized in 9 chambers enacting the physics of belief: 1 is opening. Opening naturally leads to 2, which is separating. Separating naturally leads to 3, which is changing... Also, each chamber moves from the top to the bottom cells as per the order of creation: 1) I think, 2) I feel, 3) I act and have.

BOTTOM LINE: DIVIDED ACTION SIMPLY MEANS THAT I AM YET TO DECIDE.

Code Attention - AL / LA

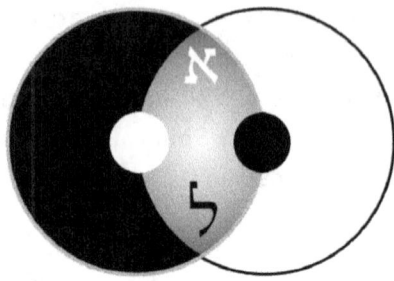

Imagine a language so pure and so sacred that it can reconcile opposites in just one pair of letters...

Top: Hebrew letter Aleph (א) → A in Roman script
Bottom: Hebrew letter Lamed (ל) → L in Roman script

Here is how S/Hebrew inscribes code "Attention" in 2 words:

- **AL:** from top to bottom, I read *El* (אל) for "toward, God."
- **LA:** from bottom to top, I read *Lo* (לא) for "no."

The Decoding: experiments in quantum physics have shown that what is being observed in nature depends on choices made by the observer (me). If I were to discipline my attention – which is the ideal use of my willpower, I would consistently focus on my goal, thinking and feeling that "I AM the AIM." I would live the future of my dream in present time, grateful that I already received it, loving it all and feeling that LOVE is One: it binds me to the vision of my soul. What am I missing? Why is it that "eye" would choose – consciously or not – to observe lack rather than plenty? Enlightenment is seeing black *and* white, empty *and* full, a dead cat *and* an alive cat, *at the exact same time*. It is to speak in the language of paradox and communicate with "God." Ah, it is the tendency to think in "either/or:" it is what limits the scope of my attention! The thing is: where I place my attention is where I invest my energy.

The Power of attention is expressed in S/Hebrew by the "God" Name *El* which also means "toward" just as the word "attention" does (from Latin *ad* "to" + *tendere* "stretch" → *attendere* for "to stretch toward"). If my goal doesn't offer me the opportunity to stretch, I will not know real change. Clearly, to reach my goal, I must learn to say **NO** to what doesn't evolve me. I must learn to say no to the past! S/Hebrew reconciles these opposites by way of *El* for "toward, deity" and *Lo* or "no." While "no!" is a whole sentence, what is the quality of my noes? Am I a false rebel, saying "no" with a vengeance as a way to withhold love? Or am I a true rebel, saying a big YES to my heart even when it means risking disappointing you with a "no?"

Finding out is easy: if I can choose peace at will, I am likely to serve *El*, *El* being the "God" Name spinning the sphere *Chesed* of "kindness" of my tree of life. Indeed, I am naturally kind when I focus on what evolves me and the whole. Since there's no part of me wanting to do what devolves me, there is also no one left to endlessly blame me for my failures. There's not even any error: no accidents! I understand, choose peace and emPower the "No." Hence, I do not let any doubt enter my mind that would delay my goal. This signifies that there is no dividedness or projection of enmity within me. I came to the LOVE that has no opposite, a love that ushers a sexual healing. **At last Cain is having what his brother had!**

WHILE "NO!" IS A WHOLE SENTENCE, WHAT IS THE QUALITY OF MY NOES? AM I A FALSE REBEL, SAYING "NO" WITH A VENGEANCE AS A WAY TO WITHHOLD LOVE? OR AM I A TRUE REBEL, SAYING A BIG YES TO MY HEART EVEN WHEN IT MEANS RISKING DISAPPOINTING YOU WITH A "NO?"

The Yesses of an Adam Aleph

"New friends may be poems but old friends are alphabets. Don't forget the alphabets because you will need them to read the poems." *Unknown*

Aleph and Beth are two worlds apart: the former is as fluid as a wave, the latter, as solid as a particle. The distinction between these two worlds is expressed in the two stories of creation of *Genesis 1* (the value of Aleph) and *Genesis 2* (the value of Beth). Understanding the difference helps me to change my script as I leave behind the self-imposed limitations of Beth's consciousness and raise my energy until I ascend into the freedom of Aleph's pure awareness. The image below illustrates how I relate to the centers of the throat (spheres 3 & 4) and the 3rd eye (spheres 1 & 2) when identified to the first Adam. Surely, these two rungs are the key players in making my exodus out of the infernal spheres of "Ego-Egypt" and my entry into the supernal spheres of "the Promised Land." Note: this vision of Adam Aleph's tree is an innovation from the rabbinical and hermetic traditions.

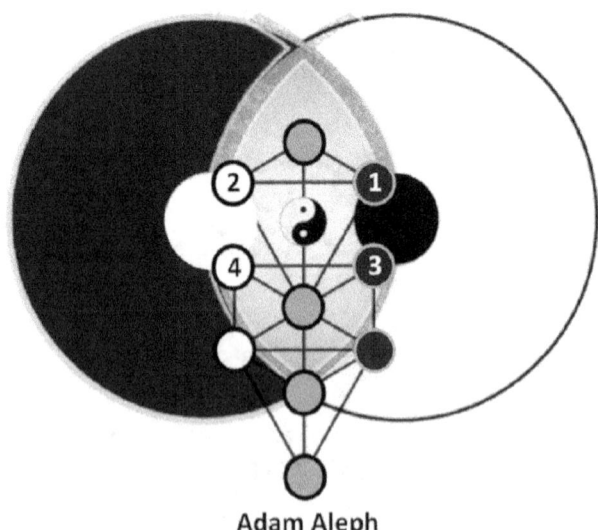

Adam Aleph

This is my story as **Adam Aleph**, as per *Genesis 1*. I KNOW I am created in the divine image, male and female. Since I have free passage through the KNOWLEDGE of good and evil (the yin/yang sphere), I neither desire nor resist this tree. I simply KNOW it is there for me – before me, behind me, above me, in me and all around me. I occupy the entirety of my tree, as I KNOW I have dominion over everything. I'm especially connected to the "God" Name that speaks through me as the Power of synchronicity. I just have to feel the energy of a word and speak it for it to be manifested as matter, with no time, no space, no mind to block it! Having it all, I suffer from no lack, no hunger, no doubt, and no betrayal. I have no need to defend or attack, to blame or to take myself down. This may be how I see the tree of life (or "God") face-to-face. Hence, my female path (the 3 black spheres) is on my right-hand side and my male path (the three white spheres), on my left-hand side.

- My 3rd eye center is wide-open: female sphere 1 is called *Binah* for the "understanding" that there is only One of us. My heart is filled with such pure Love that it reverberates through male sphere 2 called *Chesed* for "kindness." I will soon realize that the "God" Name that spins this sphere is *El* – the very Name that engraves the Power of attention. Clearly, I have no issue observing a world of abundance. The 3rd eye is also my command center: when I receive an intuitive hit, I reply with a big YES.
- My throat center is clear: female sphere 3 is called *Chokmah* for the "wisdom" that knows the difference between what I can change and what I can't. I will soon realize that the "God" Name that spins the "wisdom" sphere is *Yah* – the Name that engraves the Power of patience. Clearly, I can wait before my next word or action for the path to be clear. Such wholesomeness reverberates through male sphere 4 called *Geburah* for "Power," a Power that no longer burns me. Here is how: the throat is also my center of decision. When comes

time to decide, I CAN say "no" to what devolves me and choose to emPower the good, the true and the beautiful.

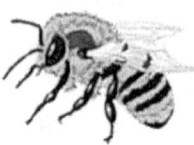

SURELY, THESE TWO RUNGS OF THE 3RD EYE AND THE THROAT CENTERS ARE THE KEY PLAYERS IN MAKING MY EXODUS OUT OF THE INFERNAL SPHERES OF SCARE CITY AND MY ENTRY INTO THE SUPERNAL SPHERES OF THE LAND OF ABUNDANCE.

THESE TWO "LANDS" ARE ALSO KNOWN AS THE FIRST TIER AND THE SECOND TIER IN SPIRAL DYNAMICS'S MODEL OF HUMAN EVOLUTION. AS FOR ADAM BETH, "HE" IS STILL WANDERING IN THE DESERT, LOOKING FOR THE EXIT DOOR...

The Nos of an Adam Beth

"The great question of philosophy remains: if life is meaningless, what can be done about alphabet soup?" *Woody Allen*

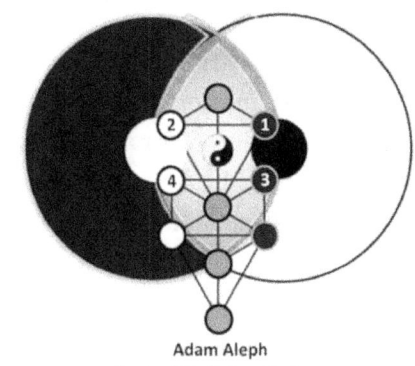

Adam Aleph
Seeing "God" face-to-face

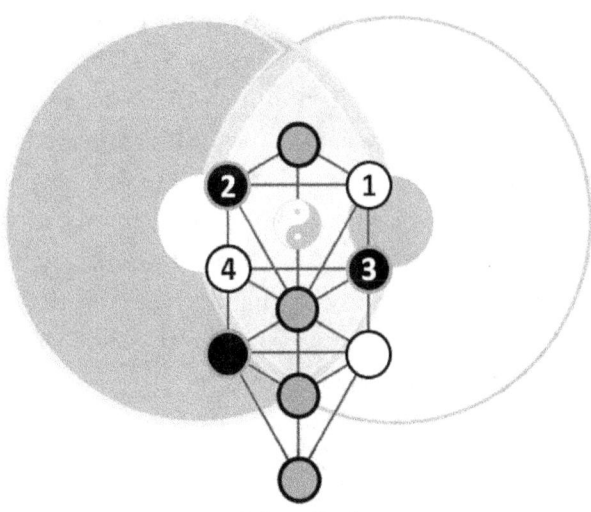

Adam Beth
Seeing "God's" back

I will now observe the same two rungs of the tree of (my) life from the viewpoint of the second Adam, a.k.a. Adam Beth. The tree of Adam

Aleph is pictured at the top, in the background, for me to see the shifts in consciousness. This second tree of life *mostly* corresponds to the teachings of both rabbinical Kabbalah and hermetic Qabalah. One exception, the reversal in polarities that is pictured here to occur at the throat.

This is my story as **Adam Beth** – as per *Genesis 2*. I no longer know. Instead, I think! Yep, I went down into the world of beliefs where problems are created. My first limiting belief is to *think* I am the body – a man! And now, I feel lonely and resist it by *thinking* "it's no good to be alone" (*Gen. 2:18*). The second limiting belief is lack: the garden in which I find myself has no water and no greenery. To top it all, I can't name and thus call my woman (meaning, my female side). And so, I'm in a complete illusion of separation: no LOVE in my heart! This explains how there is now a delay between what I desire and what I receive. As for the "God" Name that moves through me, namely YEWE *Elohim,* it is explained as the Power of HIStory: no wonder I would live in the past... This Name begins by giving me a negative commandment ("don't eat from the tree of knowledge") which sets me up to violate my own law, eat the forbidden fruit and fail. Clearly, I don't KNOW what is good or evil. As for the tree of (my) life, the positioning of its male and female paths shows that I can't see "God" face-to-face. I can only see "His" back. Indeed, my male path (crowned by sphere 1) is on my left-hand side, and my female path (crowned by sphere 2), on my right-hand side. The following concerns the larger image of Adam Beth:

- **My 3rd eye center** is closed for business since, while I am now in a fallen state, stuck in the 7 infernal spheres, and still forbidden to "eat" from the tree of knowledge (which has now become the tree of ignorance of good and evil). Moreover, since I believe that I am the body, I am now afraid to die. Male sphere 1 is traditionally called *Chokmah* for "wisdom." Female sphere 2 is still called *Binah* for "understanding." But since I don't have access to this rung, I can't hear or understand that we are One. I thus live in lack – in Scare City. The 3rd eye is still my command center: but now, when I receive an intuitive hit, I tend to resist it and reply with a "no."

- **My throat center** is unclear and ambivalent since its polarities are reversed: my male and female sides switched places in order to play the right and wrong game. Who's gonna be on top? Male sphere 3 is called *Chesed* for "kindness." However, his kindness is fake as he "tries" to compensate for the fury of a scorned woman. As for female sphere 4, it is called *Geburah* for "Power." However, her Power is *hysterical* (literally, she suffers from the "uterus") since the female side is unable to "receive." The throat is still my center of decision. But now, when comes time to decide, I often can't say "no" to what devolves me. I am also wobbly in the choice to emPower the good, the true and the beautiful.

To feel how deep the power struggle goes between my male and my female sides, I must first relate to courtship vs. marriage. In courtship, the male desires the female and the female resists the male's advances. In marriage, the female desires the male (a part of Eve's curse, as per *Genesis 3:16*), and the male resists the female's advances (a part of Adam's curse, as per *Genesis 3:19*).

These inverted polarities do not make for good sex. If I could only receive a sexual healing, I would understand that there's only One of us!

Code Sexual Healing - AL / YE

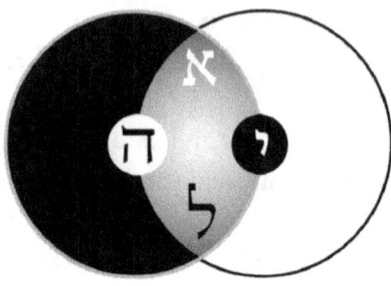

Imagine a language so pure and so sacred that it can reconcile and combine two opposite codes in just two pairs of letters...

Top: Hebrew letter Aleph (א) → A in Roman script
Right: Hebrew letter Yod (י) → I, J, Y in Roman script
Left: Hebrew letter Heh (ה) → E in Roman script
Bottom: Hebrew letter Lamed (ל) → L in Roman script

Here is how S/Hebrew inscribes code "Sexual Knowledge" in 2 codes:

- **EY/YE:** right to left and back, I inscribe code Patience by way of the Name *Yah*.
- **AL/LA:** top to bottom and back, I inscribe code Attention by way of the Name *El*.
- **AL YE:** signing (yes, doing the sign of the cross), I read *El Yah* (אל יה).

The Decoding: Patience + Attention = Sexual Healing. When I know that I can wait and continue to place my attention on the goal, I already got "the girl" – the one who completes me; the financing I need, the "God" who approves of me and heals me. Rabbinical Kabbalah teaches that the "God" Name spinning the sphere *Chesed* is *El* (אל) and that the "God" Name spinning the sphere *Chokmah* is *Yah*

(יה). *Chesed* for "kindness" is traditionally the sphere at the level of the throat which is the center of decision-making. *Chokmah* for "wisdom" is traditionally the sphere at the level of the 3rd eye which is the command center. These "God" Names are the *Koachim* or "Powers" which XPR transmits as **attention** and **patience**. *El* and *Yah* are also two of the three pairs of letters that form the Name *Elohim* (אלהים) or the Power of synchronicity (the third pair being the final letter Mem which means "pairs of waters"). Surely, within *Elohim's* Power of synchronicity, there is both attention and patience.

For me to be able to place my attention on the goal without letting any doubt enter my mind, I must have the patience to wait for the path to be clear before my next word or action. When I speak or act compulsively, I neither choose life nor peace. One day, I will understand why it was necessary that I would do harm. I will also understand how doing harm generated self-doubt, a doubt which I would use to further take me down. Understanding comes from following my folly into wisdom, which will naturally grow my patience quota.

The more patience I have, the more unwavering is the attention I can place on my goal. Equally true, the more I discipline my attention, the more patience I have. Time disappears, which means that mind disappears, leading me to experience the infinite QKosmic orgasm of being here and not here. That's sexual knowledge – *El Yah's ultimate healing!*

To understand how reading the letters of *El Yah* forms the sign of a cross, I see that the sphere *Daath* (for a "knowledge" that is sexual as it is experiential) is at the crossover point in between the throat and the third eye, involving the very spheres fueled by *El* and *Yah*.

As such, it is the mouth chakra, a transpersonal center where to consummate or die to who I *think* I am, and be reborn as the Word made flesh – honest and truth telling.

When I know that I can wait and continue to place my attention on the goal, I already got "the girl." I am whole, complete and "PAIRfectly" connected to the divine.

This chapter emanates from and inquires on the 3rd word after "in the beginning." Highlighted in the line above, its letters are read as *Et* for the untranslated particle that follows the transitive verb "created" and precedes its direct object "the heavens."

Introducing "Risking to Decide"

"The risk of a wrong decision is preferable to the terror of indecision." *Maimonides*

There is power in making a choice, which is why deciding terrifies me. There is also Power in fire and fire in language, which is why I fear [public] speaking. I'm afraid that, by making the "wrong" decision or saying the "wrong" word, I might get burned and subsequently, lose what I've got or not get what I want. Speaking is the Sacred Masculine in action. It is where the first *Et* particle resonates with the logos as the order and rationality that balances its feminine counterpart of the eros.

Hence, this chapter begins in Greek mythology, with Prometheus who stole the fire of the gods and burned himself with its Power. It continues with one of the two universal myths: the tower of destruction (the other cross-cultural myth being the flood). Known in the Bible as "the Tower of Babel," it involves the disruption of linguistic unity. This disruption is how I misuse the Power of words and must now burn in the illusion of karma. It is also what prevents me from being of One language, One speech, saying what I feel and meaning what I say. If only I could let go of the selfish desire to make a name for myself, I would not lose my voice!

This is when the Power of accountability – a Power which fuels the Four-lettered Name – shows its punishing side in four DREaM archetypes which are unconscious of being in the shadow. These four are the exact opposite of the four archetypes of LOVE which are conscious of being in the light.

This inquiry leads to the revealing of the second of SIX rows of codes which all start in patience. Newly added to code Patience are the letters of code Fire-Power. All of this leads me to the finality of making "THE" decision. On that note, is there such a thing as an integrated decision?

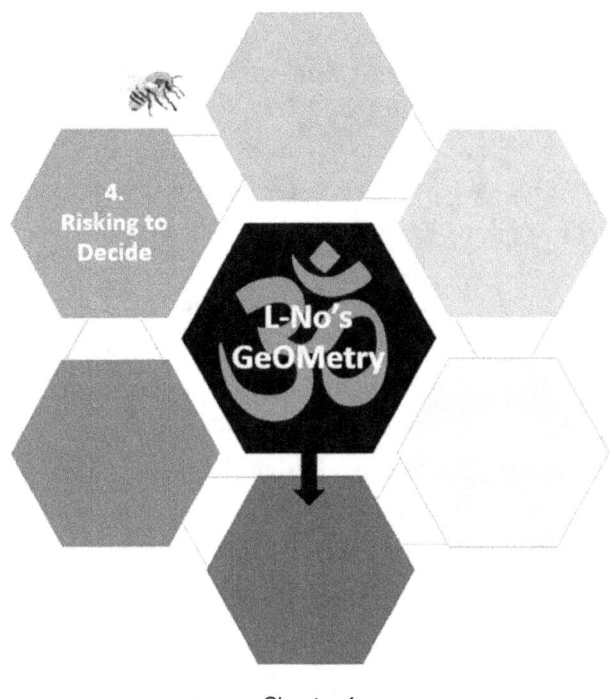

Chapter 4

The Burn of Fire-Power

"Someday, after mastering the winds, the waves, the tides and gravity, we shall harness for God the energies of love, and then, for a second time in the history of the world, man will have discovered fire." *Pierre Teilhard De Chardin*

As long as I have a body, every cell will mirror what's left of my communication problem, that is, where I repeatedly go into resistance! Cells are alive with language, which they use to work inwardly and outwardly in cooperation with other cells. Neuropeptides, for example, have receptors that pick-up signals and/or images which, in turn, affect my chemistry and my emotions. Therefore, health is the mark of clean communication within my society of cells.

This discussion reminds me of code Communication which is built around the word *Tah* (TA) for "cell" and reverses into the word *Et* (AT), the "untranslated" particle. AT/TA is the whole alphabet which is either moving forward (A to T – from the first letter to the last) or backward (T to A – from the last letter to the first). When I eventually accept to descend to letter Tav – the word for "note, sign" (the primary sign being the cross), I come to a crossover point. Deciding to turn within and take ownership of what limits me makes me "Tav-crucified." However, since there is no more resistance to my self-imposed limitations, I am now ready to ascend the alphabet until I am resurrected to my Aleph nature. Aleph is the state of flow – the "Shabbat" when I know *in my cells* that the force of Love is with me. There is no more anxiety in my space – no fear of falling, of speaking, of being rejected; no fear of burning myself with Power since I am neither pushing nor pulling against anything.

Another message given by AT the "untranslated" particle is to make conscious what I normally resist (such as darkness, my old friend). I simply "translate," if only to myself, what I tend to keep secret, e.g.; the fact that I feel bad! Feeling bad signals that fear has taken possession of me and that I lost track of the sacred.

The ultimate fear, even bigger than the fear of death, is to misuse Power and to get burned. To transcend my fear, I must learn how to honor the sacred fire of sexual energy and the potency of its spermatic word. This honoring is the subject of the Greek myth of Prometheus, a hero who stole the fire of the gods. His intention was seemingly pure: Prometheus sought to endow with a spark of life the clay he had used to create humans, a transfer of energy which could only happen through the fire of the gods. But Prometheus did more... He also tried to trick Zeus into eating bones and fat instead of the best portions of meat during a meal at Mt. Olympus. Zeus, angered by such disloyal acts, took away his fire, and sentenced him to a life of eternal damnation. Oyveh!

Fire is all about language, which S/Hebrew emphasizes through its signs which look like flamed letters. As for what the Greek says, the name *Prometheus* means "forethought." His brothers' name, *Epimetheus*, means "afterthought." Forethoughts and afterthoughts are two "brotherly" motions of the mind which negatively affect the cells. When unclear on my intentions, my hidden forethoughts anger the gods who will eventually take away from me the permission to use the fire of my sexual energy. This equates to the fear of being emPowered. If I choose to insist and push for an outcome, it is likely that I'll double-guess myself (or have afterthoughts).

As for Prometheus, his punishment as a consequence of the theft of fire was to be sentenced by Zeus to eternal torment. Prometheus was chained to a rock, while an eagle (Zeus' emblem) would tear at his liver. In Traditional Chinese Medicine, the liver is seat of anger – anger being the climax of resistance. Surely, what Prometheus resisted persisted: his liver would grow back overnight, only to be eaten again the next day in an ongoing cycle of dread. Prometheus was eventually freed by the hero Hercules. The Greek name *Hercules* means "light of the soul." The message: enlightenment is the way to free my soul from its shackles and my biology, from the tyranny of the thinking/feeling loop of sadness, shame and anger!

There is no way out: I must turn on the light by inquiring about my motivations in saying and doing what I say and do. In turn, honesty gives me the sense of being enough to handle the resistance. This emPowers me to create that which I know beyond doubt serves humanity: no forethought or afterthought on that! I stop interfering.

For if I were to believe that I am acting for your own good when I try to heal you, teach you, inspire you or save you, I would be a thief robbing you of the option to feel your pain and embrace your darkness... As long as I can distract myself by focusing on "you" as the clay I wish to endow with a spark of life, I don't have to feel my pain or fulfill my potential. I can just continue to create unconscious time, as my anger is eaten up each night to be regrown into a full blast of resisted anger the next day...

Note: the SIX days of resistance, from loneliness to anger, can be "felt" in *Chapter 6,* as a step toward "Becoming a Sentient Animal."

WHEN I DECIDE TO TURN WITHIN AND BE ACCOUNTABLE FOR THE LIMITATIONS I HAVE CREATED, I AM "TAV-CRUCIFIED." HAVING NO MORE RESISTANCE, I AM NOW READY TO ASCEND THE ALPHABET UNTIL I AM RESURRECTED TO MY ALEPH NATURE.

FROM A TO T, I COME TO MY "CURSEAFICTION" WHEN I ONLY FEEL BLESSED (NO MORE CURSE). FROM T TO A, I COME TO MY "ROSEERECTION," WHEN I FEEL THE BLOSSOMING OF MY HEART. ALL OF IT IS ORCHESTRATED BY LOVE.

THE SECOND ROW OF CODES

An English professor wrote up on the board "woman without her man is nothing" and told his students to punctuate it.

The males in the class wrote "Woman, without her man, is nothing." The females wrote "Woman! Without her, man is nothing."

As a man, I am generally raised to be a bread-winner and to compete with other men. Being artistic is frowned upon. As a woman, I am raised to make attractiveness my priority so that I could "get" a good husband – one who would provide for my children. Having a voice is not an option.

What programming have I accepted and obeyed? What conditioning did I resent and rebel against? Who am I? What do I really want?

When I have Patience, I am in the Eternal Now, not in the past and not in my conditioning. I delight in expecting the unexpected and wait for the hit of intuition to bring light on what I truly desire. I then make a **Decision** out of presence. Intuiting is going into it ("intuit"), it being **the Fire-Power**. When I do, the results will likely be more optimal than if I was reacting and had decided out of resistance.

Patience   Fire-Power   Decision

Patience + Fire-Power = Decision
When I do not get that I am "PAIRfect" as *Yah* (יה) the "GOD/dess" of
Patience, I tend to misuse my *Esh* (אש) "**Fire-Power**," as I am
possessed by the **Decision** I once made to believe that I am the body;
either a man or a woman" (יאש or אשה).

Code Fire-Power - AS / SA

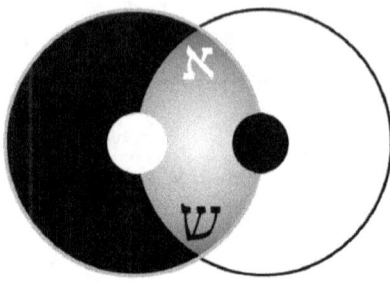

Imagine a language so pure and so sacred that it can reconcile opposites in just one pair of letters...

Top: Hebrew letter Aleph (א) → A in Roman script
Bottom: Hebrew letter Shin (שׁ) → S, Sh in Roman script

Here is how S/Hebrew inscribes code "Fire-Power" in 2 words:

- From top to bottom: I read *Esh* (אשׁ) for "fire."
- From bottom to top: I read *Sah* (שׁא) for "pardon, forgive."

The Decoding: one reason that language is holy is that it is said to have emerged around the sacred energy of fire. Daytime was given to hunting and gathering, and nighttime, to storytelling which took place around fires. There were also ancient stories – which were often sung rather than spoken – addressing a greater Power in the attempt to figure out what it wanted from us and how to negotiate with it. Both building fires and language seem to originate in humans. Both have a Power that we can use for good or bad.

Certainly, the desire to gain status and create opportunities is supported by linguistic competence: the more gifted I am with words, the more I can influence others. However, the danger of misusing the fire-Power of words is very real and so prevalent that it is the theme of the biblical myth of "the Tower of Babel." The cross-cultural cautionary tale describes how pride caused the breaking of linguistic unity.

> 'And the LORD said, "Behold, they are one people and they all have one language, and this [the desire to make a name for themselves] is only the beginning of what they will do. . . Come, let us go down and confuse their language, so that they will not understand one another's speech."' *Genesis 11:6-7*

This myth speaks volumes: first, we are confused, disconnected from life and not understanding each other when what we desire is for the little self alone. But also, there's no smoke without fire: a universal narrative about the disruption of linguistic unity presupposes the background existence of One language – a metalanguage.

Feeling its codes is to **forgive** ourselves for having misused and taking in vain the **fire-Power** of words. Such **pardon** is what returns us to being sentient, when we are so aware of our oneness that any dishonesty is unthinkable.

LNO invites such quantum leap by rediscovering the fire of language and imagining that the center of the Universe – the place where ultimate reality is created – started in a fiery jot. This jot – the letter Yod for "hand" which evolved into the letter Y for "why" – is the little flame that sparks the writing of each letter of the Hebrew alphabet. The vision is to allow me to feel and understand my own scriptures, practice enlightened justice and no longer be a victim of my biology.

THERE'S NO SMOKE WITHOUT FIRE: A UNIVERSAL NARRATIVE ABOUT THE DISRUPTION OF LINGUISTIC UNITY PRESUPPOSES THE BACKGROUND EXISTENCE OF ONE LANGUAGE – A METALANGUAGE.

Burning the Dream of Karma

"I call heaven and earth as witnesses against you today that I have set before you life and death, blessing and curse. Therefore, choose life, so that you and your seeds may live." *Deut. 30:19*

I have a choice to be in heaven or in hell. When conscious, I am awake in heaven (neither suffering nor dreaming of karma). When unconscious, I am dreaming in hell (unforgiving, eternally burning for my sins). And it makes me wonder... Who makes the decision to observe either heaven or hell, that is, to be conscious or unconscious of the true nature of the earth?

I am now reminded of the precedence of patience... Since I have experienced that making a choice out of resistance is unwise, I must own that I am yet to learn to wait for clarity before making a decision. I have not developed that skill because I don't have the courage to be honest in my speech. When my yesses and my noes (my choices) are aiming at getting your approval or disapproval, I am not choosing life; more exactly, I am not choosing to give birth to who I can be. Instead, I make myself a slave to the tyranny of appearances and to being without. The less fortitude I have in telling the truth and saying "no" to what devolves me, the more I get burned by the embers of guilt. It is a vicious circle since guilt makes it hard for me to enforce healthy boundaries. I seemingly lose my voice and suffer from a case of strangled throat chakra. I'm so used to pleasing "you" and trying to manipulate "you" that I no longer know who I am or what I want. And if I don't know what I want, how can I will it into being? Impossible!

This sense of being "not enough" is exactly how I start ♫♪ "looking for love in all the wrong places" and cause karmic consequences I would rather not have to experience. Distractions are a misuse of sexual Power (my *Esh* "fire"). It is also a misuse of emotional Power (my *El* "attention") as I now observe the curse rather than the blessing, death rather than a new way to look at life. I dream that there is an "out there" out there, someone who will complete me. When that doesn't work, I turn into Cain and am "possessed" by jealousy, believing that I am punished, and that my punishment is greater than I can bear. Just like my parents before me, I am cursed three and even four times. The decision to lie has made me vulnerable to the contamination of the following poisons. I no longer know that I am moved by "Good" and "God." Tough life being a con artist!

The Decision to Lie			
The Snake	The Adam	The Adamah	The Woman
Aversion	Ignorance	Entitlement	Greed
Broken Heart	Split Mind	Pain Body	Lost Soul

- **The poison of aversion corresponds to the snake's curse of a broken heart:** "and I will put enmity between you and the woman, and between your offspring and hers." *Genesis 3:15*
- **The poison of greed corresponds to the woman's curse of a lost soul:** "and your desire will be for your man, and he will rule over you."' *Genesis 3:16*
- **The poison of ignorance corresponds to the Adam's first curse of a split mind:** "cursed is the Adamah 'ground' because of you; through painful toil you will eat food from it all the days of your life." *Genesis 3:17*
- **The poison of entitlement corresponds to the Adamah's curse of a pain body:** "It will produce thorns and thistles for you, and you will eat the plants of the field." *Genesis 3:18*

Three "people" committed a transgression (the snake, the woman and the Adam) and four were punished (the snake, the woman, the Adam and his Adamah). All of that came from the snake's decision to lie – a decision also adopted by the woman who blamed the snake, and the Adam who blamed the woman. When taking responsibility for my transgressions, they become errors, which allows me to learn and to position myself to make conscious decisions moving forward.

The correspondences above parallel the curses of Judaism with the Buddhist teachings that identified three poisons as the mental vices that cause most of our problems, individually and collectively. Enmity is the biblical way to speak of Buddhist aversion. Yearning for Power is how the Bible speaks of greed, and forced labor, of ignorance. As for the scorched earth, it will eventually mutate into the poison of entitlement, when I wrongly defend my right to have what I believe "should" come to me.

WHEN BEING ACCOUNTABLE AND TAKING RESPONSIBILITY FOR MY TRANSGRESSIONS, THEY BECOME ERRORS, WHICH ALLOWS ME TO LEARN AND TO POSITION MYSELF TO MAKE CONSCIOUS DECISIONS MOVING FORWARD.

The Power of Accountability

> "How long, LORD? Will you forget me forever? How long will you hide your face from me? How long must I wrestle with my thoughts and day after day have sorrow in my heart?" *Psalm 13:1-2*

The real question might be: how long will I forget LOVE and play hide and seek? As long as I feel unloved, I will want to make a name for myself. And then one day, I will meet *Hashem* – "the Name" translated as "LORD" that will end up shattering my illusions (no matter how long it will take) and open me to take full responsibility for what I experience. I have seen how this Name – which is translated as the "LORD" and mispronounced as *Yahweh* – is actually best called by the name of its four letters Yod-Heh-Vav-Heh, letters which evolved into Roman script YEWE. This "God" Name is explained by *Golden XPR* as the Power of accountability: do good; good results, do harm; bad results. It is the Name that ordained that I'd suffer the consequences of my actions and that selects the sequence of activities that I must undergo in each lifetime. And while it seems that some people can get away with murder, outcomes are like debts: they can be carried into future lifetimes! So, how far will I go in compromising my climbing the ladder of success this time?

While needing to be recognized as "special," it seems that, if I dread confusion, I resist clarity even more. I don't want a full blast of light as I'm still hooked to the dark, to manipulating, to lying if I have to. I need my wound more than I do clarity – more than I do healing!

Alternatively, how willing am I to fall and fail again and again so that I would come to surrender and "unknow" my judgments of good and evil? When resisting that which I see as "no good," the four archetypes in me are no longer conscious, but asleep in the "DREaM." These four "people" resist the darkness so much that they are unconscious to be regressing. Just like the forward motion is how the **LOVE** archetypes are invoked by their initial letters (e.g.; **L** as in Leader), the backward motion is how the **DREaM** archetypes are invoked by their final letters (e.g.; **D** as in chil**D**). Surely, how will I come to the LOVE that has no opposite unless LOVE compassionately embraces its nemesis?

- LOVE calls forth the four light archetypes that are conscious to be working as One and, as such, to initiate the behavior of Love: Leader, Officer, Visionary, Engineer.
- The **DREaM** calls forth the four shadow archetypes that are unconscious of being divided, and end up doing harm as a chil**D**, a saboteu**R**, a prostitut**E**, and a victi**M**, unaware of the a-angel that watches over them in the dark.

I can now begin to relate to the Four-lettered Name first appearing at Cain's conception. Cain was born with a karmic debt he had to redeem – the very pain which his parents wouldn't feel and which became his legacy. That is how it was written for him to be a murderer. YEWE is who selected the sequence of activities that Cain was to undergo in his lifetime as the exact actions that would most favor his spiritual evolution, be they pleasant or unpleasant.

As for me, as long as I am identified with the body or the ego, I can't escape from YEWE's jurisdiction. Therefore, the only way to become free of suffering is to fully transcend the agent upon whom all suffering depends – namely, the ego and come to the LOVE that has no opposite (no dream of separation, no attachment to Scare City). The two sets of four – LOVE and DREaM – work in polarity with each other. Just like the forces of yin and yang (or of evil and good), they oppose each other in order to give rise to each other. These eight archetypes are universal. Their shadow side was first recognized by author and medical intuitive Caroline Myss.

To help me feel them in my soul, I have the help of the four ancient mythological creatures introduced earlier. As an animalistic extension of the four of LOVE, these lifeforms work in synergy to lead me to know that nothing is personal. It is only when I know that it is not about me that I stop abusing my Power and doing harm, as I now experience that the work of creation is done *through* me and not *by* me. While they belong to the myth, these creatures embody the Power of the Four-lettered Name: they will accompany me in my journey to becoming honest and being fully accountable.

Yod (Y)	Vav (W)	Heh (E)	Heh (E)
D for chilD	E for prostitutE	M for victiM	R for saboteuR
L for Leader	E for Engineer	O for Officer	V for Visionary
The Lion	The Human	The Bull	The Scorpion to be Eagle

From top to bottom: the four letters of YEWE, the four universal archetypes in the shadow, the four universal archetypes in the light, and the four creatures

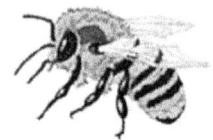

LOVE CALLS FORTH THE FOUR LIGHT ARCHETYPES THAT ARE CONSCIOUS TO BE WORKING AS ONE AND, AS SUCH, TO INITIATE THE BEHAVIOR OF LOVE: LEADER, OFFICER, VISIONARY, ENGINEER.

THE DREAM CALLS FORTH THE FOUR SHADOW ARCHETYPES THAT ARE UNCONSCIOUS TO BE DIVIDED, AND END UP DOING HARM AS A CHILD, A SABOTEUR, A PROSTITUTE, AND A VICTIM, UNAWARE OF THE A-ANGEL THAT WATCHES OVER THEM IN THE DARK.

The Power of Decision

"Nothing is more difficult, and therefore more precious, than to be able to decide." *Napoleon Bonaparte*

If life is about making conscious choices, consciousness is the job I've signed up for, whether I am conscious of it or not. :-) According to neuroscientists, we are conscious of only about 5 percent of our cognitive activity. Therefore, the majority of our decisions is sourced in the 95 percent of brain activity that is unconscious. However, to be conscious of what I *really* want and of what I decide to empower, I just have to look at my reality. Will I be big enough to take responsibility for the results of my communication?

Yes, it is that simple and also that tough! Life, the fundamental essence of being, is a moral struggle. When I have a vision, a calling, a goal, I am committed to be an agent of change, and less prone to anxiety. For me, sitting around is not an option. I must engage, no matter the odds. The potency of such dynamics of engagement was known by Noah. He was told to build an ark and he actually decided to listen, even though he must have wrestled with his guidance in the process. Response-ability is the signature of the religious instinct. It is also the mark of patriarch Abraham, and from there, of the Abrahamic religions. His answer to "God's" calling was summed up in one single word – *Hineini* for "here I am," a quality of presence he maintained even when instructed to sacrifice his son.

Conversely, when going AWOL and just "trying," I'm as Jacob; an embezzler, a liar, a con artist. Eventually, I will endeavor to walk with "God" and find the courage to see truth face-to-face. I will then be renamed "ISRAEL," the soul print of someone who "IS REAL." Meanwhile, I just need the willingness to fail until I know that there's nothing personal and that I am supported in my falls by the divine. To know that, I just need to go to the alphabet: 14th letter Nun which, as a word, means "fish" and, by extension, "fallen" is followed by 15th letter Samekh which, as a word, means "support." "LOVE upholds all who fall, and raises up all who are bowed down." *Psalm 145:14*

Yes, the letters are non-biological sentient animals that entered Noah's ark pair by pair, as the signs Nun and Samekh did, and certainly, as Aleph and Beth do. Aleph and Beth are resonances (and brain waves) that have two very different ways to decide:

- **Aleph is the ox (#1). Its primal energy is akin to pure choiceless awareness.** When in the Aleph state, I am not attached to an outcome. Instead, I trust in the harmony that infuses the cosmos while decisions are made *through* me and not *by* me. My mind has stopped moving: there is no fear in my space, no private desires to take my peace away. Aleph brain waves allow for deep relaxation. It is an optimal time to reprogram the mind and to be in touch with my intuition.
- **Beth is the house (#2). Its secondary energy is akin to consciousness.** When in the Beth stage, I am attached to having a specific result and thus, concerned by the Power of decision. I tend to worry about making a choice: shall I go right or left? Indeed, there is Power behind making a choice, which is why choosing terrifies me. Beth brain waves are associated with critical reasoning, which can also lead to stress, anxiety and overthinking.

Life is made up of an infinite number of choices, each choice being a creative act that determines which consequence I will set up. Consequently, the Power of decision is really the Power to create, and, as such, the greatest of all Powers.

When avoiding the changes that my decision might generate, I speak and act out of fear and lose connection with what I communicate. I can't be heard, which is the source of my suffering. Whether I know it or not, I am called to be authentic in my relating, saying what I feel, meaning what I say. Lying, either deliberately or not, is a way to delay the changes that a straight-forward decision would produce. Postponing a decision is also a lie: I am not being REAL with my motivations! Lucifer can now have a field day...

TO BE CONSCIOUS OF WHAT I *REALLY* WANT AND OF WHAT I DECIDE TO EMPOWER, I JUST HAVE TO LOOK AT MY REALITY.

WILL I BE BIG ENOUGH TO TAKE RESPONSIBILITY FOR THE RESULTS OF MY COMMUNICATION?

Code Decision - AS / YE

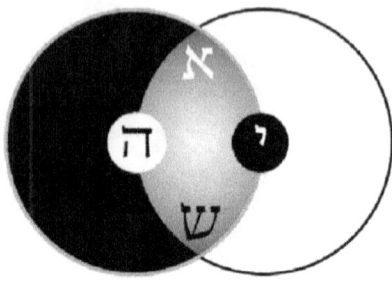

Imagine a language so pure and so sacred that it can reconcile opposites in just two pairs of letters...

Top: Hebrew letter Aleph (א) → A in Roman script
Right: Hebrew letter Yod (י) → I, J, Y in Roman script
Left: Hebrew letter Heh (ה) → E in Roman script
Bottom: Hebrew letter Shin (ש) → S, Sh in Roman script

Here is how S/Hebrew inscribes code "Decision" in 4 words:

- From top to bottom: I read *Esh* (אש) for "fire" of code Fire-Power.
- From right to left: I read *Yah* (יה) for the "GOD/dess" of code Patience.
- From top to bottom to left: I read *Ishah* (אשה) for "woman."
- From top to right to bottom: I read *Ish* (איש) for "man."

The Decoding: Patience + Fire-Power = Decision. Once upon a time, I made the decision to be born into the body. Surely, to have the biology of a boy or a girl was my first decision! Prior to that, I was just fine, having it all, understanding and feeling deep in my soul that LOVE knows no separation and even that it defies mathematics by giving the sublime and endless experience that 1+1=1. But then, the desire to make a name for myself started stirring in me until I was compelled to come out of the big Nothing and be something, some-body and some body...

To do so, I started by splitting the "**GOD/dess**" PAIRfection of *Yah* (YE) into two "ribs:" a Yod (Y) rib and a Heh (E) rib. I continued by realizing that I could form the word *Ish* (איש) for "**man**" by adding the Yod rib to *Esh* "**fire**" (אש), or *Ishah* (אשה) for "**woman**" by adding the Heh rib to the same *Esh* "fire." **Deciding** is literally to cut off one side of me as the word itself comes from Latin *de* "off" + *caedere* "to cut." No matter which side I decided to cut off, I forgot that, in *Genesis* 1:27, I was neither *Ish* nor *Ishah* but "the Adam," a being created male and female. Being made in the divine image of *Elohim,* I had within me the pair *Yah* (יה) of code Patience and the pair *El* (אל) of code Attention – two Powers that make a huge difference in my decision-making processes.

When I have the Powers of patience and attention with me, I occupy the entirety of the tree of (my) life. This means that I can fully focus on my goal while being unafraid of the speed at which my goal will manifest, since I believe and know that I already am in synchrony with it. I just do what I do in the spirit of utmost excellence, and let "God" handle the details.

But this was when I was in the mind of Adam Aleph – in *Genesis 1*. I am now in the mind of Adam Beth, I'm in *Genesis* 2, hypnotized by the belief that I am the body (either wanted as a boy or resisted as a girl), and feeling very alone as a result. To top it all, I am unable to find my partner. Hence, I now need an outside force to step in, put me to sleep and make a woman for me.

But who said that I ever woke up? After I dreamed up my woman, I soon see a snake occupying my dream time... Moreover, it's like I drank a soup of oblivion: I can't even remember that I was the one who made the decision to be somebody (one word), but also *some body* (two words). If I had perfect recall, I would again be source of my creation and deliberate in adopting a biological gender. Ideally, there would be no enmity against my "evil" female side and no yearning for my "good" male side – just the knowledge of opposites, a biblical knowledge that would actually make me gender-fluid – if only in my mind! But where else is sex but in the mind? This also means that I'd have the Power to change as I would know that deciding is how to shape my destiny. I would simply choose the goal that had the greatest impact for good (for me and others—same) and stick with my decision.

Energy follows thoughts: 1) I think, 2) I feel, 3) I have. This is the order by which I create. Thus, the question: what experiences do the following beliefs create in my life?

I am a man. | I am a woman. | I am not a man. | I am not a woman. | I am gender neutral | I am not gender neutral.

IF DECIDING IS HOW TO SHAPE MY DESTINY, WILL I RISK DECIDING TO BE CREATED IN "THE IMAGE OF GOD?"

Making "THE" Decision

"And the day came when the risk to remain tight in a bud was more painful than the risk it took to blossom." Anaïs Nin

In case I'm still delaying my blossoming, here are two ways to look at "THE" decision... First, is there a decision that has so much integrity that it is absolute? Second, might there be a personal decision that I have been postponing? I ask since, for now, I live in Scare City, endlessly agitated by the turmoil, aggravated by loads of stress hormones, fixated on and even bound to the material world, so much so that I have completely forgotten that I am energy. Yes, I am hiding my true face under my fears, hesitating to decide so afraid I am that I may lose something or not get what I want.

And then the day came when to stop postponing change and transcend the fear to be alive. At last, I made "THE" decision. This holy instant called me to the present moment, when I couldn't lie anymore and had to see the truth. Making "THE" decision may just be to decide to choose peace. Maybe my decision was prompted by a diagnosis, a divorce, a bankruptcy; either way, the reversal of fortune compelled me to take a chance and risk suffering, risk making an error, risk making a fool of myself, risk stumbling from defeat to defeat, risk dying so that I could live, and all the while, still be at peace. And ever since, I have known that I would not depart without completing a project that mattered to my soul.

This depth of peace is the proverbial peace that passes understanding when I am so surrendered that I can finally live without a why. No more "why me, God?" or "why is there evil in the world?" or "why couldn't I say no?"

Let's imagine that I decide without needing any drama to remind me of my mortality... To choose peace is also to only be inclined to do good. It is not to hesitate to tackle the next project – the one that will have the biggest impact for good in my personal and professional life, and bless the whole. If I can't choose peace, it indicates that my inquiry is not complete: there is something I do not understand. In that case, I may choose to engage on the path of becoming conscious by making the decision to strive for and acquire self-knowledge. Indeed, seeking the kingdom first is always a good beginning! But even then... What does that mean?

I am asking myself to contemplate what it would mean for me to make the decision to choose peace and see the changes that this would create... Know peace; know the Self! If spending some amount of time in ignorance, it is likely that it is when my allegiance goes to the dark. Am I aware of what I want in these times? Might my goal be directed by greed or aversion? Do I want to punish "them" and make them pay for my suffering? For greed and aversion are the main reasons why I'd spend any time in ignorance, punishing myself by resisting to do what I know I am to do...

Choosing peace is choosing a different sensory path. Moreover it is as final as an alcoholic who says "this is my last drink" and never suffers a single exception after speaking these prophetic words...

Therefore, choosing peace is asking myself to purify my energetic body from the poisons of greed, aversion and ignorance as the prerequisite to using Power wisely. Upon knowing that my soul is pure, I will then usher my dream vision with the force of such potent desire that the generosity of that decision will carry an energy that has a greater breadth than my neurological conditioning and my emotional addictions.

Then and only then, will my body follow the sound of a new mind and manifest memorable experiences that will, in turn, generate an emotion so authentic that it will rewrite my DNA: no more victim's story! And as my biology changes, I will increasingly know joy and resonate with the sacred: 'And he said to her, "daughter, your faith has made you well. Go in peace. Your suffering is over."' *Mark 5:34*

Understand. Choose peace. emPower the NOW. I just need to decide. More exactly, I just need to understand what prevents me from making "THE" decision to alter my energetic signature so that my biological fate is changed by my own actions. To allow new memories to form around me, I must surrender. This is the choice of peace – "THE" decision. And as I understand how a new belief creates a new emotion which forms into a new behavior which manifest a new "personal" reality, I give it all to LOVE – all the masks; all the personas – and enter the field of infinite possibilities. This divine field already knows the outcome. It re-members my dream and supports it!

LET'S IMAGINE THAT I DECIDE TO CHOOSE PEACE WITHOUT NEEDING ANY DRAMA TO REMIND ME OF MY MORTALITY... WOULDN'T THAT BE PURE GENIUS!

This chapter emanates from and inquires on the 4th word after "in the beginning." Highlighted in the line above, its letters read *Hashamayim* for "the heavens."

Introducing "Freeing our Genius"

"Simplicity is the most difficult thing to secure in this world; it is the last limit of experience and the last effort of genius."
George Sand

The conflict between two opposite aspects of genius – demonic and angelic – is the reason why unbridling my creativity can be such a challenge. For me to have the courage to open up, I must trust that, once coming out, my genie won't break everything in sight. Socrates was very familiar with this strange life inside him – this "daemon" which he saw as the force that made him a real philosopher. Indeed, once contended with, this force leads me to recognizing who I am.

I now come to the third of SIX rows of codes. Adding the letters of code Recognition to those of code Patience, I arrive at the end of craving and let go of demonic possession via code Transmutation. Indeed, loving myself gives me all the love, approval and recognition I have ever wanted. Hence, I no longer want: what's to want when I have it all? This readies me for the fourth row of codes – the great work by which to transmute what is left of the hatred into a LOVE that has no opposite. I can now reorient myself to feel the transmutations of code Transmutation. This is when snake-Power rises within me as the force of *Kundalini* in Sanskrit; *Mashiach* ("Messiah") in Hebrew.

I have now fulfilled my calling; my law. This also means that I transcended my name. Being free, I realize how "God" created the paradox by way of *Hashamayim* for "the heavens," a word which can also be seen as *Esh-Mayim* for "fire/water." As such "the heavens" is a metaphor for the ability to hold the tension of opposites (i.e.; to have patience). Therein is the secret of the sense of enough, and by extension, of purposiveness: to stay centered even as I go through the initiation that will end this chapter. By overcoming my either/or thinking,

I become fluent in "God's" language and move out of Scare City into a mind of abundance – the mind of a genius.

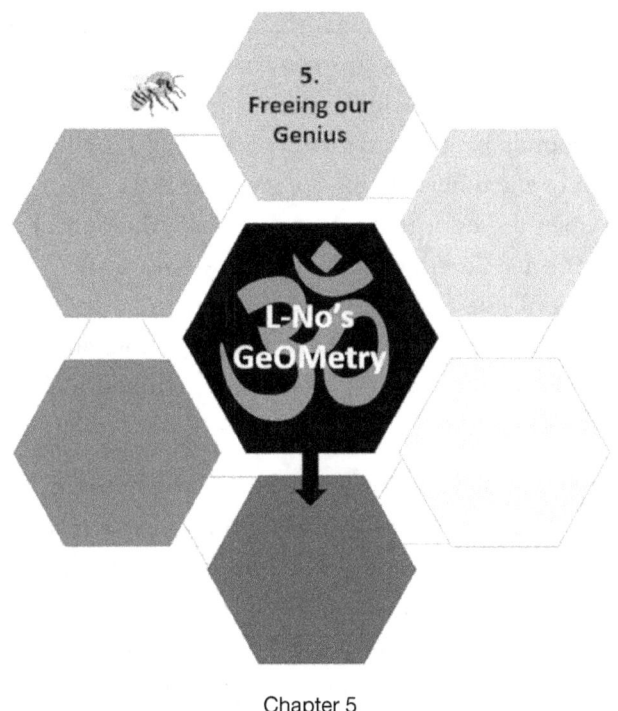

Chapter 5

The Demon behind my Genius

"If you take away my demons, you might take away my angels, too." *Tennessee Williams*

I oftentimes have the nagging feeling that I am not living up to my creative potential. Might I feel hindered by the deeply embedded programming of social conformity? Am I unwilling to cross the threshold? Do I fear that, if I really shed those shackles, I might isolate myself from my peers? Even worse, might my efforts awaken the raging genius inside me that is for now safely bottled up?

Truth be told, I'm so constrained that I don't even know what my passion is. By the same token, I can also see that not knowing is a way not to answer the call, and not to commit to my vision. I imagine that freeing my genius is like making love... I must forget that I am a separate doer and let the divine fire penetrate me. Soon I melt into the vision; time disappears, which means that mind disappears! And while that sounds beautiful, I'm still afraid that I'll either get bored with no fire or burn myself with its intensity. Ah... What will it take for me to open the door to the unconscious – the part of me that is already connected to what's missing? The only "sane" option is to befriend the evil side that I hide, deny and repress, and to transmute its darkness into light. This freeing of the genie from encapsulation is the process of making Art and of healing, both being alchemical in nature.

It is what Aladdin did: he went into a dark cave and ended up turning on the light! The tale of *Aladdin and the Magic Lamp* comes from the book of *The One Thousand and One Nights,* an enchanting collection of fairy tales of Middle Eastern origin. Aladdin is a penniless young man, who is persuaded by a sorcerer to retrieve an oil lamp from a magical cave of wonder. Yet the sorcerer double-crosses him, and Aladdin is trapped in the cave. Fortunately, he retains the magic lamp which he inadvertently rubs, causing a genie to appear. This genie will bring him home, in more ways than one. Indeed, Aladdin will become affluent, marry the daughter of the emperor, Princess Badroulbadour, succeed to his father-in-law's throne, and live happily ever after... And while the Walt Disney movie differs slightly from the original tale, the spirit is kept intact, especially when it *comes* to legitimizing our wishes. The Lucifer question now comes to a new depth: if I can wish for anything (other than taking a life, swaying someone's love, or reviving the dead), what is the most integral wish I could formulate?

My genius possesses phenomenal cosmic Powers. Yet these Powers can only be harnessed when I, the owner of the lamp, make the

only real wish there is – to free my genius from its slavery. From thereon, my genius and I can live happily forever after...

I am Aladdin and the sorcerer and the lamp and the light and the bottle that encapsulates the genie and the genie. To strengthen my container, I have a voracious hunger for LOVE I must satiate, soon followed by the attacks of doubt for me to vanquish. When I do, my genius comes out blossoming, ready to build me a palace of love. The hunger, the doubt, the betrayals -- these are true trials that I endure, along with the confusion that the ego creates around "creating." Indeed, who is the doer? How can I be at once fully responsible and aware that creation – for good or bad, in sickness and in health – happens *through* me and not *by* me? Who leads me into temptation? Even the words "taming my genius" sounds like a misuse of Power. While it is a mighty power to be reckoned with, I must find a way to befriend it so that it would get sustenance without becoming disruptive.

The fear of being fully expressed as a soul is such that the Greek word *daemon* or *daimōn* soon became "demon" as a malignant supernatural being in lieu of a presence that inspires, guides and infuses his protégé through its divine power. And yet, these spirits are endowed with a special mission: they open channels of communication between humans and gods. To this end, they can make themselves known as a voice or an image – symbols in general. Socrates had his own daemon, that is, a personal divinity which saved him while everyone else was either killed or taken by the adversary's cavalry. Socrates even suggested that it is his daemon who enabled him to become a true philosopher. Genius is the Latin name of for these presences, a name which comes from the Arabic *Djinni* by way of Hebrew word *Gan* for "garden." Indeed, giving birth to the flower of my genius is a cultivation. Even more fun: the TV sitcom, *I dream of Jeannie*, centers around a 2000-year-old female genie played by Barbara Eden (as in *Gan Eden* for "Garden of Eden")!

Not only are these lifeforms akin to nature spirits, their wood and their vegetation, but they also actively blossom from within. The flower of my genius opens when my own imaginative dreamscape resonates with a LOVE that has no opposite. I am now free and fulfilled...

My genius possesses phenomenal cosmic Powers. Yet these Powers – and especially Fire-Power – can only be harnessed when I, the owner of the lamp, make the only real wish there is: to free my genius from its slavery. From thereon, my genius and I can live happily forever after...

THE THIRD ROW OF CODES

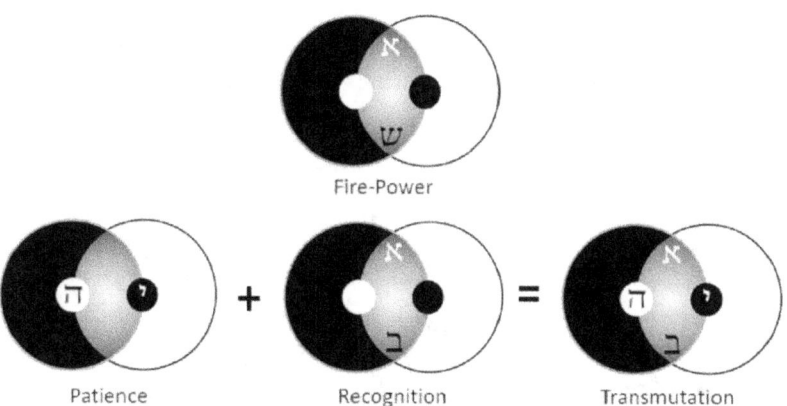

Fire-Power

Patience + Recognition = Transmutation

Patience + Recognition = Transmutation
When I know the "PAIRfection" of *Yah* (יה) as "GOD/dess," I have
Patience which allows me to come to *Ab* (אב) the "father, alphabet"
and to hear "him" speaking to me. The more I listen to my heart, the
more my self-esteem grows. The **Recognition** of who I am eventually
leads me to the **Transmutation** of hatred into Love.

Prior to understanding the root-cause of my hunger for love, approval
and recognition, I shall be introduced to the ATBaSh code by which
to substitute the letter Shin (ש) of code Fire-Power with the letter
Beth (ב) of code Recognition.

The ATBaSh Code

"It's not that the Bible is true. It's that the Bible is the prerequisite for the manifestation of truth, which makes it far more true than just 'true,' and the only way to solve the problem of perception."
Jordan Peterson

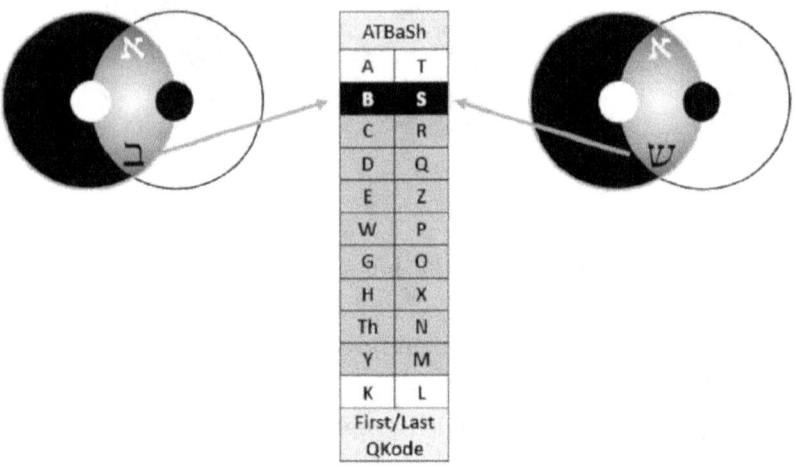

ATBaSh	
A	T
B	**S**
C	R
D	Q
E	Z
W	P
G	O
H	X
Th	N
Y	M
K	L
First/Last	
QKode	

When the ATBaSh code transfers the energy of **Fire-Power** (אש) to the **Recognition** (אב) of who I Am.

In the illustration above, the ATBaSh is used to substitute the sign Beth (ב) of code Recognition to the sign Shin (ש) of code Fire-Power, a process that is entirely kosher. :-)

The Hebrew Bible may just be an otherworldly harmonic transmission to help me to resonate with the Mystery. The Torah letters work in pairs as if in a quantum entanglement, and are affected by each other's change. The letters act as particles that can be intimately connected to each other, as revealed by ancient Kabbalistic codes such as the ATBaSh code which pairs the first letter of the first set of eleven letters to the last letter of the second set of eleven letters, e.g.; A to T, B to S, etc. As such, the ATBaSh could be called "the First and the Last" code, each word and letter association leading me closer to embodying the experience of an eternal beginning and ending. The process takes me from AT/TA to KL/LK, the goal being, once again, to understand my true motivations.

Clearly, there is Power in recognizing where I may have made an error. That is even the first step towards lasting change.

THE HEBREW BIBLE MAY JUST BE AN OTHERWORLDLY HARMONIC TRANSMISSION TO HELP ME TO RESONATE WITH THE MYSTERY.

Code Recognition - AB / BA

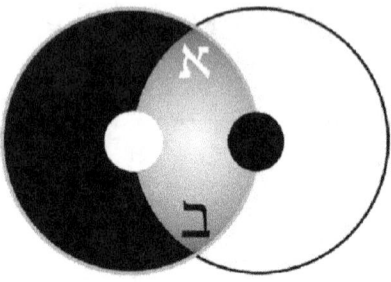

Imagine a language so pure and so sacred that it can reconcile opposites in just one pair of letters...

Top: Hebrew letter Aleph (א) → A in Roman script
Bottom: Hebrew letter Beth (ב) → B in Roman script

Here is how S/Hebrew inscribes code "Recognition" in 2 words:

- From top to bottom: I read *Ab* (אב) for "father, alphabet."
- From bottom to top, I read *Ba* (בא) for "entered."

The Decoding: this code "recognizes" that both science and religion speak the same mystical language. Starting with religion, *John 16:28* reports that Jesus said: "I came forth from the Father and have come into the world; I am leaving the world again and going to the Father." The S/Hebrew letters that evolved into AB form the word *Ab* for both "**father**" and "**alphabet**." The S/Hebrew letters that evolved into BA form the word *Ba* for "entered." What is to be entered is the sanctuary of my heart. This is where I intuitively know what to do. My "Father" clearly spells it out for me. But I don't want to hear it or see it... While I like the idea of pursuing the mystical union, I have the same condition: when time comes to cross over, I want to keep my ego intact!

Hence, I resist my guidance. This makes me a victim of my environment as I am now solely focused on the 3D world. It is therefore my resistance to change and/or my fear of death that keep me from "entering" the sanctuary of my heart. When listening to Father AlphaBet, I no longer waste my resources as a prodigal son. While "the Son" represents the mind, "the Father" represents the heart. When I resonate with it, I recognize that it is my nature to be Love. My entire being is now flooded with gratitude. And as I rise from Beth into Aleph, the perception of having made an error is replaced with the ability to suspend my judgments. Doing so sets my will free. Note: code Recognition is an expansion from *TCO—Book 2* that transmitted AB / BA as code Free Will.

As for science, the move from Beth to Aleph is the shift from Beta brainwaves (when I am constantly analyzing and judging my performance) into Alpha brainwaves (when I stop pushing or pulling, relax into peace, and let the work be done through me). But will I choose to change my brainwaves? As a precursor of Greek, S/Hebrew deepens the meaning of the lettered brainwaves. It is another way in which this alphabet can be my map to the choice of peace, a map so thorough that it traces an archetypal grid that covers all areas impressed and engraved with the pain story.

Until I can recognize how I pretend to take care of others instead of first taking care of me, I will not be able to do due diligence. I might as well look forward to lying to myself again. Recognition of truth is how to transmute dark emotions. When I do, my LOVE has nothing left to oppose it!

IMAGINE BEING SO MUCH IN MY HEART THAT I CAN'T POSSIBLY YEARN FOR LOVE, APPROVAL OR RECOGNITION. THIS IS MY EXIT FROM SCARE CITY... AND THE END OF CRAVING!

The End of Craving

"They will neither hunger nor thirst, nor will the desert heat or the sun beat down on them. S/he who has a womb of compassion will guide them and lead them beside springs of water." *Isaiah 49:10*

This inquiry invites me to enter the mystery of water, a mystery inscribed by the letter Mem (מם) which, being written with a Mem regular (מ) and a Mem final (ם), fittingly illustrates a pair. Mem is one of the five letters that take a different shape when at the end of a word (ם), which also says that it ushers an ending and/or a redemption of sorts. Mem final marks the end of desire (more on the finals in the appendix). I will now explore why it conveys this gift. I'll begin with the example of the "God" Name *Elohim* which ends in a Mem final. I have seen how it is the Power of synchronicity: when its force is with me, I can say: "let me know a peace so profound that it passes understanding," and see that such depth of peace was already here within me as I stopped asking why.

Clearly, if I had this Power, I wouldn't hunger for anything. I would know that I am enough. Feeling my worthiness would open my arteries. The blood that would flow into my heart would beat to the rhythm of such wholeness that it would be impossible for me to want. How would I want anything when I feel that I have everything? But why the connection to water? Why not air or fire? Four reasons to explain the link to water:

- **Receptivity:** water may be the ultimate of the four classical elements. First, it is the most receptive. Also, nothing can resist it, even though is it soft and malleable. Moreover, water is the element of the soul: for my soul vision to form, I just need to feel it with my inner "I." Thus, water is akin to the emotional body: when inclined to do good, I feel love, peace and gratitude, emotions that attract manifestations that are aligned with the good of all. I have a very different experience with matter when I am inclined to do evil.

- **Resistance:** the value of the regular Mem (מ) is 40. It lives in the middle row of the 4-Resisting chamber (see *Chapter 6, Resistance + Desire = the Physics of Self-esteem*). Indeed, water's resistance is a force (a.k.a. "drag") that uses friction to slow down that which moves through water. The denser the water, the greater the drag force.
- **Resting:** the value of Mem final (ם) is 600. It lives in the bottom row of the 6-desiring chamber (again, see *Chapter 6*). As such, it is the most intense experience of desiring – its climax and its end. Mastering my emotions (666) does not mean that I don't want anything anymore, but more that there is now a space in between my desire and its fulfillment, a resting space which cancels out any obsessive craving or even desperation!
- **Restoration:** water symbolizes the Tao. "The highest good is like water. Water gives life to the ten thousand things and does not strive. It flows in places men reject and so is like the Tao." *Lao Tzu, Tao Te Ching, Chap. 8.* Water also symbolizes the Torah. It is said that, just as water is cleansing and restores the soul, so does the Torah.

This is how I must jump into the ocean of my consciousness, where the fragmented self awaits cohesion. The seeds of fragmentation were planted on Day 2 (*Genesis 1:6*), when there was a division between the pairs of waters of above and of below, effectively splitting my soul from my heart (a 1st pair), and my body from my mind (a 2nd pair). This is how Adam Beth will eventually have boundary issues, and a need for protection.

As for me, in order for the energy of Love to suffuse my thinking, I must feel that I am integral. I can then change the past of my separateness. To be whole, "PAIRfect," complete and connected (integral), I must recognize that I am the one who chooses suffering by resisting to feel the emotions that smother me. This is making the choice to choose peace. **Understand. Choose peace. emPower the NOW.** This formula is how to satiate my hunger for LOVE and answer the only real question: who am I?

Will I have the courage to fish for the Piscean symbols of the dreams in the murky waters of my repressed emotions? I have seen how Mem is the middle letter of the alphabet (when written linearly). It invites me to center and be as water, adopting the path of least resistance.

UNDERSTAND. CHOOSE PEACE. EMPOWER THE NOW.

THIS FORMULA IS HOW TO ENTER THE MURKY WATERS AND THEREBY, SATIATE THE HUNGER FOR LOVE AND ANSWER THE ONLY REAL QUESTION: WHO AM I? TO HELP ME, I HAVE THE NEXT CODE - TRANSMUTATION - WHICH SPELLS OUT WHERE I WENT INTO FRAGMENTATION.

Code Transmutation - AB / YE

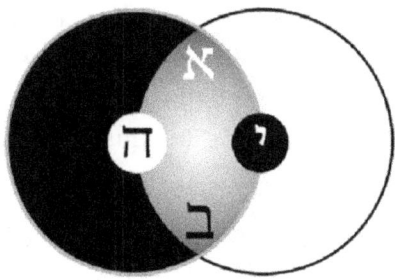

Imagine a language so pure and so sacred that it can reconcile opposites in just two pairs of letters...

Top: Hebrew letter Aleph (א) → A in Roman script
Right: Hebrew letter Yod (י) → I, J, Y in Roman script
Left: Hebrew letter Heh (ה) → E in Roman script
Bottom: Hebrew letter Beth (ב) → B in Roman script

Here is how S/Hebrew inscribes code "Transmutation" in 2 words:

- From top to right to bottom, I read *Oyeb* (איב) for "hatred."
- From top to left to bottom to left, I read *Ahavah* (אהבה) for "love."

The Decoding: Patience + Recognition = Transmutation. Transmutation is the sum of code Patience in the Name *Yah* (YE) and code Recognition via "entering father alphabet" *Ab* (AB). As a gentle reminder, hatred was the curse put on the snake. As such, it symbolizes a heart so broken that it leads me to lie so as to have "your" love, approval and recognition. The curse turns into a blessing when I know that the Power of patience, joined to the recognition of who I am, ends up transmuting the hatred into Love.

Here is how... I have seen in code Patience how Sarai traded the Yod in her name to become Sarah the matriarch (1 Yod = 2 Heh). Similarly, when I trade the Yod in *Oyeb* for "hatred" for two signs Heh, I can write *Ahavah* for "Love." Yep, *Yah* is truly a love story! And when I can't open myself to "receive" (the meaning and the sense of *QKabbalah*), I reclaim the feminine by doing shadow work, going deep enough into the abysmal waters of the unconscious to feel why I once forbade myself the desire for Love and thus the fulfillment of my own potential.

Surely, after I silenced what my heart really wanted, I am not a happy camper. Simply put, I hate "you" whom I perceive stole my bliss from me. Even worse, I'll bury the hatred so that I won't be conscious that it's there. However, when I understand that I don't take care of myself because I fear that my assertiveness may cause you to reject me, I begin making the recovery of the sensory function of the feminine my own priority.

The more I bravely speak what I truly want and give myself the permission to be me, the less hatred is in my space. The transmutation is now well on its way...

SHADOW WORK IS ALL ABOUT GOING DEEP ENOUGH INTO THE ABYSMAL WATERS OF THE UNCONSCIOUS TO FEEL WHY I WOULD FORBID MYSELF THE ONE DESIRE (LOVE) WHICH CROWNS THE FULFILLMENT OF MY OWN POTENTIAL.

TIME HAS COME FOR THE NEXT PARADOX – INVITING THE HEALING POWER OF SNAKE WHOSE VENOM IS THE ANTI-VENOM.

Vav as Snake-Power

"Just as a snake sheds its skin, we must shed our past over and over again." *Gautama Buddha*

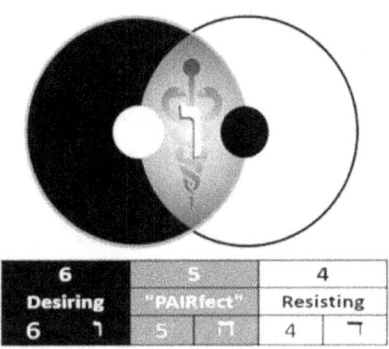

6	5	4
Desiring	"PAIRfect"	Resisting
6　ו	5　ה	4　ד

Vav is a compelling letter. Seated at the top of the **6-Desiring** chamber, it initiates the 666 mark of the beast. Henceforth, it is the sixth Word prompting the "do not kill" command, a command on which Cain completely snoozed.

Indeed, Vav has enough sexual Power – enough "Vavavoom" – to lead to misuse. This may be how the sign is not visible in the "God" Name *Elohim* (אלהים), but only in YEWE (יהוה). Vav is valued 6, as in the "created-SIX" for me to understand my beast's measurement problem, a beast which has convinced me that I am either too much or not enough.

As I have seen, there are many ways in which the sign Vav acts powerfully. Finding its meaning in the following forms is perhaps how it is considered *Vav Hachibur* or the "Vav of Connection:"

- Vav is the word for "nail."
- Vav works as the conjunction "and."
- Vav has the rare nature to be a semi-consonant. As such, it can be read as the consonant F, V, W, but also as the vowel sound O or U.

- Vav is a palindrome, since its three letters (WAW or Vav-Aleph-Vav) can be read forward and backward. This evokes its propensity to be two-sided but also to join opposites.

Snake-Power is the *Nachash* for "serpent" who seduced the woman with his silver tongue. One can argue and ask: why is there a serpent in Paradise? Why evil in the world?

Hebrew answers by linking the words *Nachash* and *Mashiach* through their equal numerical value of 358. The meaning of *Mashiach* is "Messiah." In this sense, the Bible joins the yogic teachings of Kundalini rising, to "let the snake inside you (life energy or Kundalini) dance to the tune of the universe" *Shunya*. The kundalini snake is the messiah. For it to be risen, I must shed the skins of the past, time and again, until I free myself from the suffering caused by the beast-like desires that push me to be "666-Desiring" to do harm.

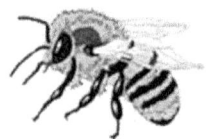

One can argue and ask: why is there a serpent in Paradise? Why evil in the world? Hebrew answers by linking the words *Nachash* and *Mashiach* through their equal numerical value of 358.

Indeed, to be in my Power, I must turn the snake into a Messiah. Therein is snake medicine of transmutation. This is also where the Vav in YEWE plays its biggest role as a connector.

THE TRANSMUTATIONS OF TRANSMUTATION

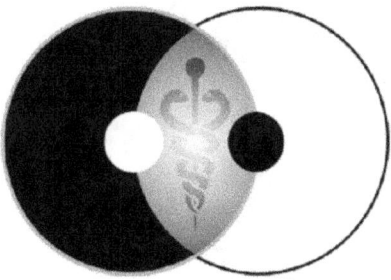

The image above initiates the transmutations of code Transmutation by featuring the caduceus, a symbol known to invoke the healing Power of snake whose venom is the anti-venom.

The caduceus is the emblem of Hermes, the Greek god of healing known to the Romans as Mercury. His volatile quality is also infused in the sign Vav, which is changeable enough to be read backward or forward. Vav has one more super-Power: as a prefix to a verb, it can change the tense from past to future. Quite the character!

Transmutation	Snake-Power	Calling

The message of this row of codes is as follows: when I add **Snake-Power** to **Transmutation**, I come to recognize and embrace my **Calling**. Due to its mercurial quality, the same message will soon be dispatched as a column, for me to "cross" over by way of a horizontal row reformatting itself as a vertical column.

The Alchemical Injunction for Shadow Work

"People will do anything, no matter how absurd, in order to avoid facing their own souls. One does not become enlightened by imagining figures of light, but by making the darkness conscious."
Carl Jung, Psychology & Alchemy

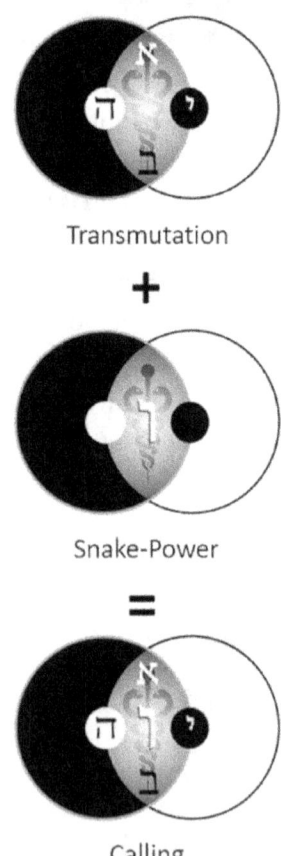

Transmutation

+

Snake-Power

=

Calling

The verticality of a caduceus is now superimposed onto code **Transmutation**, transmutation being the soul medicine of snake (as it is pictured intertwined with its nemesis). Having the courage to face my own soul involves invoking **Snake-Power**. It is how to turn the curse of aversion into the blessing of appreciation, a shift by which to answer my question about purpose and reveal what my **calling** is.

TRANSMUTING THE CURSE OF ENMITY INTO THE BLESSING OF APPRECIATION – WHICH IS ESSENTIALLY AN ALCHEMICAL PROCESS – IS HOW TO REVEAL MY CALLING, MOMENT BY MOMENT.

Calling, Purpose and Uniqueness

"All men have stars, but they are not the same things for different
people. For some, who are travelers, the stars are guides. For
others they are no more than little lights in the sky. For others,
who are scholars, they are problems... But all these stars are silent.
You-You alone will have stars as no one else has them." *Antoine de
St Exupéry – the Little Prince*

When asking about my purpose, what I really want to know is that I
will eventually hold an extraordinary position and, most importantly,
that I can support myself splendidly in my dream job. Do I see myself
more as a healer or an actor or an artist or a life coach or even an
emissary? Am I looking for a creative occupation that preferably
comes with some level of glamour and makes me feel and look "special?" The thing is: I am confused. I can't feel that my understanding
of purpose comes from my insecurities – from the belief that I am not
enough! What good would it do me to be asked to lecture on spirituality if deep down, I knew that I was judging myself and others to no
end, and that I was still "possessed" by my possessions? I'd feel like a
fake, and yearn even more for your love, approval and recognition!

Therefore, I started to accept that, possibly, my purpose and main
raison d'être was to move out of a mind trapped in Scare City and to
enter a "Promised Land" of sorts where I sustain the felt sense of
being worthy. I also came to accept that, while I want so badly to be
special, we all share the same purpose: a complete liberation from
suffering. However, it is by fulfilling it that you and I open to the
unique way we express and teach our newly found freedom – just by
being!

Upon transitioning from greed into grace, what I do for a living
doesn't really matter. What makes a difference is how grateful I am
since I feel how extraordinary it is to be awake to an entirely different

way of being – to a mind of abundance. There is no more littleness in my space. Instead, I experience the magnificence of being alive, in this body, at this time, on this earth... And if I am, by chance, to stumble upon my own burning bush, I am ready for my uniqueness as I know I will not misuse my gifts. Indeed, I can now embrace the vocation paradox: on the one hand, I once came out of the big Nothing to become somebody, that is, to make a name for myself. On the other hand, being anonymous and having no need to be recognized for my gifts is where my voice is most likely to find a trust and a hearing.

It may be that I am in fact called to teach spirituality or to be a poet. It may be that I am called to sing. It may also be that the Voice calls me to just smile and bless people while operating an elevator. Would I be willing to let my heart shine so brightly that my inner joy would help people deal with their daily stress as they go up and down with me? Would that be enough of a calling?

For now, I am thankful to be able to follow the Voice – thankful and awed that obedience took the place of impatience. I find that, as each moment calls me to a specific task, I am willing to do what LOVE would do, e.g.; clean the floor, take a walk, brush my cat's fur, write a note of appreciation to a friend, take a nap, paint the Sistine Chapel... If asked to return to corporate America after I had quit to be a healer, I appreciate the possibility to be of service and also, to pay the credit cards debts I had accumulated. Trusting that the task that is given to me is absolutely perfect, I allow myself to dance in gratitude. Hence, I no longer object to my divine bush.

So yes, my purpose is first and foremost to surrender to the light and stop telling "God" what to do. Truth be told, I don't know what's for my highest good... I just think I do.

One thing I can be certain of: the more accountable I am, the more the cosmic Powers trust me and bestow on me a calling that is commensurate with the strengths and skills I developed. My part is just to be ready to meet the Mystery unconditionally, not because of the promise of a unique calling, but just for the sake of liberation from the desire for liberation.

As for being true to my name and/or to what I am called, I wish to offer a definition: call·ing—noun: 1. the loud cries or shouts of an animal or person: "the calling of a cuckoo" 2. a strong urge toward a particular way of life or career; a vocation: "those who have a special calling to minister to others' needs." From loud cries to strong urges, being called does come with some level of intensity... Will I remain present?

ON THE ONE HAND, I ONCE CAME OUT OF BIG NOTHING TO BECOME SOMEBODY, THAT IS, TO BE "SPECIAL" AND MAKE A NAME FOR MYSELF.

ON THE OTHER HAND, BEING ANONYMOUS AND HAVING NO NEED TO BE RECOGNIZED FOR MY GIFTS IS WHERE MY VOICE IS MOST LIKELY TO FIND A TRUST AND A HEARING.

Code Calling - AB / W / YE

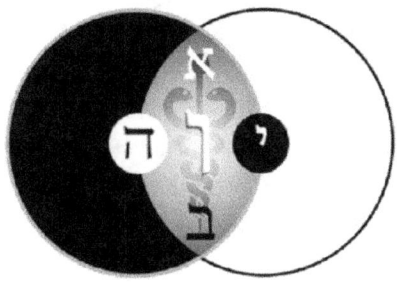

Imagine a language so pure and so sacred that it can reconcile opposites in just five letters...

Top: Hebrew letter Aleph (א) → A in Roman script
Right: Hebrew letter Yod (י) → I, J, Y in Roman script
Middle: Hebrew letter Vav (ו) → F, U, V, W in Roman script
Left: Hebrew letter Heh (ה) → E in Roman script
Bottom: Hebrew letter Beth (ב) → B in Roman script

Here is how S/Hebrew inscribes code "Calling" in 2 words:

- From top to right to middle to bottom, I read *Iyob*, (איוב) for "Job, hated."
- From top to left to middle to bottom, I read *Ahuv* (אהוב) for "loved."

The Decoding: Transmutation + Snake-Power = Calling. The merging of Transmutation and Snake-Power is exactly what Job must have had to experience in order to fulfill his calling. Naturally, I have heard about *The Book of Job!* Who hasn't? This book of the Bible focuses on the eternal problem of suffering, which it spices up with the idea that suffering is unmerited and thus hard to digest. As for its hero, Job is, by all accounts, the role model for patience, compassion and perseverance in the face of adversity as he attempts to understand the sorrows that engulf him.

While the book is named after its central character, it is rarely said that the Hebrew name *Iyob* means "**Job**," but also "**the one who is hated.**" How fickle can a destiny be?!? I can't even relate to what it would mean to be hated as my calling and my job (pun intended). Another thing that is not told or maybe realized is that *Oyeb* (or "hatred, enmity") was the curse put on the snake. As a gentle reminder, the snake is the part of me that twists the truth. As such, I am cursed with enmity after I have abused my Power and said the "wrong" words or withheld the "write" words. Ah, I pray that the revealing of this information would render me more conscious of the shadow, and encourage me to feel the hatred, the resentment, the jealousy, the anger that *factually* live in me. It lives in me because I can sense that I am lied to, but also because I lie to myself.

Hear, hear! When I know that it is my purpose (my work) to embrace the evil that is in my world, I put an end to the question: why is there evil in the world? Doing so makes me unique, and more likely to trust myself with the use of my gifts. "From everyone who has been given much, much will be demanded; and from the one who has been entrusted with much, much more will be asked." *Luke 12:48.*

I might have already recognized that my ravenous hunger causes me to hate you (since I see that you're fed and I'm not). It also triggers my dis-eased imagination of unrequited love. In that space, not only do I resist feeling rejected, but also, I don't know that it is my nature to love and be **loved**. Instead, I just keep on looking for the proof that I am not lovable. And if I look, I will find. But what if the purpose of my hatred was to lead me to know my calling by allowing me to know my deepest self? Indeed, I am not the hatred. I just identify to it. As I have the courage to take ownership of this fragment of darkness, I crack its shell open and liberate the light that was trapped in it – my light! I now have the sense of my own worth, and come to the LOVE that has no opposite.

So how did Job manage to remain compassionate after being so utterly antagonized? The answer is simple: he earned his enlightenment! While he couldn't change his genes (that is, the letters of his name), he could change his epigenetics (his reactions to life). As always, the heroes of the Bible reflect the tendencies of my soul. I am Job. For me to experience such **transmutation**, I must first master my emotions and stop identifying with the big SIX of resistance: loneliness, sadness, shame, fear, hatred and anger. I will then have the Power to discipline my attention, and to raise the energy of my **snake-Power** (my Vav of 6-Desiring). As a matter of fact, I'll have such a knowledge of good and evil that I'll feel in my gut what to do and not to do.

On that note, Vav is so central that its script is enlarged in the code above, just as it is in the word *Gahon* for "belly" in the Torah script of *Leviticus 11:42*. This Vav is the exact midpoint of all the letters in a Torah scroll. And it makes me wonder... How could the Torah know that my spiritual potential is activated by the felt sense that abides in the gut? How could it know of the brain-gut connection so far ahead of science?

Yes, I am fully *feeling* and fulfilling my calling when I do my "Job" and no longer need to narrate my victim story, even though I milked it for years by featuring me in the role of "the hated One." How could "God" do that to me? This is how I get out of Scare City and earn the recovery of my nature which is to be Love. When I feel such big LOVE in my heart, I have patience as I know that I am One with all! Instead of demanding that "you should love me," I know that you love me. I'm just not asking that you would know it.

Indeed, patience is all I need to feel the hatred and transmute it. Here is how: the day will come when I will stop asking about surrender. I will simply surrender!

WHEN I KNOW THAT IT IS MY PURPOSE (MY WORK) TO EMBRACE THE EVIL THAT IS IN MY WORLD, I PUT AN END TO THE QUESTION: WHY IS THERE EVIL IN THE WORLD?

DOING SO MAKES ME UNIQUE, AND MORE LIKELY TO TRUST MYSELF WITH THE USE OF MY GIFTS.

The Alchemy of this Book

"Our deepest fear is not that we are inadequate. Our deepest fear is that we are powerful beyond measure. It is our light, not our darkness that most frightens us." *Marianne Williamson*

This process is alchemical because it allows my serpent to ascend as a Messiah, which fulfills my purpose. Indeed, it aims at a complete recovery of self-esteem as the qualification permitting the liberation of my genius from Scare City. Its SIX steps go to the heart of shadow work by illuminating the reasons why I would want to do harm. To this end, they expose the progression of the secrets behind my problematic behaviors. They also outline how my allegiance goes to the dark when I'm afraid to give it all to LOVE. In this mental space, I know what to do to be free, but I just don't want to do it! While resisting knowing the truth, I find myself unconsciously making the following choices:

1. **Reluctance and the fear of falling:** I tell the story that I don't know what I want in order to stay confused about my heart's dictates. I know I'm going to fall. However, staging my failure by not giving it all to LOVE seems less painful than the perspective of falling after I gave it all. Withholding LOVE gives me an excuse. This is how I am reluctant to do what would evolve me and serve the good of all.

2. **Self-doubt and the fear of speaking:** I know where "God" lives. I know that to feel a LOVE so big that it has no opposite, I must do what my heart tells me to do. But since, each time I betray my word, my self-esteem takes a hit, I don't believe in myself anymore. I even doubt that I can express what I truly want... What if I said the "wrong" thing?

3. **Playing small and the fear of rejection:** I imagine that if I were to live up to my potential and actually be brilliant, talented, fulfilled and free, I would ruffle my peers' feathers.

I'm like an addict who wants to quit yet won't, because all of my friendships are based on the addiction. Oyveh; misery does love company! My self-esteem takes another hit.

4. **Incoherence and the fear of loss:** I say that I want to be free, unattached to an outcome, authentic in my relating, and just joyful for no reason at all, but I can't seem to decide to let go of the beliefs, the habits and even the "things" that possess me and block the receiving of the health, wealth and success I say I want to enjoy.

5. **Impatience and the fear of death:** unable to sit still and wait for the path to be clear, I distract myself and compulsively create unconscious time. But since my desire for immediate self-gratification actively delays my heart's desires, my self-esteem is now so low that, instead of changing (i.e.; of dying), I'll blame you and make you responsible for my lack of results.

6. **Denial and the fear of power:** I think that, if I were to be in my Power and told the truth, I would hurt people. Since I feel powerless to have what I want, my mind now generates vengeance fantasies which I must disown. Me? Jealous? No, I'm nothing like Cain! This denial is how I continue saying yes when I mean no, even when I realize that, doing so, I am actually harming myself and others.

The way in is the way out. I just have to give myself the permission to understand how one unconscious choice moves into the next level of unconsciousness and to feel each level as gently as I possibly can while remembering, this is not "I." It is just my inner demon wanting to transition into the ingenuous realm it hungers for...

THESE SIX STEPS GO TO THE HEART OF SHADOW WORK BY ILLUMINATING THE CORE SECRETS THAT ARE BEHIND MY DESIRE TO DO HARM. THEY ALSO OUTLINE HOW MY ALLEGIANCE GOES TO THE DARK WHEN I'M AFRAID OF GIVING IT ALL TO LOVE.

WHEN BEYOND THAT FEAR, I DON'T ASK WHY I AM HERE ANYMORE. I KNOW THAT I FULFILL MY PURPOSE BY JUST BEING.

THIS IS HOW I BEGIN TO FEEL AND UNDERSTAND THAT "GOD" REALLY IS "CREATED-SIX" BY PLAYING WITH THE SIX SIDES OF A DIE...

Prepare to DIE

"God does not play dice." *Albert Einstein*

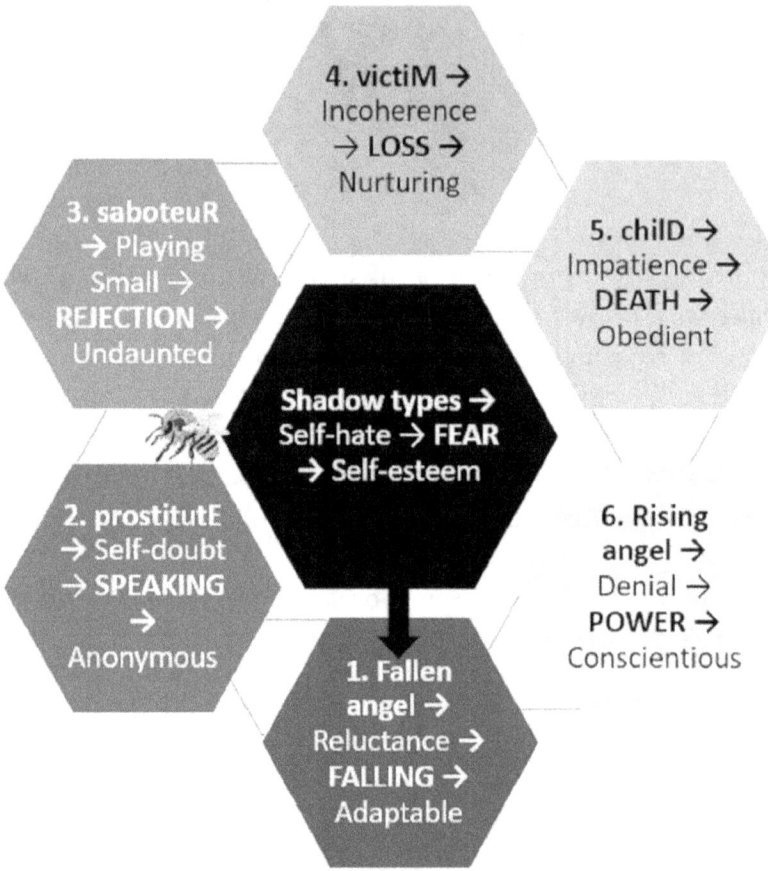

Online inquiry tool: www.goldenxpr.com/lno-self-hate-self-esteem/

In the central cell, I see the names of four creations that I am invited to experience: **Shadow types** → Self-hate → **FEAR** → Self-esteem. Around it, I see the SIX "days" or stages of each creation. The symbol → simply means that one creation moves into another. Here are the SIX steps of my process:

- **Step 1:** I fill in the blank: I want to know WHY I would choose to think I CAN'T _____ (e.g.; find a job, be patient, etc.).
- **Step 2:** I ask for truth, throw a die and generate a number from 1 to SIX.
- **Step 3:** I find my number on the map and fill in the brackets: when in the dark and expressing myself as a [**Shadow type**], I resent that I would have to deal with [**Self-hate**], which makes me increasingly afraid of [**FEAR**].
- **Step 4:** I allow myself to feel and experience the fear of [**FEAR**] and track it to the denied experience of resisting [**Self-hate**]. Yes, it is difficult. I want to run from it!
- **Step 5:** what most surprised me in this process was _____.
- **Step SIX:** what increase in being [**Self-esteem**] do I notice after beginning to own and feel my [**Self-hate**]?

YES, FEELING SELF-HATE IS DIFFICULT, SO MUCH SO THAT I WILL WANT TO RUN FROM IT!

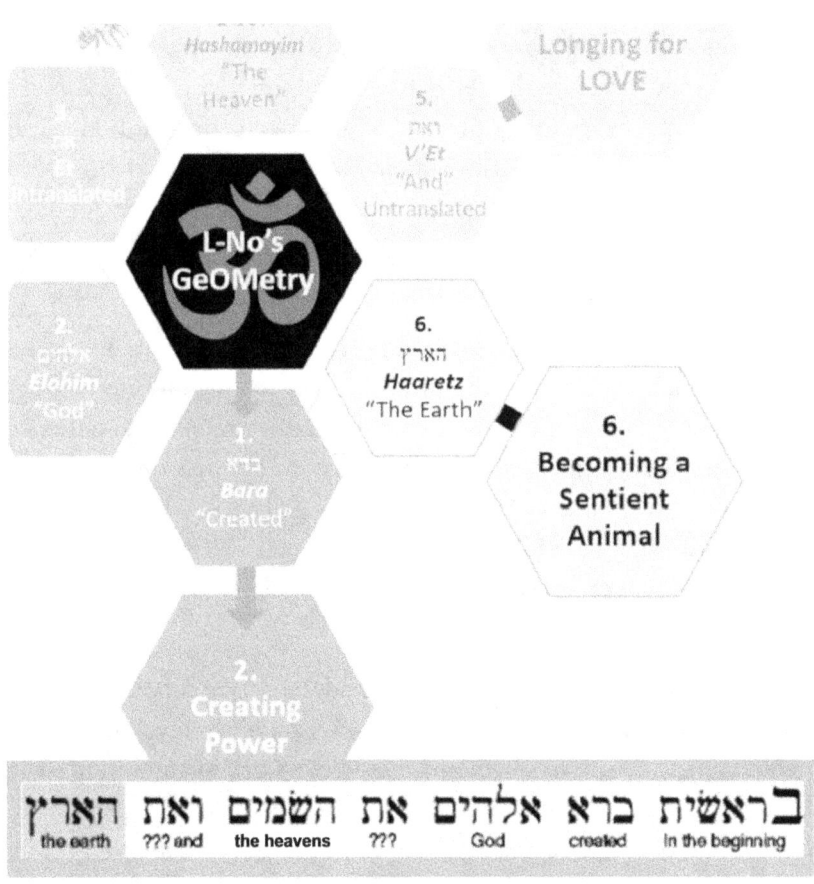

This chapter emanates from and inquires on the 6th word after "in the beginning." Highlighted in the line above, its letters read *Haaretz* for "the earth."

Introducing "Becoming a Sentient Animal"

"The soul is ever free; it is deathless because birthless. It cannot be regimented by stars." *Yogananda, Autobiography of a Yogi*

Now that I am on purpose, I need a body that can serve me well. To this end, I must restore the felt-sense of the unity of mind and body. This involves reexamining how my beliefs are affecting my body. And now, a whole retraining is in order. This is conveyed by the word *Haaretz* for "the earth" which can also be seen as *HaA-retz* for "air-running." This will unfold in code Centaur as a metaphor for the mind-body connection.

Having mastered my past, I am now ready to train my animal, a process which leads me to the fifth of SIX rows of codes; to willingness – the willingness to change. As always, this row starts in patience (in a still mind), since patience amplifies the Power to make sound decisions. With patience, I can accept my failures and begin to see their goodness as a necessary evil. I become willing to be willing when I have enough self-esteem to no longer go into desire or resistance.

The peace of a "PAIRfect" mind was already part of the plan, as shown by the alphabet that models the motion of energy when unimpeded by the ego. This is when I rest while working, and dance the rhythm of chaos while remaining still. I now come to the final row of codes – the codes on death row, helping me to die to who I *think* I am. Using an ancient cipher known as the Avgad code, I transpose the letters of code Patience into code Time in order to open to the child-like innocence that lives in the Eternal Now. More than ever, the letters walk in pairs as non-biological sentient animals that resonate with the infinity of an ouroboros and the clarity of a hawk.

From pairs of animals to pairs of animals (and from code to code), I write into being code Centaur where I use astrology in order to transcend astrology and end the superstitious allegiance to my planets –

which is to say, to my past. The less I let myself be ruled by the stars, the less I am dominated by matter and the more I recognize my unity with Spirit. I become the Word made flesh, incarnate as a teacher, One with my animal.

Chapter 6

Training the Animal

"I hated every minute of training, but I said, 'Don't quit. Suffer now and live the rest of your life as a champion.'" *Muhammad Ali*

Whether I am conscious of it or not, and whether I like it or not, I am in this body to train it to being as strong, flexible and balanced as possible. And this – being the word made flesh; a teacher incarnated – is no easy task! Training the animal begins in bringing sanity to the mind, a sanity which I know when I stop judging reality and thus, stop resisting what I see as "no good." This training in surrender is how I will one day live as a champion. The body is the subconscious mind. It is the autonomic nervous system that won't let me rest or digest when I repeatedly attach to stressful thought-forms and disruptive emotions. By making the unconscious conscious, I begin bringing sanity to the mind which then stops tormenting the body. My animal is inert in that it doesn't know the difference between good and bad. Even when it shows signs of dire abuse, it still offers it as what it is: no commentaries... I'm who does the complaining! Here are four stages to assist me in taking the mind out of the body:

1. **Identifying with the beast of burden:** when I wake up in the morning, my mind immediately remembers that I am the body and registers all the fears and other dark clouds that come with identifying with it. It is as if an invisible yoke binds me to suffering, as I go into stale routines that the body knows perhaps better than the mind. Yep, I am so afraid of the unknown that I take my yesterday and overlay it onto today! I'm so mesmerized by my pain story that I neither can think nor sync properly. I know no peace as my autonomic system is mostly out of whack. I react to everything, letting the "out there" (oftentimes, the body which became a beast of burden) tell me how to feel "in here." Mostly, I'm dissatisfied with myself: I'm never slim enough, rich enough, young enough, popular enough... enough! It seems that I'm always waiting for a messiah of sorts – someone or something "out there" that would make me happy. Unless I start thinking of new possibilities to open my heart, the body is going to live by the same schedule, which is likely to keep me hurting and wanting. And then I will call it fate... or karma!

2. **Deciding to overcome the resistance:** the retraining into joy is uncomfortable because it is unfamiliar... Dropping my story and no longer being so dissatisfied with myself does involve a few pattern interrupts. Yes, change is unnerving as it leads me to lose all points of reference: I am in between two knowns – in the unknown... And even though it is the perfect place – the quantum midst "in between" – from which to come out as an upgraded version of myself, I must

overcome the laziness of my body – I must get over it! For me to relax in the Now, I have no other option but to become willing to change. I can decide to believe that today might just be the day when my lover comes. And to believe that each day. And each day to watch my lover coming! How? I sit down with my thoughts, observe them (especially when I cannot sleep), and place my attention on my breath. I am determined to feel any possible blocks that could prevent me from blowing my heart wide open and expanding my energy field… It's okay if the body is so accustomed in the ways of laziness that it roars in anger and wants to quit. I know I am the head of the house, the one who decides when my practice is over.

3. Bringing heart and brain into coherence: when my habitual resistance weathered enough dark clouds, I change my ways, turn within and listen to my guidance. I now understand why I needed to rebel against my heart and break my own law. Through my willingness to open, I begin to feel the LOVE that has no opposite, and align with the ethics of complementarity. This is to say: I know what to do and I do it whole*heart*edly. I'll eventually notice that I feel grateful for no reason and find that I can choose peace, no matter what's going on "out there." I now have the courage to go to the level above the mind where the problem was created and move from thinking into the void and then into intuiting. Transcending the past, I receive a new heart, a new brain, a new body. It is definitely a biological upgrade in sentience as my animal and I are now more loving, more caring, more present, listening, playing – free to be at One.

4. Opening to mastery: as the master, I allow my body to serve me well while I treat it splendidly. I have found that it works each time: as soon as I surrender to my heart and go **intuit** (or "into-it" – the fire) everything lines up. My brain begins to **think** creatively, my soul **feels** peace and a kind of quiet joy that sustains

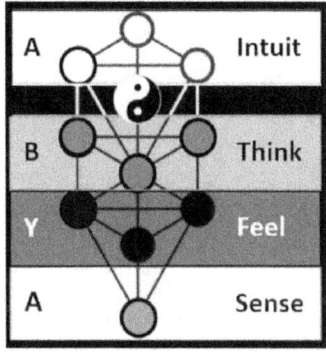

homeostasis and my animal is just
doing its thing; **sensing** it all. Every step contributes to light up the
tree of my life as I learn something about who I am. Being incarnated
has never felt so good – so awesome good!

WHETHER I AM CONSCIOUS OF IT OR NOT, AND WHETHER I LIKE IT OR
NOT, I AM IN THIS BODY TO TRAIN IT TO BEING AS STRONG, AS FLEXIBLE
AND AS BALANCED AS POSSIBLE. THIS IS BEING THE WORD MADE FLESH; A
TEACHER INCARNATED...

AND IT IS NO EASY TASK!

Code Training - BL /O/ LB

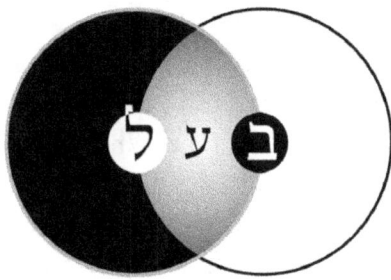

Imagine a language so pure and so sacred that it can reconcile opposites in just three letters...

Right: Hebrew letter Beth (ב) → B in Roman script
Middle: Hebrew letter Ayin (ע)→ O in Roman script
Left: Hebrew letter Lamed (ל) → L in Roman script

Here is how S/Hebrew inscribes code "Training" in 5 words:

- From right to left, I read *Bal* (בל) for "do not!"
- From left to right, I read *Lev* (לב) for "heart."
- From right to middle to left, I read *Ba'al* (בעל) for "master"
- From middle to left, I read *Al* (על) for "upon, above, over," but also *Ol* (על) for "yoke."
- From middle to right, I read *Ab* (עב) for "dark cloud."

The Decoding: in looking at the image above, the first place of focus is the pair of non-biological sentient animals (the two letters) that occupy the dots. These two form the pairs BL/LB that partner to convey the entirety of the Torah's wisdom teaching. Practically, they encompass the whole of the law by being the first letter and the last letter of the Five Books of Moses. As for transmitting wisdom, here is what "the First and the Last" are saying:

- **The letter Beth (ב)** begins the first word of the Torah, a word which is read as *Bereshit* and means "in the Beginning." This B is also the B of Boundaries that I create with each word I speak, for good or bad, in sickness and in health. As a word, *Beth* means the "house" or that which begins to define my creation of mind, space and time. What story will I tell today?
- **The letter Lamed (ל)** ends the last word of the Torah, a word which is read as *Yisrael* for "Israel." Hence, the last wisdom I am impressed with is the call to become s/he who IS REAL – authentic in my relating as I come from my heart. As a word, *Lamed* means "ox-goad" and also "learn/teach," i.e.; train my animal in the ways of Love.

I shall continue by reviewing the points made by the previous section *Training the Animal,* yet this time exploring how the codes inscribe the exact same insights. To do so, I will let the pair BL/LB interact with the animal in the "midst," namely the letter Ayin (ע | O) which substantiates my training as follows:

- **The pairs OL/OB (עב/על)** for **identifying with the "beast of burden:"** when I identify with the body, my fears are like **dark clouds.** It is as if an invisible **yoke** binds me to suffering, as I go into stale routines which the body knows perhaps better than the mind. And then I will call it fate... or karma!
- **The pair OL (על)** for **deciding to "overcome" the resistance:** the retraining into joy is uncomfortable since I must go into the unknown where a new version of me (my lover) awaits. I am determined to get **over** any possible blocks to a heart wide open... It's okay if the body roars in anger or if it wants to quit! I am the one who decides when my practice is over.
- **The pairs LB/BL (בל/לב)** for bringing **"heart and brain"** into **coherence:** when I have suffered enough, I will change

my rebellious ways of doing what I am told **not to** do, and turn my **heart**. I transcend the past and receive a new heart, a new brain, a new body, more loving, more caring, free to be at One – coherent.

- **The triad BOL (בעל) for opening to "mastery:"** as the **master** of the house, I allow my body to serve me well while I treat it splendidly. I have found that it works each time: as soon as I surrender to my heart and go into it / intuit, the heart-brain coherence is reestablished, which makes it possible that body and soul would work as One.

At last, I am LOVE, my Leader's heart intuits (goes "into it" – the fire), my Engineer's mind thinks (or syncs), my Visionary soul feels (or heals), my Officer's body senses (via the SIXth sense of enough).

FOR ME TO RELAX IN THE NOW, I BECOME WILLING TO CHANGE. I AM DETERMINED TO FEEL ANY POSSIBLE RESISTANCE THAT COULD PREVENT ME FROM BLOWING MY HEART WIDE OPEN AND EXPANDING MY ENERGY FIELD...

THE FOURTH ROW OF CODES

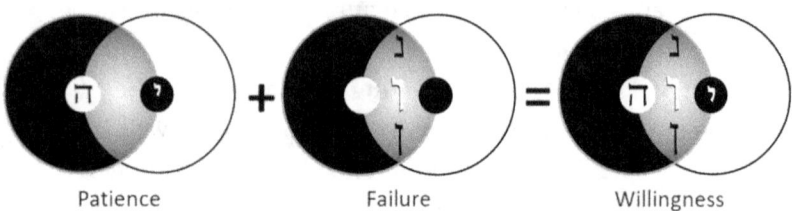

Patience   Failure   Willingness

Like the previous rows, the fourth row also begins with code Patience, a virtue which I acquire by *gently* asking myself: how does it feel to resist knowing the truth? Indeed, when ready for how truth will change my life, I am filled with patience and *compassion*, a word saying that I am "with my pain." I willingly encounter this pain of mine, willingly and concretely. I feel the punishment, the repression, the denials. And I forgive myself for doing it all wrong, since I realize that it is my folly and my failures that have allowed me to fall into "God's" hands. Yes, it is the failures, the betrayals, the rejections, the pain that open the door to "God's House."

Therefore, when failure strikes again, there is no one to react. In that sense, failure is my best friend. As for its code, it writes its letters vertically – as a fall. At the core, I recognize the letter Vav (ו) of snake-Power. At the top, I see the regular letter Nun (נ). At the bottom, the final letter Nun (ן). While both letters evolved into the same Roman letter N, Nun final is called "final" as it takes a different shape when at the end of a word (like the word *Nun* itself for "fish, fallen"), but also when ushering the end of a world (more on the finals in the appendix). The world that it brings to an end is the world of resentment that has me making you my enemy from the belief that I owe you, or worse, that you owe me. Failure, whether I like it or not, is my training in the willingness to let go of my judgments. I don't come to God by doing it right. I must deal with my "errors," until I see that there is nothing wrong.

Henceforth, **Patience** + **Failure** = **Willingness.**

When I turn the wound into a sacred wound, I pass my initiation as I allow for the reciprocity of a win/win. This is when a spirituality of imperfection becomes utterly "PAIRfect!" The next section and the image to the right show me the centrality of failure by revealing how the letter Nun (the top letter in code Failure) can be the exact center of the S/Hebrew alphabet – the place of forgiveness and of humble self-emPowerment.

5	
"PAIRfect"	
5	ה
50	נ
500	ך

I WILL FORGIVE MYSELF FOR DOING IT ALL WRONG, SINCE I WILL REALIZE THAT IT IS MY FOLLY AND MY FAILURES THAT HAVE ALLOWED ME TO FALL INTO "GOD'S" HANDS. YES, SUSPENDING MY JUDGMENTS ON THE FAILURES, THE BETRAYALS, THE REJECTIONS, THE PAIN IS WHAT OPENS THE DOOR TO "GOD'S HOUSE."

Resistance + Desire = the Physics of Self-esteem

"I care for myself. The more solitary, the more friendless, the more unsustained I am, the more I will respect myself." *Charlotte Brontë, Jane Eyre*

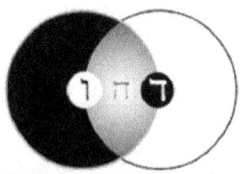

9		8		7		6		5		4		3		2		1	
Completing		Ordering		Engaging		Desiring		"PAIRfect"		Resisting		Changing		Separating		Opening	
9	ט	8	ח	7	ז	6	ו	5	ה	4	ד	3	ג	2	ב	1	א
90	צ	80	פ	70	ע	60	ס	50	נ	40	מ	30	ל	20	כ	10	י
900	ץ	800	ף	700	ן	600	ם	500	ך	400	ת	300	ש	200	ר	100	ק

This table is an offshoot of what the elders called "the Kabbalah of the 9 Chambers," a version that comprises the wisdom of the Hebrew alphabet. The intelligence of its 27 signs (22 regular letters + 5 final letters) can be sensed via the 9 chambers that organize these signs on 3 rows (3 x 9 = 27) to elucidate the physics of beliefs. Since Hebrew is read from right to left, the first chamber is to the right, and the ninth, to the left. The associated value is marked next to each letter, e.g.; 2 | ב. The first row contains the letters equal to single digits (the mental realm); the second row, to the tens (the emotional realm), the third row, to the hundreds (the physical realm).

Golden XPR takes an additional step by revealing the physics of belief as the energy moves from 1-**Opening** (when I am as one dot in the infinity of time) to 2-**Separating** (when my two dots draw a line) to 3-**Changing** (when my three dots allow me to triangulate) to 4-**Resisting** (when my four dots make me "fair and square"). The energy continues to progress one step at a time by adding one dot (or one Aleph) until I come to 9-**Completing**. This effectively merges the physical laws with their metaphysical counterpart, both sets of laws governing the behavior of energy.

An entire book could be written on this table. For now, here is what to notice:

- **To the right:** three black chambers of 1-Opening, 2-Separating, 3-Changing. The message: everything comes from the mother. First is yin-female-evil-black.
- **In the middle:** three grey chambers of 4-Resisting, 5-"PAIRfect," 6-Desiring. I see that reality is "PAIRfect" when I want all I have and have all I want, since I am simultaneously desiring what I resist and resisting what I desire.
- **In the exact center** (right to left, top to bottom): a white rectangle around the letter Nun. The message: I stop suffering when willing to fall and fail, as many times as necessary.
- **To the left:** three white chambers of 7-Engaging, 8-Ordering, 9-Completing. The message: everything goes to the father. Last is yang-male-good-white.

Lastly, the letters in the geometry above the chambers spells the word *Hod* (הוד) for "majesty, splendor, appreciation." These three letters are also in the top row of the grey chambers. *Hod* names the 8th sphere of the tree of life (solar plexus – female side), an energy and information center which is spun by the "God" Name *Adonai Tzevaoth,* a name explained by *Golden XPR* as the Power of self-esteem. I have self-esteem when I can hold the tension of opposites – especially between desire and resistance – as it is when I master the present moment, the body, the environment and ultimately, myself. Such coherence soon leads me to increasingly trust myself. Radiating the energy of enlightened justice, I vibrate with the sense of enough.

THE VALUE OF *HOD* (ד + ו + ה) IS 15, WHICH IS EQUAL TO THE VALUE OF
YAH (ה + י) OF CODE PATIENCE.

SURELY, SELF-ESTEEM COMES WITH PATIENCE, JUST AS THE ABILITY TO
WAIT TAKES SELF-ESTEEM.

Code Willingness - NN /[W]/ YE

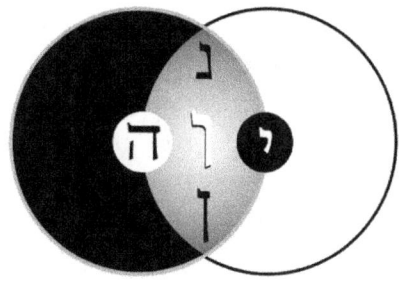

Imagine a language so pure and so sacred that it can reconcile opposites in just two pairs of letters around Vav, the central sign of the Torah...

Top: Hebrew letter Nun (נ) → N in Roman script
Right: Hebrew letter Yod (י) → I, J, Y in Roman script
Middle: Hebrew letter Vav (ו) → F, U, V, W in Roman script
Left: Hebrew letter Heh (ה) → E in Roman script
Bottom: Hebrew letter Nun final (ן) → N in Roman script

Here is how S/Hebrew inscribes code "Willingness" in 5 words:

- From right to middle to top to left, I read *Yonah* (יונה) for "Jonah, dove."
- From top to right to top to middle to left, I read *Nineveh* (נינוה) for the city of "Nineveh."
- From top to middle to bottom, I read *Nun* (נון) for "fish," and, by extension, "fallen, miscarriage."
- From right to top to middle to bottom, I read *Yenun* (ינון) for "he endured."
- From left to top (twice) to right, I read *Hineini* (הנני) for "here I am."

The Decoding: Patience + Failure = Willingness. Once upon a time, "God" told **Jonah** to go the great city of Nineveh and preach to them and let them know that they ought to change their evil ways. Jonah might have jumped at such opportunity, for **Nineveh** was the capital of the Assyrian empire. However, instead of rising to the call, Jonah went in the opposite direction, and ran for cover. He eventually boarded a ship that would take him to Tarshish, a city on the other end of the Mediterranean. Once on board, a great storm arose, leading the sailors to sense some sort of divine retribution against someone on the ship. They ended up casting lots to see who the culprit was, and the lot fell on Jonah. But it was Jonah himself who confessed his disobedience and asked the sailors to cast him overboard to save the rest of the crew – which they finally did.

But "God" wasn't done with Jonah. Rather than condemning him, "He" mercifully appointed a huge **fish** to swallow him. There, in the belly of the whale (a symbolic and abysmal place where to do shadow work), Jonah had time to contemplate his reluctance to obey as well as "God's" claim on his life. The belly of the whale is also known as the dark night of the soul, a "time" which I must be willing to **endure** to go on the other side, until I am at last spit out on the shore, scared certainly, and maybe even smelly and humiliated, but alive and authentically grateful for "God's" mercy in spite of my resistance starting with the word "obey!"

The moral of this story is for Jonah, for the people of Nineveh, but also and foremost for me who, like Jonah, is also a reluctant prophet/ess.

Indeed, I know what to do, I just don't want to do it, even though I suspect that my surrendering would serve the good of all. Using my will to delay the common good may just be the extent of my arrogance. Redemption occurs naturally, when I have the courage to stay three symbolic days in the belly of the whale (or the womb of the tomb), to rise again with a clean bill of health, forgiving of my own stubbornness.

It now is clear why the reading of *the Book of Jonah* is part of the ritual of *Yom Kippur* – 'the day of "At-ONE-ment."' It prepares me for the initiation to come, when I have the opportunity to respond to the call with a big fat YES, as Abraham did in *Genesis 22:1*. This is when "God" put him to the test and Abraham answered without a single hesitation *Hineini* "**here I am!**" Presence is how to break open the seals placed on my own name and begin to feel the grace, like Jonah did when he realized his name also meant "**dove**," a symbol of peace, love and renewal.

USING MY WILL TO DELAY THE COMMON GOOD MAY JUST BE THE EXTENT OF MY ARROGANCE. REDEMPTION AND THE SUBSEQUENT STATE OF FLOW OCCURS NATURALLY, WHEN I HAVE THE COURAGE TO STAY THREE SYMBOLIC DAYS IN THE BELLY OF THE WHALE (OR THE WOMB OF THE TOMB), TO RISE AGAIN WITH A CLEAN BILL OF HEALTH AS I FORGIVE MY OWN STUBBORNNESS.

Resisting Nothing

"To fly we have to have resistance." *Maya Lin*

Online inquiry tool: www.goldenxpr.com/lno-resisting-nothing/

In the central cell, I see the names of the four creations that I am invited to experience: Shadow types → **RESISTANCE** → Fear → DESIRE. Around it are the SIX "days" or stages of each creation. The symbol → simply means that one creation moving into another. Here are the SIX steps of my process:

- **Step 1:** I fill in the blank: I want to know WHY I would choose to think I CAN'T _____ (e.g.; find a job, be patient, etc.).
- **Step 2:** I ask for truth, either throwing a die or going to an online random number generator and generate a number from 1 to SIX.
- **Step 3:** I find my number on the map and fill in the brackets: when in the dark and expressing myself as a [Shadow types], I resist feeling that I am overwhelmed by [**RESISTANCE**] and subsequently led into the fear of [Fear].
- **Step 4:** I allow myself to resist feeling my [**RESISTANCE**] and track it to an increase in my fear of [Fear]. Yes, feeling is difficult. Yes, I want to run from it!
- **Step 5:** what most surprised me in this process was _____.
- **Step SIX:** am I beginning to trust that my desire for [DESIRE] could be fulfilled? What changed?

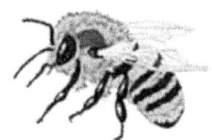

Yes, feeling is difficult. Yes, I want to run from it! As much as I can, I give myself the permission to resist wanting to know the truth. I also notice that resisted loneliness turns into sadness; resisted sadness, into shame; resisted shame, into fear; resisted fear, into hatred, until finally, resisted hatred becomes pure unadulterated anger, begging to be recognized...

The ABCaD Code (a.k.a. Avgad)

"Time flies like an arrow; fruit, like a banana." *Groucho Marx*

The Avgad code is a classical code used by Kabbalists. It was renamed "ABCaD" by *Golden XPR*, since the first four Hebrew letters, Aleph, Beth, Gimel and Dalet, evolved into Roman script A, B, C, D. Indeed, many Kabbalists miss the fact that the third Hebrew letter Gimel became C and not G – C as in "camel," an oversight which creates all sorts of confusion. And while Beth, the second letter, can be read as a soft V, calling the code ABCaD rather than Avgad restores the integrity of the original geometry, and thereby eases the "receiving" of the alphabet as the law of LOVE.

As for its working, ABCaD replaces each letter of a given word by the next letter, as if to facilitate a process of becoming. First letter Aleph (A) becomes second letter Beth (B). Second letter Beth (B) becomes third letter Gimel (C). The opposite operation is also used. Fourth letter Dalet (D) becomes third letter Gimel (C). Third letter Gimel (C) becomes second letter Beth (B).

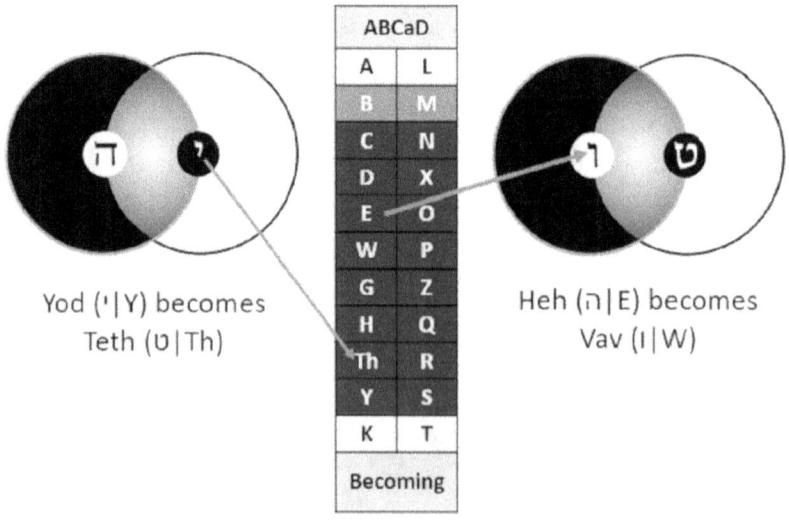

ABCaD	
A	L
B	M
C	N
D	X
E	O
W	P
G	Z
H	Q
Th	R
Y	S
K	T
Becoming	

Yod (ʼ | Y) becomes
Teth (ט | Th)

Heh (ה | E) becomes
Vav (ו | W)

In the illustration above, the two letters of code Patience (יה) morph into the two letters of the new code to the right (טו), a code soon to be identified as code Time. The message is no less than emotional mastery. Indeed, just like a letter passes into another, this dark feeling too shall pass!

On that note, it is Jean de La Fontaine who said "patience and time do more than strength or passion." In looking at the image above, I recognize code Patience to the left. Using the ABCaD grants me patience by changing my perception of "time" (more to come). Who would I be if I could learn to wait? Might this newfound Power make me less afraid of falling?

THE MESSAGE IS NO LESS THAN EMOTIONAL MASTERY. I CAN JUST IMAGINE HOW WISE AND POWERFUL I'D BECOME IF I KNEW THAT, IF I COULD FEEL MY LONELINESS, MY SADNESS AND MY ANGER, I WOULD REALIZE THESE TOO SHALL PASS, AS EASILY AS ONE LETTER PASSING INTO ITS NEXT OF KIN...

THE FINAL ROW OF CODES: ON DEATH ROW

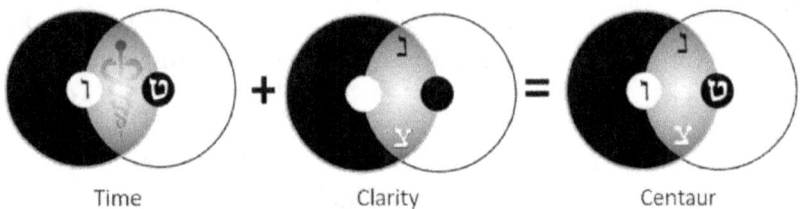

Time Clarity Centaur

Time + Clarity = Centaur Consciousness

Only the first code has a caduceus whose intertwined snakes evoke the knowledge of good and evil. As for the other two codes, their animal nature and the refinement of their instincts places them beyond the need for the wisdom that knows the difference between good and evil, and the subsequent need for patience. These two codes that involve animal wisdom can only lead to centaur consciousness.

Code **Time** merges human and animal wisdom by beginning in an ouroboros (a snake that eats its tail). Code **Clarity** speaks of the medicine brought by hawk. Combining both codes, I come into **Centaur** consciousness – when my soul is released. This means that I can finally inhabit my body as an incarnate student/teacher.

The animal presence confirms C.G. Jung's sense that religion is an instinct, as are creativity, aggression, sexuality and hunger. Instincts are innate patterns of behavior in animals in response to certain stimuli. As long as I have a body, I will have an animal life. The question is: may I stretch my consciousness to be as human as many "animals" are or will I continue to abuse Power as I kill with no real hunger, just being moved by the desire to distract myself by killing?

Code Time - ThW / WTh

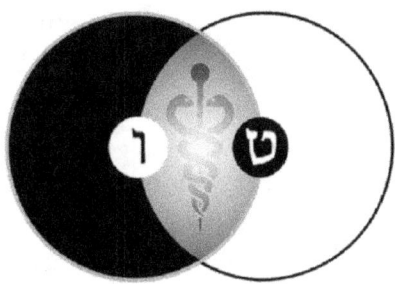

Imagine a language so pure and so sacred that it can reconcile opposites in just one pair of letters...

Right: Hebrew letter Teth (ט) → Th in Roman script
Left: Hebrew letter Vav (ו) → F, U, V, W in Roman script

Here is how S/Hebrew inscribes code "Time" in 2 words:

- From right to left: I read *Tu* (טו) for "15" – the value of *Yah* (יה) in code Patience.
- From left to right: I read *V'Teth* (וט) for "and Teth the snake."

The Decoding: to understand the shift from code Patience to code Time (or from YE/EY to ThW/WTh), I must be made aware of the codification of the fifteenth verse of each chapter in the Hebrew Bible (which is an application of the ABCaD code). Ideally, the information generated by the two pairs of letters will inspire me to feel what remains of my impatience, and thus to transcend time.

The verses of the Hebrew Bible are not numbered, but "lettered." Hence, verse 1 in the King James Bible is verse א in the Torah, since Aleph (א) has the value of 1. Verse 2 is marked by ב, since Beth (ב) is 2. Jumping to verse 12, it is marked by the two letters יב since Yod (י) is 10 and Beth (ב) is 2. Therefore, one would expect for verse 15 to be marked יה since Yod (י) is 10, and Heh (ה) is 5. But no, it is marked by

טו, which is still 15 since Teth (ט) is 9, and Vav (ו) is 6. The shift aims at respecting the Power carried by the "God" Names, in this case, *Yah* (יה), a Name of such great Power that it is recommended (and even commanded) not to use it in vain. As for the number 15, it marks time in several ways:

- *Tu B'Shevat* or "the 15th in the month of Shevat" is a special holiday which occurs around the midpoint between the winter solstice and the spring equinox. It celebrates the birthday of trees and their early blossoming, and as such, is a renewal of time.

- The 15th day in each month marks the full moon, since each month of the Hebrew calendar begins on the new moon. The full moon is when most Jewish holidays occur, serving as witnesses to a specific season and purpose. The end goal is to have the Power to choose peace and abide in the Eternal Now. Meanwhile, these 15th days of the months act as portals for me to transcend time and stay present, in my body, regardless of my circumstances. They are a *Shabbat* and a "rest" because, being full, Madame Moon is neither waxing nor waning.

Such is the magic of 15, a reminder to "be still and know that I Am," which is made possible by *Tu* substituting for *Yah*. Note: the simple gematria of 15 is 6 (1+5=6), as is the measuring of time which is shown in the next BEE wisdom to be "created-SIX," e.g.; the 24 hours of each day (24=2+4=6).

As for the letters Teth and Vav, they also inscribe code Time by allowing me to come into snake-Power. Not only does the word *Teth* mean "snake" (which makes it a natural counterpart for Vav's snake-Power) but also and foremost, its hieroglyph (ט) resembles an ouroboros – a snake eating its own tail. If every great story begins with a snake, it also ends in one, a cycle epitomized by the Egyptian symbol of the ouroboros. The term comes from Greek *oura* "tail" +

bora "food." It is a literal "feedback" process, meant to at once kill me and restore me. The more I devour and assimilate my illusion of free will (and any subsequent acting out), the more I open to the LOVE that has no opposite... and to a wholesome use of my creative Power. When that happens, there is no more mind which also means that there is no more time.

As for now, just how much patience have I really come into? When the rubber meets the road, am I able to stay quiet until the path is clear, or will I force a decision out of resisting the challenge I'm in? The next code – code Clarity – answers me.

BESIDES MONEY, TIME IS MY MOST POTENT CREATION: WHETHER I LIVE IN NEW YORK CITY OR BANGKOK, AM YOUNG OR OLD, TEACH MUSIC OR SELL PAPER CLIPS, I HAVE AN EQUAL 24 HOURS A DAY, 60 MINUTES AN HOUR, AND 60 SECONDS A MINUTE TO REACH MY GOALS.

THIS BEGS THE QUESTION: HOW WILL I USE MY FAIR SHARE OF TIME?

Code Clarity - NZ / ZN

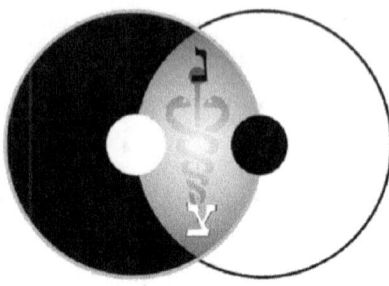

Imagine a language so pure and so sacred that it can reconcile opposites in just two pairs of letters...

Top: Hebrew letter Nun (נ) → N in Roman script
Bottom: Hebrew letter Tzaddi (צ) → Z in Roman script

Here is how S/Hebrew inscribes code "Clarity" in 2 words:

- From bottom to top: I read *Zin* (צן) for "desert area."
- From top to bottom: I read *Netz* (נץ) for "hawk."

The Decoding: just like the belly of the whale or the dark night of the soul, the **desert** is a place of initiation, where I am divested of the power trips of my ego. The desert is thus symbolic of the terrain in which I unlearn my Power misuse and surrender to the cosmic Force. In the desert experience, the motives of the false self can be seen clearly, sometimes for the first time.

Such sight is when my soul receives the medicine granted by **hawk**, asking me to leverage my confusion and take immediate action to clarify a situation. Hawks are often seen as a symbol of Power in Native American cultures. In some tribes, such as the Cheyenne, hawks are associated with protection from enemies and/or as a warning of danger. Like eagles, they show courage and strength when the time comes to observe the desert I am in, with unrelenting honesty.

Flying with hawk comes naturally after I dare entering the desert of my soul. It is how I answer my question about patience and the Power to choose peace; how I shift from counting time to making time count.

Note: both letters – Nun and Tzaddi – are part of 5 letters which are "final" for two reasons: 1. they take a different shape when at the end of a word, 2. they usher a redemption of sorts – an end. Nun final (ן) – the last letter of the word *Zin* (ןצ) for "desert" – marks the end of resentment, as it is when I for-give it all: no debts/no debtors. Also, the word *Netz* (ץנ) for "hawk" ends in a Tzaddi final (ץ) which marks the end of confusion as in the crystal-clear vision of a hawk. I was confused: I really thought it was all your fault, and I realize now that I was responsible! More on the end games of the final letters in the appendix (*The TWIN Trees*).

In the desert experience, the motives of the false self can be seen clearly, sometimes for the first time. Such sight is when my soul receives the medicine granted by hawk, asking me to leverage my confusion and take immediate action to clarify a situation.

Centaur Consciousness

"Hence, centaur – mind and body are both experiences of an integrated self." *Ken Wilber*

Integrating mind and body is like doing a jigsaw puzzle which, once complete, grants optimal health. The difficulty comes from my being so obsessed with the physical pieces that the body now becomes the mind. It is how I *think* I am the body (or that which is dying) and the personality (or that which fears death). Henceforth, I can never complete the puzzle by which to connect mind and body. But how do I stop identifying with my thoughts, my emotions and my actions, and instead, become source over them?

Understand. Choose peace. emPower the NOW.

The centaur brings a whole lot of understanding. As a mythological being with a horse's body and a human chest, arms and head, the centaur is a metaphor for the integration of the animalistic body and the divine mind. I integrate it when I am compassionate or "with my pain," feeling the feelings that emanate from my soul and sensing the sensations given by my body. This is how I become source over them. This experience – named by Ken Wilber "centaur consciousness" – is a stage that terminates the compulsive thinking of the prostitutE archetype and the dissociated acting of the victiM archetype. This new way of being feels quite different: free from the mind, I no longer lose touch with *the unity* of body and mind. I also no longer distort the clarity of the sense impressions I receive. Said differently, I am able to remove my focus from lack and place it on abundance, which is much less stressful.

The experience of the mind-body connection existed in *Genesis 1:1* as the creation of *Haaretz* for "the earth," working in parity with *Hashamayim* for "the heavens." That was before the beginning of time (i.e.; the beginning of mind).

Indeed, time did not begin in *Genesis 1:1*, but in *Genesis 1:5* with Day 1: "and *Elohim* called the light Day, and the darkness He called Night. And there was evening and there was morning, Day 1." Although it was never said that darkness was "bad," the judgment "this is good" which is throughout *Genesis 1* was bound to be followed with "this is no good" (in *Genesis 2:18*), a perception that could only invite a "no good" resistance. :-) The way out of this predicament is, of course, to surrender my judgments. Doing so is what gives birth to the centaur, a consciousness known in the Bible as "the Word made flesh." The same *Basar* for "flesh, nourishment" turns into *Besorah* for "good tidings" and then *Mevashereth* for "announcer of good tidings," literally s/he who allows for the Holy Word to be made flesh.

There is no escaping it: unless I am true to my word, I can't open to the sense of enough. This is how I prevent myself from extending Health (Health with a big H) to all levels of communication. As a gentle reminder, code Communication joins AT (the "untranslated" logos) to TA (the eros of the "cell"). This code also existed in *Genesis 1:1*, before the beginning of time. It is in fact the *Et* (AT) particle that precedes the creation of the heavens and the earth.

- *Et Hashamayim* for "the heavens" is best understood when I realize that the word *Hashamayim* is formed by *Esh/Mayim* meaning "fire/water." Surely, the experience of "the heavens" comes from the ability to hold the tension of opposites; fire/water being the most potent antagonists of all elements. It is to speak in "God's" language – in the paradox.
- *Et Haaretz* for "the earth" follows as the mind-body connection. Just as *Hashamayim* holds a pair of elements, so does *Haaretz*. The letter Aleph (A) of *Aretz* is a mother letter recognized in classical Jewish mysticism to invoke the element of air. As for the *Retz* part, it is the earth that "runs" as a fluid wave before it solidifies as a particle.

I have seen how I know where "God" lives. However, since if I don't really want to give it all to Love – to a LOVE that has no opposite, I just have to "run" as fast as I can in the "opposite" direction. It thus makes sense that the Hebrew word *Retz* for "run" would branch into *Ratzon* for "will." Indeed, it is only when I stop running and become willing to do what I know I ought to do (heart and soul, mind and body) that I begin to see that my goals on "earth" are no longer running from me. From waves of potential, they became actualized particles.

This introduces code Centaur which will substantiate the keywords of the four creatures as follows: when what **I desire** aligns with what **I have**, **I know** that I made a divine use of **will**.

Leader's Heart	Engineer's Mind	Officer's Body	Visionary's Soul
GOD	SIN	LAW	SEX
The Lion	The Human	The Taurus Bull	The Scorpion to be Eagle
"I will"	"I know"	"I have"	"I desire"

Elohim created the heavens as the **fire/water** paradox before the earth could be created as the **mind-body** connection.

<small>Surrendering my judgments is how to give birth to centaur, a consciousness known in the Bible as "the Word made flesh."</small>

The Book of Formation

"The emotions have been seen as the center of woman's soul. For
that reason, emotional formation will have to be centrally placed
in woman's formation." *Edith Stein*

Prior to entering code Centaur, I owe it to myself to introduce *Sepher
Yetzirah* or the "Book of Formation." It speaks of the creation of the
universe, time, of sentience and symbolic Power itself. According to
modern historians, the origin of the text is unknown and hotly
debated. Some scholars believe it might have an early medieval
origin, while others emphasize earlier traditions appearing in the
book. Whether it comes from the Mishnaic period (2nd century BCE)
or from Adam, and was from there "passed over to Noah, and then to
Abraham, the friend of God," nobody knows. However, it is generally
believed that the book is only to be used for spiritual purposes, and
only accessible by the pious.

This book itself is a conundrum. On the one hand, it is one of the
founding works of Jewish mysticism; on the other hand, it has never
really been felt. And if there is one book among all the books on the
Kabbalah that ought to be felt, it is *the Book of Formation*, especially
since elevating my soul out of survival mode and feeling gratitude is
how to "receive" my heart's desire. And yet, its codes have remained
unexplored psychologically since the understanding of its six short
and dense chapters has thus far remained very abstract. This is how,
having never been seen in the center of the soul, it can't touch the
soul. And if it does not touch the soul, how can it help me?
Impossible!

**To make matters even more curious, while the book's title does
mean *the Book of Formation*, it is often translated as "the Book of
Creation," as if its Hebrew title were *Sepher Beriah* and not *Sepher
Yetzirah*.**

To understand the difference between *Beriah* and *Yetzirah*, I can review the four worlds of the tree of life (a.k.a. the ABYA) which were first pictured in the preface in *The Level Above*:

- **The first world is "transmission"** – A as in *Atziluth* in Hebrew. It is the intuiting realm that I visit when I am in my heart.
- **The second world is "creation"** – B as in *Beriah* in Hebrew. It is the thinking realm that I visit when I am in my mind. It is also the level where the problem is "created" when I attach to a limiting belief or two.
- **The third world is "formation"** – Y as in *Yetzirah* in Hebrew. It is the feeling realm that I visit when I am in my soul. It is also where my beliefs are trans-forming into e-motions (energy in motion). How good will I *choose* to feel? Unless I inquire on my limiting beliefs, they will transfer into smothering emotions which I will resist feeling and hide in the unconscious!
- **The fourth world is "action and manifestation"** – A as in *Assiyah* in Hebrew. It is the sensing realm that I visit when I am in my body. This is where I can either be bound to the material world as I attach to the fruit of my actions, or be free to do what love would do and manifest accordingly as I have nothing left to prove or to lose.

I decode my own "Book of Formation" when I can give myself the permission to FEEL my pain and, for example, transmute the hatred into love. Finally, I can get out of the fear I tried to ignore while in the emotional realm of *Yetzirah*, and stop the feeling from being acted out in the physical realm of *Assiyah* as fight and flight, a response which only amplifies the pull of Scare City.

I know that emotions yield a formation. I can feel that. To transcend my fears and exorcise any demonic lifeforms, I just have to realize that emptiness is form and form is emptiness. However, this is easier said than done, since to do so, I must have the courage to detach from the familiar forms of the past and enter the unknown – the void which I avoid with all my might! A-void-dance is how I ignore this level, although the void is just beyond the mental world of *Beriah* where I create problems for myself.

This "level" and all-encompassing realm is the *Ain,* Hebrew for "nothingness." It is both in between and beyond *Beriah* and *Atziluth* (or between and beyond the world of creation and the world of transmission). While it is empty, it is also simultaneously full with infinite possibilities. For me to re-member a more fluid response to life, I must go into the nothingness of the etheric and quantum "un-knowledge" of *Daath* where matter is energy. As I change the way I feel and vibrate with a different energy, I make contact with a higher frequency that becomes my new reality.

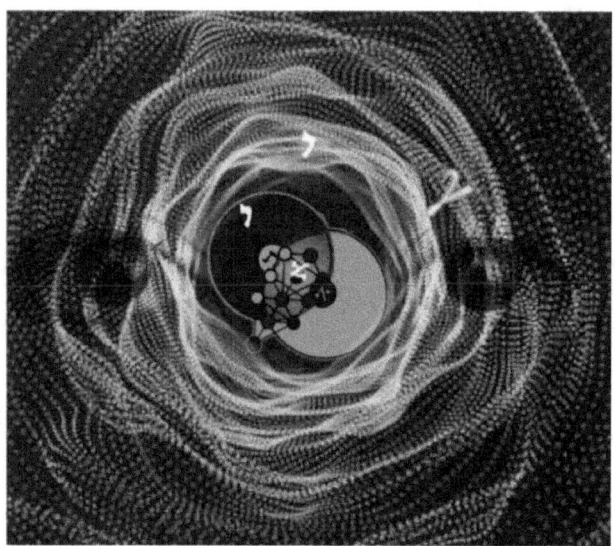

Me, myself and "eye" taking a cleansing dip in the Void

While riding the waves of the etheric empty-fullness of the Void, I am also communicating with my *Yetzirah* waters. The more I immerse myself, the more I nullify the toxic/talk-sick thoughts, and the more my negativity trans-forms into pure joy and gratitude. And then (and only then), I am patience, since I know beyond doubts that I "received." I made contact with a future version of me that already has the health, the wealth or "the girl" I once sought, and brought it into the Now– in my *Assiyah* of manifestation, a felt-sense which continues to magically alter my biology. Surely, I am now energetically connected to the LOVE that has no opposite – alive, vibrant, heart and soul, a sane mind in a sane body. What a trip this is!

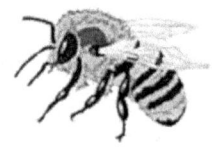

THE TRUE PURPOSE OF *THE BOOK OF FORMATION* IS AND HAS ALWAYS BEEN TO CONVEY THE IN-FORMATION THAT ALLOWS FOR TRANS-FORMATION.

I AM IN-FORMED BY PATIENCE, WHEN I KNOW BEYOND DOUBT THAT I "RECEIVED" MY TRUE SELF. I MADE CONTACT WITH A FUTURE VERSION OF ME THAT ALREADY HAS THE HEALTH OR THE WEALTH OR "THE GIRL" I ONCE SOUGHT. I BROUGHT IT INTO THE NOW, A FELT-SENSE WHICH CONTINUES TO MAGICALLY ALTER MY BIOLOGY.

Code Centaur - NZ / ThW

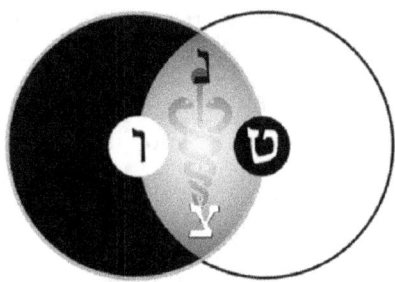

Imagine a language so pure and so sacred that it can reconcile opposites in just two pairs of letters...

Top: Hebrew letter Nun (נ) → N in Roman script
Right: Hebrew letter Teth (ט) → Th in Roman script
Left: Hebrew letter Vav (ו) → F, U, V, W in Roman script
Bottom: Hebrew letter Tzaddi (צ) → Z in Roman script

Here is how S/Hebrew inscribes code "Centaur" in 3 words:

- From top to bottom: I read *Netz* (נצ) for "hawk" of code Clarity.
- In the middle, I read *Tu* (וט) for "15" of code Time.
- From top to left to bottom, I read *Nootz* (נוצ) for "to flee away, to bud forth."

The Decoding: Time + Clarity = Centaur. To relate to the centaur, I must start in the word made flesh and open to the hieroglyphs or "sacred signs" of the S/Hebrew alphabet which are organized as per the formula of 3+7+12=22, as clearly announced in *Sepher Yetzirah, Chapter 1:2:* "10 spheres of awareness (nonlocal), and 22 foundation letters: 3 mothers, 7 doubles and 12 simples." Like Sanskrit's three *matrikas* or "divine mothers" that form the supreme syllable *Om*, S/Hebrew also has 3 mother letters. Each of these lettered "wombs" invokes twin elements (e.g.; sign Mem invokes water and ether). 7

letters of the 22 are called double, as they have two sounds, two shapes and invoke the seven classical planets which are dualistic in nature since the solar system has two foci (e.g.; Beth can sound as B or V, depending on whether or not it has a dot inside it. It invokes the moon). 12 letters of the 22 are called "simple" as they invoke the twelve basic signs of the zodiac (e.g.; Yod invokes the astrological sign of Virgo).

The signs that form code Centaur are the four "simple" letters that invoke the four fixed signs. No matter what my birth sign is, these are of concern to me if I want to transcend my stars and thus, not to be a victim of my biology. The fixed signs of the zodiac are invoked by the letters **Vav** (ו) for Taurus, **Teth** (ט) for Leo, **Nun** (נ) for Scorpio, and **Tzaddi** (צ) for Aquarius. Owning my desire and befriending the **Nun** of my Scorpio self is where to start. Indeed, questioning my motivations is so essential to consciousness that it may be how the letter Nun is at the core of the 9 Chambers. Surely, to no longer be condemned to repeat the same pain story, I must transition from obligation to *pleasure* and ask myself: do I truly want what I want or am I trying to *please* or even *displease* "you?"

Answering the Lucifer question ("what do you really want?") liberates the "I desire" of my Nun Scorpio for it to be born in the soul. It then stands the best chance to be heard as it is spoken as a true desire.

Besides being first seen by Ezekiel and being studied by philosophers as various sets of four, these four creatures of the zodiac support my being successful in my creation. How? They lead me to recognize that it is not about me, as I increasingly feel that the work of creation is done *through* me and not *by* me. When I know that what I want evolves not only me but also the whole, I am in a state of flow; neither pushing nor pulling, which allows the four keywords to enter in synergy.

Heart-Soul Paradox	
Leader's Heart	Visionary's Soul
The Lion	The Scorpion to be Eagle
"I will"	"I desire"
Mind-Body Connection	
Engineer's Mind	Officer's Body
The Human	The Taurus Bull
"I know"	"I have"

The Heaven of the Heart-Soul Paradox and the Earth of
the Mind-Body Connection

I experience heaven on earth, when what **I desire** aligns with what **I have**. **I know** that I made a perfect use of will. Scorpio is now sublimated into eagle (or LOL, might it be a hawk?), showing me that patience may just be the last desire.

When I know beyond doubt that I have what I prayed for, I am out of Scare City and I can wait. And when I know that I can wait, I transcend **time** and **mind**. Indeed, "Siddhartha does nothing; he waits, he thinks, he fasts." This is how I reach my goal: I wait before my next word and action to have the **clarity** that knows where to walk. The willingness to know the truth makes room for my coming out, as I **flee away** from the desert, my genius now being free to **bud forth**.

HEAVEN IS "HAVING!" WHEN I KNOW BEYOND DOUBT THAT I AM CEN-
<u>TAURUS</u> AND <u>HAVE</u> WHAT I PRAYED FOR, I CAN WAIT. AND WHEN I
KNOW THAT I CAN WAIT, I TRANSCEND TIME AND MIND.
THE END

APPENDIX

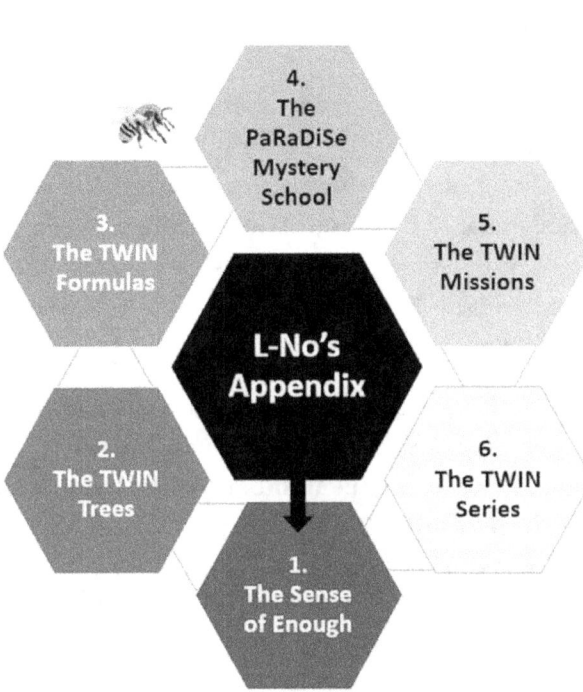

"Twins don't go through life searching for their other half. They were born with it." *Anonymous*

1. The Sense of Enough as the Deliverable
2. The TWIN Trees and the Mouth Chakra
3. The Two Keys to LOVE and the TWIN Formulas
4. The PaRaDiSe Mystery School
5. Meet M&M and their TWIN Mission
6. The TWIN Series

The Sense of Enough as the Deliverable

"Come, all you who are thirsty, come to the waters. And if you have no money, come, buy and eat. Come, buy without money for this wine and milk are unsalable!" *Isaiah 55:1*

Satiety is a mystery. Hunger seems to be physical, and yet it is not. So, what is EAT? I want to say that it is an initiation into a realm where matter is not solid, and earthly foods are like the manna, imbued with a heavenly quality. But this just deflects the question: what is the manna? The word first appears in *Exodus 16:15,* not as a noun, but as the question *Man Hu* "what is IT?" I answer "IT" when I see the letters of *Man Hu* reordering as *Emunah* for "faith."

Faith is what satiates me, as it is when I am 100% certain that my prayer is received. Thus, faith is how I move out of Scare City – a "land" where I'm a slave to the number of bills I have in my wallet and/or the calories I ingest. Surely, the trick to having faith is to be 100% and thus have 0 doubts.

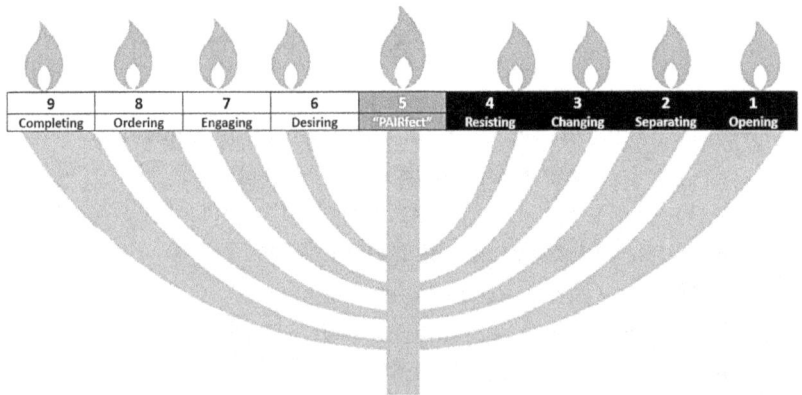

The 9-branch candelabrum joins the pairs of animals into a 10 (1+9, 2+8, 3+7, 4+6) for my heart to understand the one (1) of us, and my mind to have zero (0) doubt that my hands serve enlightened justice.

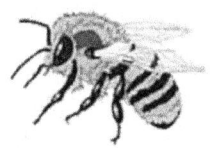

Satiety is a mystery. Hunger seems to be physical, and yet it is not. So, what is EAT? I want to say that it is an initiation into a realm where matter is not solid, and earthly foods are like the manna, imbued with a heavenly quality. But this just deflects the question: what is the manna? The word first appears in *Exodus 16:15*, not as a noun, but as the question *Man Hu* "what is it?" I answer "it" when I see the letters of *Man Hu* reordering as *Emunah* for "faith."

Ask and Ye Shall QKabbalah!

Is there a part of the Bible or of *The LOVE that has No Opposite* that puzzles you, which you would like to better understand? You may either:

- **Post** your question(s) at www.empoweringnow.com/ask
- **Join** a live community gathering: www.empoweringnow.com/calendar
- **See** articles and podcasts at www.empoweringnow.com/blog

The TWIN Trees

'Then Jesus said to his disciples, "again, I tell you, it is easier for a GIMEL to go through the eye of a needle than for a rich man to enter the QKingdom."' *Matthew 19:24*

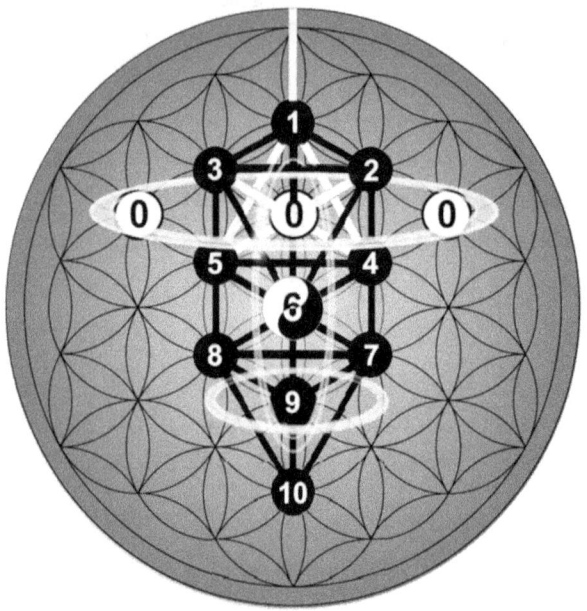

The letter Gimel (for "camel") passes through the eye of the needle, in the unknown of sphere 0, as it walks from sphere 6 to sphere 1. As such, its meridian is the straight path to "God."

The integration of the TWIN trees is an innovation brought forth by *Golden XPR*. This vision merges the tree of life and the tree of the knowledge of good and evil which are both in the midst of the garden. It joins what tradition sees as the 32 wondrous paths of wisdom to the newly revealed 13 infinite paths of Power, in order to allow the Adam in me to transcend the mind of duality and to identify to the LOVE that has no opposite. 32 + 13 = 45, which is the value of the *Adam* (אדם) whose potential is to be supernatural.

<u>Black</u>: the tree of life and its 32 wondrous paths of wisdom, which encompass the 10 numbered spheres (1 to 10) and the 22 meridians (the 22 regular letters) that circulate the light in between the spheres. 10 + 22 = 32

<u>White</u>: the tree of the knowledge of opposites and its 13 infinite paths of Power, which encompass the 3 voiding spheres (0.0.0) and the 10 lettered meridians (5 finals, doubled) that stabilize the passage between the 7 infernal spheres of "Ego-Egypt" and the 3 supernal spheres of "the Promised Land." 3 + 10 = 13

Below are the names of the tree of life's 10 spheres as "chakras" and/or centers of energy and information (to review the shifts from traditional placement, see *Chap. 3, The Yesses of an Adam Aleph*):

1. *Kether* for "crown" as IS-REALity – crown chakra.
2. *Binah* for "understanding" – third eye (female side).
3. *Chesed* for "kindness" – third eye (male side).
4. *Chokmah* for "wisdom" – throat chakra (female side).
5. *Geburah* for "Power" – throat chakra (male side).
6. **Tiphereth for "beauty" – heart chakra as the absolute center of the garden of life.**
7. *Hod* for "appreciation" – navel chakra (female side).
8. *Netzach* for "perseverance" – navel chakra (male side).
9. *Yesod* for "foundation" as honesty – sex chakra
10. *Malkuth* for "QKingdom" – root chakra.

Below are the names of the newly identified 3 spheres of the tree of the knowledge of opposites as the transcendental mouth "chakra:"

- 0—center: known traditionally as *Daath* for [sexual] "knowledge" – mouth chakra (neutral).
- 0—right: *Okhel* for "eating" – mouth chakra (female / evil side).
- 0—left: *Dibri* for "my word," and by extension, speaking – mouth chakra (male / good side).

Gimel the "camel" – value 3 – walks directly to "God." When embodying its consciousness, I have no resistance to giving it all to LOVE. Also, I now have 10 more lettered paths that are surely final, as they usher a redemption of sorts and lead to THE END of suffering.

The Mouth Chakra

"I humbled me, causing me to hunger and then feeding me with a manna which neither I nor my ancestors had known, to teach me to not live on bread alone, but on every word that comes from the mouth of LOVE." *Transmission of Deuteronomy 8:3*

The mouth chakra is a portal into the *Ain* – the field of "nothingness" where all possibilities exist as frequencies. Its central sphere named *Daath* for the "knowledge" of good and evil is conjointly the "unknown" of good and evil. This is how rabbis have said about such center that it is "here and not here;" or in scientific terms, "non-local." Indeed, when I no longer obsess on the knowns of my past or worry about the unknowns of the future, I let go of my reference points, which is to say, I surrender my judgments of good and evil. Finally, I allow myself to enter the "NOWthingness," and know that I don't know. Surely, it is only when I stop trying so hard to be "somebody" that I can become "nobody" – a selflessness which is the key to being One with "everybody." Similarly, it is only when I stop attaching to "something" that I have "nothing" left to lose – a freedom which is the key to being One with "everything."

This passage into boundlessness is facilitated by the 5 final letters that are doubled. Indeed, coming to "THE END" of my self-imposed limitations opens the door for a new beginning. For now, here are the 5 final letters, "finally" explained in their reversed and ascending order (moving from Tzaddi final into Kaph final):"

1. **Sphere 5 to 2** (throat to 3rd eye; Power to understanding) are linked by Tzaddi's meridian: *Tzaddi* means "hook." When final, it is THE END of confusion as I understand that I was in a projection: I thought it was your fault; I now see it was mine. Indeed, I "hooked" enough particles of darkness to take full responsibility for my results. Note: THE END of confusion marks the beginning of awe.

2. **Sphere 5 to 1** (throat to crown; Power to IS-REALity) are linked by Peh's meridian: *Peh* means "mouth." When final, it is THE END of dissatisfaction as my judgements of good and evil are at last consummated and fully metabolized. I can now be in the present moment without attempting to control it. Note: THE END of dissatisfaction marks the beginning of integrity.

3. **Sphere 4 to 3** (throat to 3rd eye; wisdom to kindness) are linked by Nun's meridian: *Nun* means "fish, fallen." When final, it is THE END of resentment as I forgive all errors: yours and mine. Hence, I stop feeling that I owe you and/or stop wanting to make you pay. At last, wisdom descends and kindness ascends. Note: THE END of resentment marks the beginning of simplicity.

4. **Sphere 4 to 1** (throat to crown; wisdom to IS-REALity) are linked by Mem's meridian: *Mem* means "pairs of waters." When final, it is THE END of desire and of the hopelessness behind it since my emotional body is no longer yearning for love, approval and recognition. I observe that reality rules

and am One with all that is! Note: THE END of desire marks
the beginning of fulfillment.

5. **Sphere 1 to the *Ain*** (crown to boundlessness) are linked by
   Kaph's meridian: *Kaph* means "to coerce." When final, it is
   THE END of Power misuse since I am no longer trying to
   force an outcome. I travel from the crown to the *Ain*
   "nothingness," and connect to the quantum field. Note: THE
   END of Power misuse marks the beginning of creativity.

Note: the mouth chakra may just be what the Bible calls "the red sea."
It is to be crossed in order to be REAL! *Yam Soph* for "the red sea" is
more accurately translated as "THE END sea," since crossing over is
knowing the finality of decisiveness, as traced by the final letters.
However, if this center of energy and information is truth, it ought to
be found in the East as well.

The Hindu scriptures of the Brahmanas and Puranas recognized
twelve *adityas* or "expanses," which entered the womb of mother
Aditi, so that they would again enjoy the rank of gods. Formed from *a*
— "not" + *diti* "bound" from the verbal root *da* "to bind," *Aditi* means
"free, unbounded."

In the Rig-Veda, goddess Aditi is recognized as the power of mystic
speech and voice. As the womb of space, she is the essence of divine
wisdom and the first Logos. Aditi has the honor of being one of the
few goddesses mentioned by name in the Rig-Veda (Hindu religious
& mythological text). She is held to be the impersonation of "infinity,"
especially the boundlessness of heaven, in opposition to the finite-
ness of earth. She is wave-like instead of particle-like.

The Sanskrit root verb *Da* is exactly the same as Hebrew *Da*, a root-
verb which branched into *Daath*. With the prefix *a*—, *da/diti* is "free"
to go unencumbered. With *Daath*, I am free to part the sea of my
emotions. Seeing beyond boundaries and coming to the END of the
path is a NDE – a Near Death Experience. An unbounded LOVE
washes over me, taking everything from me; names, objects, hungers,

opposites... It leaves me with a body (what grace; what gratitude!) to receive "God's" thoughts. I now become an informational field inscribing a new narrative that eternally transmits the beauty and the bliss of a felt "biblical knowledge..."

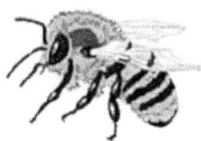

IT IS ONLY UPON ENTERING THE "NOWTHINGNESS" THAT I KNOW THAT I DON'T KNOW!

The Two Keys to LOVE

"True love begins when nothing is looked for in return." *Antoine de Saint-Exupéry*

To know such big LOVE, I am given the two keys of inquiry and surrender:

- **Inquiry leads me to no longer resist the DREaM of karma, free will and destiny:** upon encountering any problem, I can ask myself why I judge my problem as "bad" until I realize that only the ego is bound by judgments, and that the ego is non-existent. As long as I judge this or that to be "no good," I will resist it, which says that my understanding is not complete and that my will is not free.
- **Surrender opens my heart to LOVE by saving me from forbidden desires:** I can admit my powerlessness and say at all times (as Jesus did); "not my will, Thy Will be done," giving up all sense of "I" and "mine" and leaving it to the Universe to do as it pleases with me. As long as I desire this or that, I am not surrendered. Surrender is loving LOVE for the sake of love and nothing else, not even for the sake of liberation.

Yep, this is a big bite. And what else is there to do under heaven besides coming to THE END of dissatisfaction? Here is a practice which is admittedly not for the faint of heart. However, it will return me to LOVE by showing me how I create something or someone as my opposite: **I look forward to trying to take care of you instead of taking care of me. This way, I can continue to nurture the story of unrequited love (subtext: "after all I've done for you?").** Acting out of obligation and not having any pleasure, I have all the forced labor I need to justify fueling the hatred for "God."

I'll eventually be so miserable that I'll recognize that I only pretend to give it all, but don't *really* give it all to LOVE. And on that day, I will feel my grief and my grievances. And then, poof; as if by magic, I'll realize that I was dreaming of karma, free will and destiny. I can now open to my real destiny – which is to be free to love, love, looove the LOVE "God" with all my heart, all my soul and all my might!

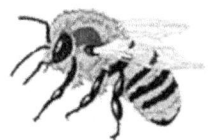

UPON ENCOUNTERING ANY PROBLEM, I CAN ASK MYSELF WHY I JUDGE MY PROBLEM AS "BAD" UNTIL I REALIZE THAT ONLY THE EGO IS BOUND BY JUDGMENTS, AND THAT THE EGO IS NON-EXISTENT.

The TWIN Formulas

THE FORMULA OF INQUIRY:
UNDERSTAND → CHOOSE PEACE → EMPOWER THE NOW

Understanding myself – and therefore being able to feel and clearly express WHY I once chose to do harm – is understanding everyone and everything. Such sentience is also what guides me on the path to transformation.

Understand: understanding is to feel the order inherent to chaos. This sense is helped by an inquiry that is sourced in sacred geometry. As such, it is universal (it relates to the whole and not just parts of me), credible (I can trust it), and radical (it takes me to the root).

Choose Peace: choosing peace is the step beyond understanding. It is the ability to foresee the consequences of my words and actions, and thus not create results I would rather not have to experience.

emPower the NOW: emPowering the NOW is an active listening. It hears the heart and answers "**ROGER** that" (Received Order Given), as the compassion that does what it takes to heal. Expecting different Results is no longer insanity. It is wisdom.

THE FORMULA OF SURRENDER:
DECIDE → DO AND UNDERSTAND

Decide: deciding begins in my acceptance of what needs to change. It continues with the responsibility to change for good. It ends in the recognition of the following integrated goal: to acquire self-knowledge and/or self-emPowerment. Not only will that decision best serve the whole, but also it will ease the attainment of all other goals by allowing rest while I work to reach them.

Do and understand: "do and understand" is the meaning of *Naaseh V'Nishma* – the ancient saying given to you and I on Mount Sinai along with the mosaic law. Enlightened action is doing the next perfect thing, one moment at a time, without arguing with my heart or having to ask why. When I "do" and take action toward a goal, the decision is made. However, not being able to sustain my momentum indicates that I am yet to decide. In that case, when I know what to do and immediately practice the opposite, I ought to move back to the formula of inquiry above: understand [the necessary evil]. Choose peace. emPower the NOW of enlightened action. I will then naturally do good, or, at the least, do no harm!

DECIDING BEGINS IN MY ACCEPTANCE OF WHAT NEEDS TO CHANGE. IT CONTINUES WITH THE RESPONSIBILITY TO CHANGE FOR GOOD. IT ENDS IN THE RECOGNITION OF THE FOLLOWING INTEGRATED GOAL: TO ACQUIRE SELF-KNOWLEDGE AND/OR SELF-EMPOWERMENT.

NOT ONLY WILL THAT DECISION BEST SERVE THE WHOLE, BUT ALSO IT WILL EASE THE ATTAINMENT OF ALL OTHER GOALS BY ALLOWING REST WHILE I WORK TO REACH THEM.

The PaRaDiSe Mystery School

"I have always imagined that Paradise will be a kind of library."
Jorge Luis Borges

The *PaRDeS* – the S/Hebrew word for "orchard" – is also a theory first advanced by Spanish rabbi and kabbalist Moses de León (c. 1240 – 1305). As such, it is an acronym formed by four words describing four levels of biblical interpretations. These words are: the *P'shat* or the "surface, plain" meaning; the *Remez* or the "hint" beyond the literal sense; the *D'rash* or the "inquiry" as a possible commentary, and the *Sohd* or the "secret" esoteric and mystical, as given through revelation.

The problem with the classical approach is that it views the text as being "out there:" I am here, and the Bible is there. I have just ignored that it is my consciousness that does the reading.

But what If I took a quantum jump and reversed PRDS into **SDRP?** After all, this "turnaround" and turn within happens to be the meaning of *Teshuvah* – one of the three pillars of Jewish religion, next to *Tephillah* for a "prayer" of felt gratitude, and *Tzedaqah* for a "charity" generous enough to give it all to Love – the LOVE that has no opposite.

Back to innovating, I will also go to magical English to transmit the four letters in such a way that I could better understand myself. The letter **S** for "Secret" comes first since secrets warp the intuiting function, preventing me from receiving any possible revelation given by my heart. As a result, my thinking mind no longer knows the **D** of **D**ifference between good and evil, my soul is no longer feeling the **R** of **R**eflection and my body is no longer sensing the **P** of **P**racticality.

Consider: when I live in **PaRaDiSe**, I understand myself so completely that the fulfillment of my own law is a pleasure and not an obligation. Indeed, I am the Torah. I am the Law!

The WHY of the PaRaDiSe Mystery School ™ **is to end** my suffering by clearing the confusion induced by the "God" label, whose abstraction keeps me lonely as I run from the Mystery, and angry as I won't own the Truth that I am creating IT all!

The HOW of the PaRaDiSe Mystery School ™ **is to own** my projections (what I deny and repress) by using *Golden XPR* as a scrying mirror, at once shocking and sobering, and see that the places in the decoding where I go in limbo exactly reflect where my shame-based secrets are at work.

The WHAT of the PaRaDiSe Mystery School ™ **is to will** with a Power that cannot be corrupted; to keep silence as both the practice and practicality of self-mastery; to dare wielding energy to solve problems, to have the wisdom to know the difference moment to moment.

The problem with the classical approach is that it views the text as being "out there:" I am here, and the Bible is there. I have just ignored that it is my consciousness that does the reading. But what if I took a quantum jump?

Meet M&M...

Behind any great woman, there is a great man – and vice-versa!

I go by Maha. As the author (and a poet), my job is to make the conversation real. To this end, I speak as an "I" and dare (as much as possible) to be honest. As long as I remember, I longed for my gifts to be recognized. The hunger for Love eventually became so ravenous that I knelt in prayer and received the following counsel: "reveal that S/Hebrew is the tongue of Nature, and you'll heal your mind. The sacred frequencies open lines of communication to the heart, granting the coherence to turn within so as to find the recognition you sought without." What the heck?!

Although riddled with doubt, I couldn't help painting the Hebrew letters or writing on their wisdom. As I came to a place where the work showed some promise, I prayed (yep) for a partner who could help me bring this monumental project to the world. A week later, I met Michael, a curious mix of salesman, technical guru, energy healer, system analyst and community leader. I had no clue he was about to become my editor, not only in pointing out typos, but also and foremost in mirroring the errors of my way – altogether a very surreal partnership.

While we are polar opposites in numerous ways, Michael, just like me, prayed for a path of full awakening. Also, just like me, he yearns for recognition. Our egos have clashed so often that the day came when we realized that the book that begged to be written was *The Code of Opposites* – the series that follows LNO. In our desperate attempts to dominate the other, we were oftentimes conscious of being trained on how to embody wisdom and acquire wholesome Power. Would we ever reconcile the conflicting parts of us: the part that wants to offer its gifts freely, and the part that obsesses on "what in it for me?"

Trust was a big issue. We were two beings who alternated between loving each other as true friends and hating each other as sworn enemies. And, surprisingly, the day came when *The LOVE that has No Opposite* was mutually felt and ready to be published...

To wind down the right and wrong game, we had to transmute the shame-based gender identities. To let the other win, we had to learn that forces oppose each other in order to give rise to each other. This compassionate listening of the other is how we succeeded in fulfilling our deepest desire: to have a voice that can make a difference in freeing what may be a universal desire – to let our light shine in service to the good of all.

To let the other win, we had to learn that forces oppose each other in order to give rise to each other.

M&M and their TWIN Missions

"Feeling the rage and staying in the fire with the other M to fulfill this mission impossible was THE most surreal and sacred adventure imaginable. Surprisingly, ending the war of the sexes marked the beginning of integrity." *M&M*

The Mission of *Golden XPR* ™ is to reveal the order inherent in the chaos of knowledge. When I perceive that there is a universal code to hearing and seeing the soul of perennial truths, the visible and the invisible merge (I stop doubting), the hunger for LOVE is satiated (I have nothing left to lose), integrity is naturally embodied (I do no harm), and an enlightened civilization emerges (I love IT all).

The Mission of *emPowering NOW LLC* ™ is to test, experience, and bring forth *Golden XPR* as a path to transition from a world of **GR**eed that splits **G**iving and **R**eceiving by communicating fear, confusion and domination, to a world of **GR**ace that unites **G**iving and **R**eceiving by communicating wisdom, understanding and kindness.

www.GoldenXPR.com
www.emPoweringNOW.com

The First TWIN: *TCO—The Series*

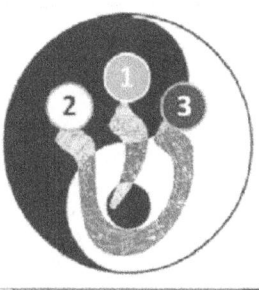

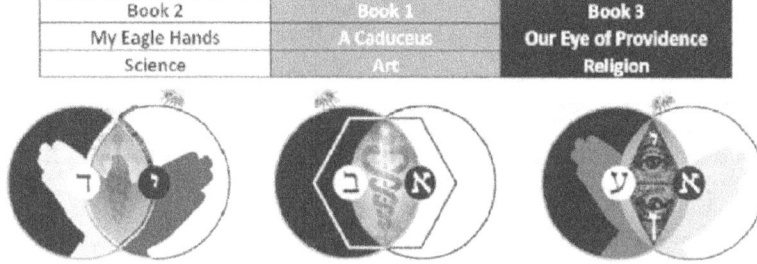

Book 2	Book 1	Book 3
My Eagle Hands	A Caduceus	Our Eye of Providence
Science	Art	Religion

Is TCO "write" for me? this booklet is a free resource. It begins in a good faith estimate of all the reasons to engage (or not) in the Great Work. It continues with Simplifying Consciousness – a synthesis of what the Work entails. It concludes with the basic elements positioning *Golden XPR* as a path to THE END.

Book 1—no push/pull invokes a caduceus: in the beginning was the end, when I deliberately choose peace and rest while working. This book lays the foundation for me to recognize the existence of a meta-language as a sacred guide to using Power. Power is a big deal. It is wholesome when I am unbridled in my expression, and yet, do not need to accuse myself of either speaking too much or not enough. Therein is the healing I seek.

Book 2—no self-doubt now superimposes "my eagle hands" over the caduceus. Eagle teaches me to return to childlike innocence. The same eagle who inspires me to reach for the sky grounds my action by suggesting a master code. Its head and wings are the digits of my two hands united in giving/receiving. When I feel the freedom of reciprocity, I know the kind of faith that makes everything well. This book invites me to inquire on why I do not trust myself.

Book 3—*no yearning* positions "my eagle hands" under "our eye of providence." This book marks my return to the WE perspective of collective Power. For me to have the certainty that you and I can work together, I must first stop asking for "your" love, approval and recognition. Such longing is at the foundation of desire itself. Consider: when I accept that I can only control my *inner* responses to "you" and not "you," I yearn for nothing. Such acceptance communicates the felt sense that I do contribute to the whole. Indeed, there is a tiny crack in existence that cannot be filled by anyone but me.

To learn more about *TCO—The Series* or purchase your copy, visit: www.thecodeofopposites.com.

Is TCO "write" for me? this booklet is a free resource.

www.thecodeofopposites.com

The Second TWIN: *The Path of Golden XPR*

1. Golden XPR
2. Golden XPR Distilled
3. Opening to the heART of XPR
4. The Genesis Pattern - book 1
5. The Genesis Pattern - book 2
6. This Year: EZ to Digest
7. Tweet tweeT
8. The LOVE Code
9. Sooo... I CAIN'T and you're ABEL!
10. The Creation Tool
11. The Expire Tarot Advanced
12. Victim of my GENESis
13. The WHYS Bite
14. The ThREE of Sapphires
15. The 7x7 Count
16. PaRaDiSe Circle
17. TABU: The Anarchist Book of Understanding
18. The GR-Code
19. This Year in Jerusalem
20. Welcome to the PaRaDiSe Mystery School
21. The Sapphire Book
22. Mercury REDROgrade

B'Siyata DiShemaya: "with the help of the heavens!"
September 1, 2023 – 15th of Elul, 5783